EMPTY CRADLES

Empty Cradles

Margaret Humphreys

Doubleday

LONDON • NEW YORK • TORONTO • SYDNEY • AUCKLAND

The publishers have made every effort to trace the owners of photographs used in this book. In any cases where they have been unsuccessful they invite copyright holders to contact them direct.

TRANSWORLD PUBLISHERS LTD
61–63 Uxbridge Road, London W5 5SA

TRANSWORLD PUBLISHERS (AUSTRALIA) PTY LTD
15–25 Helles Avenue, Moorebank, NSW 2170

TRANSWORLD PUBLISHERS (NZ) LTD
3 William Pickering Drive, Albany, Auckland

Published 1994 by Doubleday
a division of Transworld Publishers Ltd
Copyright © Margaret Humphreys

A catalogue record for this book is available from the British Library

0385 404522

Typeset in 11/13pt Linotype Sabon by Kestrel Data, Exeter

Printed in Great Britain by
Mackays of Chatham, plc, Chatham, Kent.

*To all the child migrants and their families,
particularly those who have suffered in
silence for so long,
with respect and admiration.*

ACKNOWLEDGEMENTS

Many individuals and organizations have helped me directly or indirectly through their support for the Child Migrants Trust.

In Australia, I wish to thank the Federal Department of Immigration and Ethnic Affairs in Canberra and Melbourne; the Department of Community Development, Western Australia; the Australian Federal Police; the Melbourne Support Group; the ex-Nazareth House, Geraldton group of women around Perth; Oliver Cosgrove (research); Barnardo's Australia; the Parmelia Hilton Hotel, Perth, and Qantas Airlines. For their deep friendship and support, Richard and Susan Minc, Juliett and Tom Tootill and Jeanette and Julian Abrahams.

In Britain, I am especially grateful to all the staff and trustees of the Child Migrants Trust, including Yvonne Barlow, Norman Caudell, Manfred Dessau, Joan Kerry, John and Penny Myles, Colyn Pietzsch (C.M.T. Australia), Beverly Rutter and David Spicer.

I have received similarly consistent and much-appreciated support from the Hon. Joan Taylor, Chairman, Nottinghamshire Social Services Committee, and her colleagues on the committee from the very beginning of the work of the Child Migrants Trust. I am also most grateful for the support of David White, Director,

Social Services Department, and Michael Lyons, Chief Executive, Nottinghamshire County Council.

I wish to thank the City of Liverpool Social Services Committee, Rotary International, Britain and Ireland, especially Division 1220, and the Department of Health, for their interest and assistance in promoting the work of the Trust.

Many individuals have given much time and devotion to the work of the Trust and helped me in many different ways. I wish to thank David Barlow, Jan Hesketh, Pauline Ireland and Marie Wood for their many contributions.

I am also indebted to an increasing number of Members of Parliament who have brought the position and needs of child migrants to the attention of both Parliament and the wider community. In particular, David Hinchliffe MP has been a very articulate and active advocate in promoting and pursuing the interests of child migrants.

I am particularly grateful to all those whose experiences as child migrants or as members of their families are described in the following pages.

Mark Lucas, my agent, and Michael Robotham, who assisted with the writing, have both shared the growing pains and teething troubles of this book for longer than they care to remember. My thanks to both for their inspiration, caring and support. I am especially indebted to Mervyn Humphreys for his invaluable research.

At Transworld, my thanks to Patrick Janson-Smith, Marianne Velmans and their colleagues for all their commitment.

Finally, I must thank the members of my family, in Nottingham, London and across the world, who made it all possible. But especially Mervyn, Rachel and Benjamin, whose love and understanding has sustained me throughout.

AUTHOR'S NOTE

This account of my work with Britain's child migrants is neither an academic nor a social work text. Instead, it describes seven of the most difficult, demanding and exciting years of my life. I hope it will interest a variety of readers, including those who have never heard of Britain's unique history of sending its children overseas.

I have witnessed so many tears of joy and sadness, so much laughter and sorrow in my work that it has been a daunting challenge to do justice to the range and intensity of emotions involved. This has not been an easy or enjoyable book to write. Indeed, at times, it has been extremely painful. It has also created many personal and professional dilemmas which I have struggled to resolve.

For legal and ethical reasons, some of the accounts of children's experiences of abuse have not been described in fine detail. Similarly, I have respected the wishes of those who have asked to remain anonymous and changed certain names and details to preserve confidentiality. It is highly unusual for a professional social worker to write about her clients, due to a strict code of confidentiality. I have had to bear this in mind from the very beginning.

Sadly, this means that those concerned cannot be acknowledged by name in public but will be thanked by me in private.

At a time when empty cradles are contributing woefully to empty spaces, it is necessary to look for external sources of supply. And if we do not supply from our own stock we are leaving ourselves all the more exposed to the menace of the teeming millions of our neighbouring Asiatic races.

In no part of Australia is settlement more vital than for Western Australia, which, while it contributes only one-twelfth of the total population, occupies one-third of the whole commonwealth . . .

The policy at present adopted of bringing out young boys and girls and training them from the beginning in agricultural and domestic methods . . . has the additional advantage of acclimatizing them from the outset to Australian conditions and imbuing them with Australian sentiments and Australian ideals – the essential marks of true citizenship . . .

His Grace the Archbishop of Perth, welcoming British boys
arriving in Australia on the SS *Strathaird*, August 1938

PROLOGUE

Perth, 1988

Opening the door, a woman asked me: 'Are you the lady from England?'

'Yes, I think so.' I smiled.

'You must be with that pale complexion. So what's the weather like in the old country.'

'The old country?' I asked.

'Much colder than here,' she said. 'Oh, it was cold when I left.'

'And when was that?' I asked.

'November 1950. We had gloves and scarves.'

'We? How many were you?'

'Oh, there were about sixty of us on the boat. We were collected from all over England. There were kids from Scotland and Ireland too. It was very hot when we arrived here. A bit like today.'

Outside it was already forty plus.

'You'd better keep out of the sun,' she said. 'My God, we burnt. Our arms were burnt raw within days.'

I arranged a settee and two armchairs in the sitting-room and began explaining why I was in Perth.

'I've come to talk with people who were child migrants; people who arrived in Australia without their parents.'

'You mean you've come all this way to see us?' the woman asked.

'Yes, I've come to see you.'

I could see the physical relief on her face.

She asked, 'Can I hold your hand?'

I was taken aback but sat down beside her on the settee. She took my hand.

'Where do you want to start?' I asked.

'Do you think I've got any family? Cousins, anybody. I'm not fussy. Anybody. They told me that my parents were dead. Do you think that's true?'

'I don't know, but I can find out. I'll need your help.'

'How can I possibly help you? I don't know anything about myself. Until I married, I didn't even have a birth certificate. I felt ashamed.'

The tears began flowing down her face. We sat there for a long time until I had to go out and get tissues because her skirt was becoming soaked with the tears. She kept saying to me, 'I'm sorry, I can't stop. I'm sorry. I'm sorry.'

The flood of tears washed away any thoughts that the interviews could be given a specific time limit. Even the most basic questions were charged with such emotion.

'What did we do wrong?' she asked. 'Can you find out why they sent me? What did I do wrong?'

'You did nothing wrong.'

She looked at me as if I was being kind to her.

'Do you know how old you were when you came to Australia?'

'Eight.'

'What could an eight-year-old possibly have done that was so bad?'

She smiled a little and squeezed my hand. 'Do you mind if I ask you some questions?'

'No, that's why I'm here. Ask anything you want.'

I thought she was going to ask me about something I wouldn't be able to answer. I knew so little about the child migration schemes.

'Do the daffodils and violets still grow on the side of the streets, and are there still chimney pots?'

I laughed, it came as such a surprise.

'You see, I remember the chimney pots and I've never seen a chimney pot in Australia.'

'Yes. Yes. Yes.' I told her all the daffodils and tulips were out on the day I left, and all the blossoms on the trees. She was just mesmerized. She wanted me to describe how things looked and smelt and felt.

'You see, when I was in England we used to walk to school and home at night and I was very happy there. But when we came here . . .' She began sobbing. 'When we came here . . .' She took a deep breath. 'When we came here we were prisoners. We didn't have that freedom.'

Although it seemed a silly question, I asked, 'Did you want to come to Australia?'

She looked at me incredulously. 'I thought I was going on holiday. They told me I was going on holiday. Said I would be away for six weeks. I didn't know where Australia was.

'I felt very strange on the boat and I can remember looking at the English coast and I thought, I'm never going to see this place again. I think I knew really – deep down – that I wasn't meant to come back.'

I had never seen such pain and sense of loss. Until now, in my work with adoptees, I was used to talking with people who had a small piece of their identity missing. It was just a slice. But the child migrants weren't missing a slice. Their lives were blank sheets of paper. If I had handed this woman a sheet of paper and said, 'Write down everything you know about yourself,' she would have handed back a blank sheet of paper.

As she wiped away tears, I explained to her: 'We have to view this like a journey. You have to help me understand, somehow, the milestones of your life so far and from there we will take another journey. Neither of us knows where it's going to lead. I know it's going to be painful but you have to help me.'

She nodded her head.

I asked, 'What are your earliest memories? What can you remember about leaving England?'

'When we were on the boat, somebody told me that we would be going to families. I knew it wasn't a holiday then. They said there was a family especially chosen for me who were waiting for me in Australia. But that wasn't to be. No-one was waiting.

'We were taken by bus to an orphanage miles out of the city – all the land looked burnt and dry and it was hot and there were flies everywhere. I just hated it.

'I arrived with only a suitcase. In the children's home in Liverpool I'd had a few toys, not much, but I wasn't allowed to bring anything with me.'

'What about photographs?'

'Nothing.'

'Any letters?'

She shook her head.

'We slept in dormitories. They didn't let us go out to school. Lessons, if you can call them that, were at the orphanage. There were about sixty girls – some Australians but most of us were English. The Australian girls used to poke fun at us because of the way we spoke.

'For the first few months I was there I used to cry myself to sleep every night. I wasn't the only one. We used to put the sheet over our mouths to muffle the sobs.'

'What were the differences between the children's homes in England and Australia?' I asked.

'Within two days of arriving at the orphanage I was scrubbing floors on my hands and knees. The people in charge didn't know who I was, they didn't seem to care where I came from. Back then I had lovely long hair that was plaited and fell down my back. I loved my hair. In that first week I was called on to the veranda and a woman told me to turn around. I was scared because I didn't like being singled out. She picked up my plait and tugged on it. Then I heard the scissors. "You can't have long hair," she said and then she hacked it off.'

It had been two hours since we began talking and her voice was beginning to show the strain. When she got up to leave she threw her arms around me and gave me a hug.

'We knew you'd come. I knew that some day, somebody would come and ask about us. What took you so long?'

I couldn't answer her. Where would I start?

'Why do you think you came to Australia?' I asked her.

She paused and thought for a moment.

'It must have been that nobody wanted us. I've never forgotten England. It's my home. It's my birthplace, but they just didn't want me.'

1

My family had been rooted in Nottingham for generations. My grandfather was an astute businessman who owned several houses in one of its leafier suburbs. My parents survived the Depression there, and then the uncomfortably close attentions of the German *Luftwaffe*. Bombs fell on the well-known football and Test cricket grounds on either side of Trent Bridge, not far away, but the house I was to grow up in was spared.

My two older sisters were already teenagers when I came into the world in 1944, but they were not old enough to be conscripted into the war effort. My father dealt with the casualties of the conflict as an ambulance driver.

My parents were very close. Their lives revolved around the family and each other, with the local church providing an added sense of rhythm and purpose. As committed Methodists who attended church regularly, their religion was woven into the fabric of their everyday existence. My father had sworn a pledge of abstinence, and nothing stronger than a well-brewed cup of tea ever passed his lips. Although his liver must have enjoyed excellent health, his lungs consumed at least a full packet of cigarettes a day.

From an early age, I found my parents' fellow Wesleyans a very bland collection of people: pleasant and easy-going, but unwilling to take a view. They lived in a genteel world where bodily functions didn't exist and the closest they came to intimacy was shaking hands in church. Nevertheless, I enjoyed Sunday school every week and put some pocket money in an envelope for the National Children's Home to help deprived children. I wrote long essays on the perils of drinking and gambling and the joys of a sober, honest life. What remained a mystery to me, however, was that while I was being told that drink was the source of most human misery, many neighbours seemed to enjoy themselves immensely in noisy and cheerful pubs like the Sherbrooke Arms at the end of our street. Many was the night I heard a raucous rendering of 'When Irish Eyes are Smiling' resounding from behind its profane doors, and wondered what devilry was going on inside. Was this what he meant when the minister said, 'Why must the devil always have the best tunes?'

My parents owned a large Edwardian terrace house on a long road near the river and the playing-fields. Since my grandfather had been well known in business circles it was natural, perhaps, that my father had inherited his outlook as a Conservative voter. It wouldn't have mattered, had we not been in a predominantly Labour constituency: everyone around us lived in rented accommodation or new council houses. When it was voting day I didn't dare go outside. All the other people had their red Labour posters on display, while our sitting-room window sported a large, provocative, blue rosette.

'Why aren't you going out?' my father asked me during one General Election.

It never occurred to him that I ran the risk of grievous bodily harm from my school friends! At times I felt isolated in our neighbourhood, but its saving grace was the presence of my wonderful grandmother. Selflessly devoted to her sense of public duty, Grandma had served the St John Ambulance Brigade in a senior role for many years. On Saturdays, I would accompany her as a cadet to local events at the skating-rink or football ground. It was expected that my uniform would be immaculately clean, my badges shining, my black shoes gleaming with polish and my white cap starched so fiercely that it almost cut your hand. Her high standards were softened by her calm temperament and warm, accepting smile. I adored her.

I attended good local schools and my parents were proud and pleased when I passed exams. They believed that hard work should be rewarded; their maxim was: There's no such word as can't. The word is: you can, you will. They drummed this into me day and night, especially my father. I was very shy, and quite happy at home reading books or going for a ride to the Embankment on my treasured Raleigh bicycle. In those days, my bike could be left outside the sweetshop for a few minutes without it being stolen.

I didn't want to mix a lot. I'd say, 'I don't want to go to that party.'

'You must go, and you will,' my father would say, in a firm but caring voice, followed by a smile and a wink.

In his book, there was no such thing as failure. You had to grasp every opportunity with a positive approach. However, I have never felt that I reached my full potential at school. As children growing up in the post-war period, we were expected to breathe life into other people's hopes and expectations for us. Yet I was too young to remember the war and I had no idea of the hardships earlier generations had endured.

Although our home enjoyed few modern amenities, it was comfortably furnished with large, dark oak sideboards, cushioned sofas and big open fires. In the evenings we'd listen to *The Archers* on the radio and when it finished my father would always say, 'It's up the wooden hill to bed, young girl.' Every year, as a family ritual, we'd all listen to the last night of the Proms and feel proud and patriotic.

I inhabited a secure and relatively restricted little world with my home, school, library and church all within ten minutes' walking distance. Occasionally, at weekends, I would venture beyond this familiar territory. My father's saloon car, a black Austin Seven, was his pride and joy. It provided one way of broadening my horizons, though many of our family outings ended with roadside repairs on Trent Bridge rather than the intended picnic in the countryside.

My parents believed strongly in helping those in less fortunate circumstances. My mother would not hesitate to knit five school jumpers for a local Catholic family whose mother was expecting another baby.

They both worked hard. Father was an engineer with the

Electricity Board, Mother ran her own haberdashery shop. She often let local families have considerable amounts of credit before their bills were eventually paid – long after they were due. My father was not amused.

Another key figure influencing my outlook, as a child and in later years, was George O'Gorman, a firm and trusted friend of my parents, and our family doctor. He often came to dinner on a Sunday. An Irishman and a Catholic, he would tease my parents about their more traditional, conservative views and habits. Dr O'Gorman had an open mind, an extroverted personality, and a wicked sense of humour. He helped contribute to the feeling I had that, all in all, my childhood was secure, ordinary and quite predictable, as if it rested on solid foundations.

When I was twelve years old, however, that ground began to shake. Gradually, I realized that my father seemed to be at home more and more when I returned from school in the afternoon. He would tell me he was tired, but none the less he'd always help me with my homework.

'I can't do it,' I'd say, knowing full well what the answer was going to be.

'No such word as can't.'

Soon he began to take whole days off work. It was not long before cancer was diagnosed.

One night, I heard my mother tell Dr O'Gorman that she would not allow my father to be admitted to hospital. 'No-one's taking him away from home,' she said.

'Well, Margaret can't stay here then,' replied Dr O'Gorman.

Within a few days, I was sent to stay with my mother's sister. As I left, my mother said, 'When you go to school in the morning and when you go to Aunty's at night, you mustn't call in here.'

'Why on earth not?' I asked. 'I want to pop in to see you.'

'You must get straight on the bus to Aunty's, you see.'

I didn't see. I didn't know what my mother was thinking of by sending me into exile at my aunt's house on the other side of Nottingham.

It was only much later that I realized my mother probably hoped that I would retain a memory of my father at his best. Or perhaps she simply felt unable to care for my father at home and cope with my reactions. However, this was not explained to me at the time. I was just aware of everyone telling me, 'Your dad is getting worse.' I didn't need anyone to tell me that. I knew he was very ill but I felt powerless to help and marooned by my family's good intentions.

Then one day I came home from school and Aunty looked very serious and solemn as she put her hands on my shoulders. In a soft voice, she said, 'You know what we said was going to happen? Well, I'm afraid it's happened.'

My mind struggled to find the right answer to this puzzle. 'What has? What's happened?' I asked.

'Your mother will ring you in half an hour.'

When the telephone rang, my mother said simply, 'Your daddy died this morning.'

'Oh dear,' I replied, 'what do we do now?'

'You can come home after the funeral.'

I wanted to go to my father's funeral but my mother had clearly decided against it. I felt strongly that it was wrong for me not to be there, but I did not urge Mother to let me go. She was busy trying to appear as if she was in control of her emotions, though her voice betrayed the true extent of her sadness and confusion. I guessed that she wanted to shield me from the grief, but instead it only made it more difficult for me to come to terms with my father's death.

Nobody told me when it was the day of my father's funeral. I must have gone to school as usual that day, because every morning my first thought when I woke up was: I have to go to school, but perhaps it's the day when the phone will ring and Mother will tell me she's ready and I can go back.

The call came two weeks later. Returning home was very strange. I went back to a mother who had lost her husband, her life partner, and along with him all their hopes and dreams. Her life changed completely; she dressed only in black and lilac and took little interest in her shop. It wasn't just his life which had been cut short, but hers as well. I didn't know how to help her and she didn't know how to comfort me, perhaps because we had not shared the ordeal of my father's last days together.

There was one question, however, that I felt compelled to ask.

'Mother,' I said, 'is Dad going to come home?'

My mother looked at me in amazement.

'What a strange question. What do you mean?'

'I want to know if Dad's coming home, because his hat and coat are still on the stand in the hall.'

'Don't be silly, dear, that's to let people think there's a man in the house. You know he's gone to heaven.'

That might have been part of the truth, but I was sure she felt, too, that as long as his hat and coat were still there, then so was he. For a while I was genuinely uncertain about whether my father had really died; after all, I had neither attended his funeral nor said goodbye.

Like most children, grief was a mystery to me. But I had learned three important lessons about death: when parents died you never talked about them any more; you kept their hat and coat in the hall, and you sang their favourite hymn – 'When I Survey the Wondrous Cross' – every Sunday at church.

Many, many things confused me. As the day of my parents' wedding anniversary approached, I said to one of my sisters, 'Do I have to go and buy a card for Mum now that Dad's died?'

'Don't be stupid,' she snapped. 'Of course you don't, there's nobody to celebrate it with.'

'There's me,' I said.

'She doesn't want to celebrate it with you!'

Over the next few months, the foundations continued to crumble. The sudden death of both Dr O'Gorman and my grandfather dealt two powerful blows to the body of our family.

Those next few teenage years remind me of the English weather on an unpredictable early-summer day: a weak sun shines fitfully, but only occasionally pierces the gloom of a dark sky, heavy with threatening clouds. Two generations of my family died during this time, including my mother and grandmother. Both of these losses shook me to the core.

I had made a child's assumption that because my parents had been a permanent feature of my early years, they would remain as reliable, consistent figures in the future. I had never had reason to see my parents as being on loan to me for a limited but unspecified period. The foundations which I had assumed to be built of solid rock crumbled beneath me like moist sand.

Shortly after my mother's funeral, one of her longstanding

customers innocently asked me in the street, 'How's your mother, Margaret?'

'Oh, she's fine,' I replied, hurrying on my way to avoid both embarrassment to her and the possibility that she might feel sorry for me.

I went with my sisters to help clear my family home before it was sold.

'Mum said that whatever you want here is yours,' they said. 'One day, you will have a place of your own – you've got to be practical. Anything can be stored.'

'I don't want anything,' I said.

'Perhaps you don't today, but later on you will.'

We were standing in the bedroom.

'Well, I'd like Mother's scarf,' I said, spotting it draped over the back of a chair. 'But that's all I can cope with now.'

Although I had attended my mother's funeral, it was simply too much for me to deal with my grandmother's death. I didn't appreciate this until I was in one of the funeral cars on my way to the church. When the car stopped, I dashed out and began running as fast as I could.

I ran down to the river, across the suspension bridge where I had spent so much of my childhood, and into our old street. I was drawn to places that had meant a lot to me – familiar places where we had all been happy together. There was too much grief, with too little time to absorb it all. When was it all going to stop? And why was it happening to me?

When I left school at sixteen after passing some of my examinations, I had no definite career plans. I really needed time and space to work out some answers. So many familiar faces and landmarks had disappeared that I had difficulty contemplating the fact that I had a future. The world seemed an absurd place, one where you couldn't count on much to last for very long. The only thing that offered me solace was classical music: it was a comforting reminder of times spent listening with my parents to concerts on the radio. There were occasions when these memories carried me through difficult times.

My father had instilled in me an aversion to a defeatist approach to any of life's problems. This seemed even more relevant after his death than during his life. On a material level my life was fairly comfortable. I had a variety of jobs which paid for occasional holidays abroad and a series of small cars, most as unreliable as my father's. With the passing of time and the healing support of close family and friends, I began to enjoy life again. I felt that I had laid the more painful times in my past to rest.

During my twenties, I felt settled and mature enough to decide upon a career in social work. There were several options to work as a trainee within the Children's Department of Nottingham City Council and later attend university for professional training.

The hours were long, but I felt totally committed to the people I was working with – whether they were children who'd had to leave home because they were abused, or parents who were unable to care for their children.

The Social Services Department in Nottinghamshire was a close-knit group. We'd work until late and then find a pub still open, talking shop and complaining about the decision-makers. Social work was different back then and I remember during the coal miners' strike we loaded up our cars and at nine o'clock at night we were still delivering bags of coal to the old and vulnerable.

By my late twenties, I was qualified, married to a fellow social worker, Mervyn Humphreys, and had a baby daughter. As the midwife put Rachel in my arms I looked at Mervyn and said, 'Please God, don't let me die until she's forty!'

'Whatever do you mean?' he asked.

'I don't want her to be lonely,' I said. 'I couldn't bear to think of her having nowhere to go at Christmas, or not receiving birthday cards from her mum and dad.'

'But our children will always have somebody,' Merv said.

'It's not that, Merv,' I said. 'It's not having your mum and dad . . .'

I was one of the first women to take maternity leave in the department, and returned to work with a very young baby. I was part of the new wave of women who were going to have children and continue with their careers.

I worked full time, which sometimes included weekends on emergency duties.

Mervyn and I devoted every spare minute to Rachel and then Ben, who was born in 1980. There was very little energy for anything else. Many people we knew were moving around the country for promotion, better jobs or more money, but Merv and I decided early on that we weren't going to move our kids from pillar to post and risk disrupting their education. We resolved to stay put in Nottingham.

In those far distant days, a few optimistic souls imagined that the new, all-purpose social services departments would herald a brave new world of exciting opportunities and extra resources. If some of these hopes proved to be illusions, it was certainly not due to a lack of effort on the part of my enthusiastic and dedicated colleagues.

Working with children and families had become perhaps the most important and largest area of social work. It was also, without doubt, the saddest. By the mid-eighties, I had a heavy workload of high-risk cases – children at severe risk of injury or grave neglect if allowed to stay with their families.

If I could help a family stay together, whatever it took, it was worth while; but sometimes there was little choice. There is no social worker who does not feel great sadness when children have to be moved permanently from their families. If we felt any other way, we would be less than human.

I remember having to take a new-born baby from her mother, a woman with severe learning difficulties, who I knew could not possibly have coped. It was the second time I had taken a child from her and it affected me deeply. I was driving away with a colleague holding the baby girl on the back seat of my car and I wondered, What will she think, years from now, about the decisions being made for her? What will she want to know about her mother and father? What will I tell her, if, in the future, she seeks me out and asks me why I took her away from her mother?

These are questions that every social worker asks themselves. This kind of intervention requires enormous compassion and skill because you are dealing with the most fundamental and important aspect of our well-being, our families.

In 1975, a change in the legislation meant that, for the first time, adopted adults had access to their birth certificates – and, in turn, a part of their identity that had been missing. It made me consider the importance of an individual's identity and of knowing how we define who we really are. It's an issue that hasn't been well researched.

I counselled many adults who had been adopted as children and now wished to take advantage of their new rights to information by obtaining their original birth certificates. They faced many new and difficult dilemmas. The most common is feeling torn between the need to find their roots and the fear that the search will upset their adoptive parents. This conflict can create an enormous level of anxiety which can dominate every waking hour.

Although some people avoid this problem by waiting until their adoptive parents have died before researching their family background, there is still nearly always an underlying fear of rejection. What if their birth parents find it difficult to deal with the past? What if they don't want to be reminded of it?

There were literally thousands of mothers and fathers in Britain who were affected – a large, silent group of people – and from a social-work perspective we had no knowledge of how they would respond to these new developments.

Nationally, there was a reluctance to fund adequate services to cope with these issues, and many social workers had to face the tasks without the necessary training or adjustments to their workload.

In 1984 I decided to establish a small project to explore this area. I thought it would be helpful to bring people together to talk about their experiences of adoption from their different perspectives. I wanted to find out what adoption had meant to them at different stages in their lives.

I put a small ad in the local paper, having no idea if anybody would respond, and eventually received a handful of replies – one from as far away as Surrey. Because it wasn't an 'official' department project, I had no funds and had to arrange meetings outside work hours.

My bosses at Nottinghamshire Social Services were quietly supportive but feared I was stepping into a minefield.

I called the service Triangle, since it was open to all the adult members of the adoption triangle: birth and adoptive parents, as well as adults who had been adopted as children.

We met every fortnight in an attic room in a building shared with other self-help organizations. The furniture was sparse but there were just enough chairs for the seven or eight members who attended the Thursday evening meetings. It was adequate, but cold in winter. However, at least it provided a forum: adoption was one of those vital issues like sex or death which seemed to be rarely discussed in a relaxed atmosphere. We'd sit there with our coats on, deep in debate, until the caretaker asked us politely to leave the building. 'I don't know what you talk about in here,' he used to mutter, 'but none of you seems to want to go home.' Sometimes the conversations would continue on the pavement, or in the pub if we finished reasonably early.

The group had been running for two years when, one winter night in 1986, something happened that was to turn my world completely upside down.

2

My home town boasts many attractive features, but the evening rush-hour traffic is not one of them. Nor, at the unfestive end of December, is the weather. As my car crept slowly across Trent Bridge, thunder rumbled overhead and lightning flashed across the dark sky. By the time I reached the city centre, rain was hammering against the windscreen and the wipers were finding it hard to cope.

I turned up the radio to catch the news headlines. 4 December 1986 was dominated by two major scandals. Admiral James Poindexter had just resigned as the American president's National Security Adviser, and Lieutenant-Colonel Oliver North, a member of the National Security Council staff, had been dismissed. President Reagan had been forced to admit that he had been involved in secret negotiations with Iran for eighteen months trying to free American hostages, and that he had authorized the transfer of 'small amounts' of arms to Tehran. It had also emerged that 'Ollie' North not only made a profit on the deal, but passed it on to the Contra rebels fighting the left-wing Sandinista government in Nicaragua when Congress cut off official US funds. Reagan pronounced: 'I was not fully informed of one of the activities undertaken in connection with this initiative.'

The second major news item concerned progress in the Spy-catcher trial. Sir Robert Armstrong, Britain's cabinet secretary, had apologized to an Australian court for unintentionally giving mis-leading evidence. He said that he had been 'economical with the truth'. Sir Robert was the Government's chief witness in the action to try to suppress publication of the memoirs of Peter Wright, the former MI5 officer. In a courtroom clash Mr Wright's lawyer demanded of him, 'Can any of your evidence be trusted?' It seemed the case was going badly for Her Majesty's Government.

I found myself shaking my head in disbelief. Government-sanctioned conspiracies and cover-ups were a long way removed from the everyday life of a forty-something wife, mother and social worker.

I turned off the news and listened to the wipers on the wind-screen. My mind drifted back to a letter that had been waiting for me when I got home from work. The envelope bore an Australian stamp which surprised me.

A few weeks earlier I'd received the first letter from Madeleine, a married mother in her forties who lived in Adelaide. She'd heard about the Triangle group from a friend of hers visiting Nottingham, and turned to me for help.

'I was four years old when I left England,' she wrote. 'I was living in a children's home because my parents were dead, and was put on a boat with other children and sent to Australia. I don't even know if my name or birthdate are right. All I know for certain is that I once lived in Nottingham.'

Although I sensed her desperation immediately, my first reaction was that this couldn't be right. Surely Madeleine had been adopted or had left these shores with a guardian. I couldn't see how it was possible for a four-year-old to have been sent off alone 12,000 miles across the world.

I wrote back to Madeleine saying that she must be mistaken.

Now a second letter had arrived and her swift reply was positive and definite. I quickly found myself accused of being arrogant and uncaring. Yes, Madeleine was sure about her facts. 'You don't forget things like that,' she wrote. 'I still have nightmares. I simply want to discover my roots.'

Madeleine had spent forty years in Australia and still felt she didn't belong. She had no sense of background or heritage. A key part of her identity had been left behind somewhere in Britain. Now she wanted to find it.

As I slipped her letter into my pocket, I was still sure Madeleine was mistaken, but this time I would complete some basic research before writing back to her. She believed it was the truth and deserved some answers.

Outside the rain had eased slightly as I found a parking spot outside the large Victorian house in Mansfield Road. I switched off the engine, grabbed my overcoat and made a dash for the doorway.

3

The chairs were arranged in a circle around an old wooden coffee-table. Few of them matched, and some had sagging seats, but the room was quite comfortable and what it lacked in heating was made up for by the warmth of the company.

Marie was talking as she spooned coffee into the mugs. A quiet woman of about fifty she had been adopted when she was young. She often spoke in short, apologetic sentences that tailed off, as if she could never quite believe that anybody was listening to her. Her eyes were downcast as she spoke now, fixed on what she was doing; she didn't have the slightest idea of the impact her words had on the group.

'All my life, I felt something was missing,' she said. 'I was brought up as an only child, left home, and trained as a nurse at a London hospital. Then, one day, out of the blue, I remembered I had a brother. The more I thought about it, the clearer it became to me that he was younger than me and his name was Harold.'

Every person in the group was entranced. Normally so quiet and reserved, Marie had told us more about herself in those few sentences than in the previous twelve months.

'What can you remember of your own childhood?' I asked gently, wanting to keep her talking.

'I know I was adopted somewhere in England, though not in Nottingham, when I was about ten years old. It's hard to explain, but I know my adoptive parents changed my Christian name to Marie.

'I lived with them in the South of England and when I eventually left home I went straight into nursing training. Nobody hid the fact I was adopted and I always wondered, and thought about, who I was.

'Then from somewhere – who knows where these things come from – I remembered I had a brother. Somewhere I had a brother.

'I didn't know where to start looking for him, but eventually I began trying to trace his birth certificate.' Marie paused and for a moment I feared that she wouldn't finish.

'I found it,' she whispered as if it came as a complete surprise to herself.

'His name was Harold and he was just eleven months younger than me. He hadn't been adopted so I thought that maybe he was still with our mum and dad.

'I put Harold's certificate in my bag and kept it there for ages. I often took it out and looked at it wondering, Where is he? Will I ever find him? Sometimes I used to run my finger over his name.'

'Did you ever try to trace him?' somebody asked.

Marie smiled sadly and nodded.

'For all I knew Harold could have lived around the corner from me. I had no idea where he was or how to find him. I turned to the Salvation Army which had arranged my adoption.

'I sent off a letter, unsure of what would happen. I expected them to write back, asking for more information – information I didn't have. In the meantime, I tried hard not to build up my hopes. A letter did arrive, but not from the Salvation Army. It was post-marked from Australia and when I opened it the first words were: "Dear Marie, I'm Harold Haig and I think I'm your brother." '

'That's amazing,' said someone.

'You must have been thrilled,' echoed another.

Marie's face told a different story. There was no sign of joy or a happy ending.

'Did you get to meet him?' asked a chorus of questioners.

Marie lowered her head and explained that Harold's letter had arrived almost twenty-five years ago, just as she was about to marry. As part of their honeymoon they were going to New Zealand to visit her husband's brother and decided to return home via Australia so she could meet Harold.

'It wasn't easy,' said Marie. 'We had nothing to fill in twenty-five years except a handful of letters. I arrived on the doorstep with my husband and, from first sight, I knew it was true. It was lovely to see Harold, my brother.

'But the visit was very brief. My husband and Harold were from different worlds. Harold was artistic and unconventional, my husband was very English and reserved. They didn't get on and we weren't there long before my husband decided we should leave.'

'Harold and I didn't write – not after a time, anyway. Perhaps my husband was jealous. Raising children and nursing took over and although we weren't in contact I thought about Harold a lot. And then one day in the Seventies, it was Christmas Eve, my husband answered a knock on our door and there stood Harold.

'I was shocked and thrilled at the same time, but again it was difficult. I wanted to talk to Harold, I wanted a brother, but there were tensions between Harold and my husband. They argued and Harold stormed back to Australia.

'Periodically I wrote to him, never sure if he got the letters, but I have always held out the hope that we'll meet again.'

Marie seemed exhausted and drained, sitting on the edge of an armchair and close to tears. I didn't want to press her but I couldn't let it rest.

'How exactly,' I asked, 'did Harold get to Australia?'

She shrugged. 'Somebody just sent him as a child.'

'Who sent him?'

'I don't know. He said somebody put him on a boat.'

'With your mother and father?'

'No. He went on his own.'

'This is bloody ridiculous,' somebody said, and several

conversations seemed to spark up at once as people shook their heads in disbelief and fired off more questions.

But I didn't join in; I didn't say a word. All I could think about was the letter from Madeleine in my overcoat pocket. It suddenly seemed far more significant and disturbing.

4

I had visited St Catherine's House dozens of times before. It was always the first step in any search for the relatives of adopted people who sought my help. Headquarters of the General Register Office, and a Mecca for genealogists, the building houses some 260 million records of births, marriages and deaths in England and Wales, indexed in 8,500 bulky volumes.

Three days after Madeleine's second letter arrived, I took the early train from Nottingham, to take advantage of the cheap return fare and make the most of a day's research in London.

A day spent at St Catherine's had never been my idea of fun. The journey took 100 mind-numbing minutes on British Rail, followed by a mad scramble on the London Underground in the middle of the early-morning rush hour. Then two short stops and up and out into the wind tunnel of a walk along Kingsway to the grey, bleak building commanding one of London's busiest junctions.

The building itself was not designed with the consumer in mind. This is a world of harsh electric lighting and poor ventilation, where the bureaucrat is king. In the summer, crowds of schoolchildren and American tourists are nearly suffocated as they attempt to assemble the branches of their family trees.

St Cath's is like a medium-sized library without the peace and quiet. There are up to two thousand visitors a day frantically searching through the indexes, a strange mixture of people, some of whom simply need a copy of their own birth certificate for administrative reasons, and others in the painful grip of a search for lost relatives. I can recognize the latter because their faces are so anxious and they lean low over the pages.

Eye strain, backache and sore arms are the occupational hazards of regular visitors who must wrestle with the large, cumbersome volumes stored in an endless series of metal racks. Every day brings drama and disappointment, but like some patron saint of lost souls, St Catherine rewards patience and diligence.

An orderly queue already snaked around the side of the building when I arrived. A man was selling roasted chestnuts near the entrance and the warmth of the burning coals and his smile contrasted totally with the bleak, grey surroundings. I caught sight of a newspaper headline – the Government had successfully applied for an injunction against *Spycatcher* and the British press was not at liberty to publish extracts.

Once inside, I crossed the lobby and quickly took my place among the rows of colour-coded volumes where I was hoping to find the registration of Madeleine's birth. With this, I could order her birth certificate which, in turn, would give me details of her birthplace, the names of her mother and father, their address and their occupations.

The volumes for the 1940s are arranged in quarters for each year, with surnames in alphabetical order. If Madeleine had given me the correct details, I might only have five volumes to search.

After looking through three, I found Madeleine's entry. She was right: she had been born in Nottingham. I breathed a sigh of relief as I completed the pink application form to order a copy of the full birth certificate.

There were about eight people in the queue to order certificates, each clutching their forms and their cash or cheques. The clerical staff behind the glass screens became irritated with a man who hadn't completed the form correctly and the queue became restless.

I felt my own search had had a positive start, but my confidence was tempered by the frustration of knowing that it would take three days before a copy of Madeleine's certificate would arrive in the post. Experience taught me not to be impatient. Discovery often comes in a series of sudden leaps forward punctuated by lengthy delays or complete halts. It was like driving a car for the first time, the results are quite unpredictable.

I knew that I would have to come back: Madeleine believed she was an orphan which meant that ultimately my search would take me to the bleak black records of death to discover when her parents had died.

The Australian High Commission is only a short walk from St Catherine's House on a landmark site at the corner of Aldwych and the Strand. I had no idea what I wanted really, but decided it wouldn't hurt to ask a few questions.

All week I'd tried to find any reasons why Madeleine and Harold might have been sent to Australia without their families. None of my colleagues could help. A few thought I was joking when I asked them and one looked wistfully at me and said, 'No, but I can think of one or two joyriders I'd happily nominate for a free passage.'

In truth, I still found it hard to believe myself. Perhaps they'd misunderstood what had happened, or had had a guardian caring for them. Maybe they were sent out to stay with relatives.

It was mid-afternoon and already the day had provided a look at all four seasons. Now it was raining and I dodged the puddles along the Strand, staying clear of the sheets of water thrown up by passing cars.

The colourful travel posters selling sunshine and tropical beaches seemed to mock rather than entice as I arrived at Australia House and walked past the visa section towards a young man who dealt with general enquiries. His Australian accent surprised me on such a typically English day.

'Hello. I wonder if you can help me. Is it possible for children to migrate to Australia without their parents?'

'Yes,' the official said, 'if the parents or guardian give their written consent, complete the necessary paperwork, and arrange for a close friend or relative in Australia to take responsibility for the child.'

'Well, do you have any records of children who were sent to Australia just after the war, in the late nineteen-forties, without their parents?'

'That was before my time,' the young man said. 'I'll have to ask upstairs.'

I stood back from the desk and he turned slightly away from me to telephone for advice.

Slowly I watched his demeanour change. It seemed that the enquiry wasn't exactly routine.

'Just another few minutes,' he said, dialling a new number. I began to feel uneasy. Maybe I'd asked the wrong question. Perhaps I didn't know what I was talking about.

Eventually he apologized and said, 'Someone is coming down to speak with you.'

Ten minutes later an older man appeared. His more authoritative air matched his formal blue suit. I was afraid that he was going to ask me far more questions than I would ask him. I had to think quickly and look confident despite my ignorance.

'My name is Margaret Humphreys. I'm a social worker from Nottingham. Do you hold the records for all the children who were sent to Australia in the nineteen forties and fifties?'

The man stiffened.

'I'm sorry,' he said. 'Those records are no longer held at Australia House. They were sent to Canberra several years ago.'

Although he might have been taken aback by my enquiry, I was absolutely stunned by his response. There was a moment when we both just stood there looking at each other. I couldn't gather my thoughts quickly enough to respond.

To break the silence, he repeated himself. 'The records of the children have been sent to Canberra.'

I knew that Canberra was the capital of Australia, but little more. 'Well,' I said, 'are there any records here in England?'

'I think that's the sort of enquiry that you should address to your own government, don't you?'

Long after he'd turned on his heels and left, I stood in the doorway trying to make sense of his answers. Outside, the rain had eased and been replaced by a crisp wind that tugged at the open umbrellas of commuters spilling out of offices.

I found a coffee house near the underground station and ordered a hot drink and a slice of cake. It was my first food since breakfast. My train was at 6.30 p.m., an hour away, and suddenly I felt desperately tired. My mind flitted from half-formed images of

Madeleine and Harold on a boat to the face of the Australia House official.

I was still confused nearly three hours later when I reached Nottingham and Mervyn picked me up from the station for the short drive home. He knew me too well to start asking questions. Instead, he told me about his day and what the kids were doing.

'And you?' he asked after a long silence.

'I found Madeleine's birth entry,' I said. 'But I wish she was in England. There's something more to this than I imagined. I need to ask her some difficult questions and I don't even know what she looks like.'

'Why don't you ask her to send a photograph?' he suggested. 'And when you get her certificate, you can send her a picture of the house where she was born.'

Rachel and Ben were pleased to see me, both talking at once and eager to have some attention. I listened to their pleas and chatter, fighting tiredness, and later disappeared upstairs for a warm bath, with medicinal gin and tonic close at hand.

What was it the Australia House official had said? 'The records of the children have been sent to Canberra.'

His openness had stunned me. I don't know if I touched a raw nerve or sent alarm bells jangling, but every time I closed my eyes I saw him again. It wasn't his tone of voice or attitude, it was simply the fact that, by his own admission, there had to be far more children involved than just Madeleine and Harold.

5

When Madeleine's birth certificate arrived I finally knew that she hadn't been formally adopted. On every birth certificate there is a column in which the word 'adopted' appears if applicable. No such word appeared on Madeleine's certificate. One of my theories had gone out the window. There was also no reference to her father, but at least I had her mother's full name and I returned to St Catherine's House to check the marriage records.

Sliding out the first green volume, I opened it on a desk and ran my finger down the names.

I had decided to check marriages over a twenty-year period. Madeleine's mother was called Vera, and I assumed that if she had married it would have been some time between her seventeenth and thirty-seventh birthdays. If she had remained single, of course, she could be much harder to find.

From a researcher's point of view, it would have been ideal if Vera had married someone with an exotic, unusual surname, never changed her address and had a child every year until the menopause. I would be facing a series of major headaches if she had married an infertile member of the Smith, Jones or Brown family.

The first task was to remove and replace about eighty volumes which covered the twenty years of marriages following Madeleine's birth. Each quarterly list of surnames had to be examined for any entries which might correspond to the name and other details which I had obtained from Madeleine's birth certificate. I wrote each likely entry in my notebook and then cross-checked against the relevant surname of the husband.

It was slow progress, but speed is less crucial than accuracy. At the end of the day my notebook contained five possible marriages; the assumption that Vera had married in the Midlands or the North of England reduced the figure to just two. I ordered both certificates.

In the week since I'd been to Australia House, I kept reminding myself of what the official had said when I asked whether records for children might be kept in England. 'I think that's the sort of enquiry you should address to your own government, don't you?'

Right, I thought, I'll do just that.

None of the social services departments or professional associations could help me, so finally I rang the Home Office and asked about the records of British children sent overseas in the forties. After being cut off twice and put on hold for an eternity, an information officer told me he had no idea what I was talking about.

There was little else I could do except wait for the marriage certificates to arrive and hope one of them would reveal a link with Madeleine.

Friday's post brought the answer. One certificate did indeed correspond to Vera's full name on Madeleine's birth certificate. There was, however, a major flaw.

Vera had married after Madeleine had been sent to Australia. I couldn't understand this. If Vera and Madeleine were mother and daughter, how had they become separated in this way? Why did Madeleine think she was an orphan? And who took her to the other side of the world?

Suddenly I had more questions than answers.

I wrote a carefully worded letter to Madeleine, aware that I was going to challenge her recollections. I still couldn't accept that a four-year-old could have been put on a boat and sent to Australia. Gently I told her that I'd found the marriage certificate of a woman who had the exact name of her own mother.

Her reply came within a fortnight.

'Look, I was sent to Australia because I was an orphan,' she wrote. 'My parents are dead, so how can my mother have married *after* I left Britain?'

This threw me into a state of confusion. Her version of events just didn't appear to add up. There had to be some reasonable explanation – but where? Had I got my facts wrong? Perhaps I'd just found the marriage of a woman who happened to have the same name as Madeleine's mother?

I decided to check the registration of deaths for the four years after Madeleine's birth, to see if somebody with that name had died. I found no trace of Vera.

By now, it was nearly a month since I'd received the marriage certificate and I was frustrated at feeling so near and yet so far from real progress. I decided to telephone the children's home near Nottingham which Madeleine remembered leaving to be sent to Australia.

'I'm a social worker, based in Nottingham, and I'm interested in finding out if you have the records of a woman I believe was in your care many years ago. I understand she left your care as a young child and went to Australia in the nineteen forties.'

'Sorry, but we no longer have the records for that period.'

'Perhaps you still have the admissions and discharge registers?' I persisted.

'No. There are no registers. I don't remember any children going to Australia.'

'Are you sure?'

'Listen, unless you have some authority, what business is it of yours?'

The conversation ended abruptly. It had been like talking to a brick wall.

Where to now? I knew Madeleine was a Catholic, so there should be a baptismal record. She'd been born in an area with two or three Catholic churches and I went to see the parish priest. After explaining my search, he understood Madeleine's need to find out about her mother and helped me look through the baptismal register for the relevant dates.

Quite quickly we found Madeleine's name. The dates and

addresses were all correct and there was one additional piece of information – the details of her godmother.

This, I knew, was a very important new link with Madeleine's past. Her godmother, Kathleen, wherever she might be, had to have seen Madeleine and held her as a child. She also had to have known Vera.

A week later, I took another day's leave and another early-morning train to St Catherine's House. I decided to change tactics and concentrate on finding Kathleen. After checking half a dozen marriage volumes covering two or three years, I found her marriage and cross-checked it against her husband's surname. Thankfully it was an unusual name with three Christian initials. This increased my chances of finding them.

Late that afternoon, I visited my local library which had a full set of telephone directories for the UK. I was prepared to look through all 106 of them, but found Kathleen's husband in the same district in which they'd married. The address was in a mining village near Doncaster but instead of a house it was a pub, The Lion and Unicorn.

Having found Kathleen, I was moving into a different area altogether. How and when did I approach this woman? Would she remember Madeleine and her mother? Would she know what had happened to them?

The issue was far too sensitive and personal to discuss on the telephone. I didn't know if Kathleen and Vera were still friends; or were in contact with each other. Whichever approach I took, I would have to be careful to make it discreet and confidential.

I waited until the middle of the week when I thought the pub might not be too crowded. Mervyn drove the car and we arrived in the early evening, shortly after seven, having map-read our way through the minor roads of Doncaster.

The Lion and Unicorn was at the end of a narrow lane and looked to me surprisingly drab and uninviting. We walked into the lounge and could see four men in the saloon bar playing darts. A woman on her own in this local pub would have raised everyone's eyebrows. Mervyn ordered a pint of bitter for himself and a grapefruit juice for me.

'You need to keep a clear head,' he said with a smile.

I was self-conscious about the fact that I was in a pub and not in someone's house. If Kathleen was here, I would be approaching her in public which is much harder. I might unwittingly embarrass her in front of others.

As the barmaid brought our drinks, Mervyn glanced at me. We were both thinking the same thing. She was the right age, probably in her late fifties, and spoke in a local accent. She had a very open face and laughed easily with her regulars. I half hoped one of them would call her by name.

Back behind the bar she joined a well-rounded man who I assumed was the landlord and might well be her husband. They both seemed relaxed in each other's company and laughed easily together.

A few minutes later, two middle-aged men walked into the bar and one sang out, 'Two pints of best bitter please, Kath.'

Mervyn looked at me and said, 'I think it's time for another drink.'

We moved and found two stools at the bar, waiting for the barmaid to be free. When she turned to us, I leaned closer and explained that I was a social worker. 'Can I talk to you about something private and personal that happened many years ago? It doesn't have to be here or now. Any time that suits you.'

I could see her cheeks flush and anxiety crease her forehead. Her voice was soft, almost conspiratorial. 'Oh no, not now. I can't talk now. But, if you wait, my husband will go into the other bar. I'll come and talk to you then.'

Merv and I sat near the bar and nursed our drinks. At every opportunity, as she cleared glasses or wiped trays, the barmaid would look across at me with an intensity that made me slightly anxious.

After almost an hour she joined us. Merv rose and left us alone.

Kathleen said quietly, 'I think I know why you're looking for me.'

This took me aback. She was only the godmother. How could she possibly know why I'd come?

'You are looking for me, aren't you?' she asked.

My whole rehearsed speech suddenly fell apart. I was expecting to spend a good half an hour explaining why I was trying to locate her friend of forty years ago.

When I mentioned Vera's name, Kath immediately said: 'No, it's not her, it's me you're looking for, isn't it?'

She stared at me intensely and finally said, in a voice that was almost a whisper: 'Are you my daughter?'

Her face crumpled as I told her, as gently as possible, that I was sorry, but I didn't know her daughter.

Kath lit a cigarette and fought to compose herself. Her voice shook as she explained that she and Vera had been good friends a long time ago. 'It was terrible then, you know, there was no help. It was an awful struggle. People looked down on you if you were an unmarried mother.'

Kath and Vera had both been single mothers. 'We wanted to keep our babies but it was just not possible. We did what we thought was best for them. I didn't see my baby or Vera after that.'

She faltered, not far from tears. 'I've never been able to tell my husband about my baby. I don't know what he'd say if he found out now.'

'It's all right, I understand,' I reassured her. 'Your secret is safe.'

For twenty minutes we talked, Kath smoking one cigarette after the other. She gave me the names of places where she and Vera had stayed together, and just before we parted she brightened a little.

'If you see Vera, tell her to come and see me. She had a lovely baby.'

It was late when we returned to Nottingham. Mervyn gave our babysitter a lift home and I went upstairs to check the children. They were both sound asleep. I tried to read in bed but could not manage more than a few pages of an uninspiring novel. I was asleep before Mervyn got home.

The most significant thing Kath had told me was that both their babies had been placed for adoption. Yet I knew in Madeleine's case this hadn't happened. It added a new sense of urgency to the search because I kept thinking to myself, Is Vera like Kath? Is she still waiting for her daughter to find her? Does she believe that Madeleine was adopted?

The next day, I used my lunch-break to check the telephone directories at the Central Library. Using the address from her marriage certificate as my starting point, I began looking for Vera.

Occasionally my prayers are answered. I discovered Vera's name, address and number in the very first directory I picked up. She was living in Harrogate. To be certain, I called the nearest library and discovered from the voters list that she was the only adult registered at her address. The telephone directory had been printed only four months ago.

Although I was getting closer, I felt uneasy. One of the major difficulties was distance. In the past when I'd traced parents, I always involved the adoptees as much as possible in their search. But Madeleine was in Australia. She wasn't taking this journey with me and I couldn't tell if she was ready for the news that her mother was still alive.

A few evenings later, she telephoned me at home.

'I'm coming to England for a holiday,' she said. 'Do you think you'll have some news for me about my family?'

'I hope so,' I replied, my tone as non-committal as I could manage. 'I've made some progress already.'

It was a brief conversation, just a few minutes long and it ended with Madeleine promising to keep in touch. As I put the phone down, I thought that she seemed to be a person who didn't give her trust easily and her voice, full of hesitancy, suggested fragility.

I looked at the photograph she'd sent me. She was small in stature and quite slim, almost like a little girl in adult's clothing; and I wondered whether the look in her eyes was sadness or resignation.

My professional training told me that I needed to find out more about Madeleine. I needed to know her strengths and weaknesses; her level of self-esteem; whether she had people around her to support her. Was she forgiving or did she harbour resentments?

Although I had my professional skills and experience to rely on, I felt isolated and exposed. In the past I had approached a birth mother or father on behalf of an adopted son or daughter. This was different from anything I'd done before.

I didn't know if Vera had given her baby to people she knew and trusted; or if she realized Madeleine had been sent to Australia.

My normal practice was to write an informal card, explaining that I was a professional social worker who was looking for a particular person about something that happened many years ago. I would give the child's birth date but not the full name and invite the person to telephone or write to me.

I had never just arrived on somebody's doorstep, but this case was different. If Vera was elderly and living on her own, I wanted to ask her about Madeleine in person.

It was almost a three-hour drive to Harrogate and I spent the time rehearsing what I'd say. I chose a weekend when I had plenty of time and left early so I could drive through the streets getting a feel for the area. Every piece of information could help.

I parked a little way from the house and sat for a long time, rehearsing the scene over and over. It was a Victorian house that had seen better days but the neighbourhood seemed friendly. Two children were kicking a white plastic ball on the road.

An elderly woman came out of the house with a dog, and I watched her disappear down the street and then return. She was in her seventies and moved slowly, obviously unsteady on her feet. I saw her go back into the house.

This is it, I thought, taking a deep breath as I got out of the car.

A light was shining through the stained glass of the front door and I heard the dog barking and footsteps in the passage.

The door swung open and the woman stood there and almost shouted, 'Yes, what do you want?' The voice seemed far too loud for such a tiny figure.

There was a brief moment when we both simply looked at each other. I was wondering whether to be formal or informal with her but didn't get the chance.

Before I could say a word, she said quietly, 'I know why you're here. You're here about my baby.'

We walked down the narrow passageway with the dog nipping at my ankles. 'Come into the kitchen, it's warmer,' she said. As I passed the living-room I noticed a bed, and assumed that she had trouble tackling the stairs.

She tried to make a cup of tea but her hands were shaking too much to fill the kettle. She let me take over as she needed to sit down. As I arranged the milk and sugar, I saw that Vera was still looking at me, waiting for confirmation that I'd come about her baby. I wanted to reassure her but first I needed to be certain of my facts.

'Vera, can you tell me when your baby was born?'

'Of course I can. How could I forget it?' she said, as she gave me the date of birth.

'And where was she born?'

'Of course I know that.'

Again the information matched.

Peering over my shoulder she said, 'Have you got her with you? Is she here? Has she been happy with her family? Have they looked after her? She's all right, isn't she?'

It was clear that Vera had no idea that Madeleine was in Australia. I didn't want to tell her. I had to deal with her anxiety. Her questions kept coming, and suddenly she began to sob. Her whole body was shaking.

For a long time I sat holding her hand and she told me about her life, especially the sad times.

'I tried hard to keep her but my baby was placed for adoption. I was working, trying to get money together, but I wasn't well after the birth. I just couldn't cope.'

Finally she asked, 'Well, what's happened to her? Where is she?'

I took a deep breath. 'I don't know all the answers. All I can tell you is that Madeleine seems happy, but she is desperate to find her family.'

'Did her new family treat her well? Did they love her?'

'I'm sorry, but it looks as if she wasn't adopted. For some reason which I don't understand, Madeleine went to Australia as a young girl where she lived in a children's home.'

Vera's whole body stiffened. Her lips narrowed and her knuckles grew white. She suddenly turned away from me and I saw her shoulders begin to shake. Her whole face was buried in a large white handkerchief.

'How could they?' she sobbed. 'How could they?'

6

After waiting more than forty years, Madeleine finally met her mother on a Saturday morning in January 1987. Although I'd brought them together and both needed the security of my presence, I couldn't intrude on such a private moment. I took Madeleine to her mother's house in Harrogate and then left them alone together while I found a quiet corner in another room.

There were countless emotions that mother and daughter had to work through. The experiences of a lifetime were distilled into a few days and hours. It was difficult to imagine how it felt for both of them. For Vera the joy at being reunited with Madeleine was tempered by an enormous sense of guilt. Even though Vera had little choice but to give her baby for adoption, and had played no part in her being sent to Australia, I knew it would be difficult for her not to accept the burden of responsibility for these decisions.

Seeing them together, I had mixed feelings. On the one hand, I felt enormous satisfaction at having helped achieve this reunion, but I also felt sadness. It was not what they'd found that touched me, but what I could see had been lost. Madeleine could never recover her childhood while Vera's faith had been shattered.

What would it be like for Madeleine going back to Australia, leaving her mother behind? Would she go back fulfilled, with a sense of identity and family, or confused and bewildered about her past?

Something wonderful had happened but it might only serve to remind Madeleine of everything that had been taken away from her. Until then, she simply hadn't known what she had missed both as a child and as an adult. She had always believed that she was an orphan. Some nameless, faceless person had told her that.

Somebody had sent her overseas and denied her even the most basic truths about herself. She had no foothold on the world; not even a birth certificate to tell her that she belonged to a family and a country.

Why had Madeleine been sent overseas? What could justify such an act? Why send a four-year-old from a children's home in England to another in Australia? What was the reason for all these lies?

The Australia House official had implied that many children had been involved when he mentioned that files were in Canberra. Indeed, Madeleine remembered travelling to Australia with other orphans.

When I explained all this to Merv, he was intrigued. He has a very analytical mind and cannot leave a question hanging unanswered. With very little prompting, he decided to see if Nottingham University library held any answers.

Meanwhile, I still had my full-time job with Nottinghamshire Social Services and the fortnightly meetings of the Triangle group.

Marie also wanted to find her mother but I knew that I couldn't start that search without Harold. Their relationship had to be resolved and I needed to know if both brother and sister would take the journey together. This meant talking to Harold face to face, not across the oceans.

'Is there any chance Harold would come to England?' I asked Marie at the next Triangle meeting.

'I don't know where he is,' she said. 'He's disappeared and is somewhere in the Northern Territory working with the Aborigines. He has a friend in Melbourne and I've been sending letters to her in the hope she can forward them to Harold.'

'I need to talk to him,' I explained. 'I would like to know if he also wants to find his mother.'

'Oh, he does, I'm sure he does. His letters used to talk about almost nothing else.'

Marie felt as though she'd abandoned Harold. She had promised when they last met, on that troubled Christmas Eve years earlier, that she would visit him in Australia. But as time passed, Harold began believing that Marie was never coming. He'd given up on her and his depression had deepened.

Eventually, one day he took all his paintings to the banks of the Yarra River in Melbourne and, one by one, threw them into the murky water, watching them float away. Then he packed a few possessions and disappeared.

'He thinks he'll never know me properly,' Marie said, looking from face to face in the circle of armchairs. 'He says that I'll never keep my promise to go out there. But wouldn't it be lovely – so lovely – to see him again?'

'So what's stopping you, for God's sake?' someone asked.

'I don't know,' she shrugged shyly.

'I know that if I had a brother in Australia, I'd be out there – with or without my husband,' someone else declared.

Marie smiled defensively. I could see the panic on her face.

'Does your husband have brothers and sisters?' somebody asked.

'Yes.'

'Does he see them?'

'Oh yes.'

'Why can't you be with your brother then? What's the difference?'

I suggested that Marie write a letter to Harold, care of his friend in Melbourne. 'Tell him I would like to meet him. Perhaps I can help him. But there's only one way to get him out of the desert, Marie. You have to go to Australia. He'll come out to see you.'

'I can't do that!' said Marie.

'Why not?' the group chorused.

'I can't afford it.'

'Look, life is short. You're miserable,' somebody said. 'You won't feel any better, and nor will Harold, until you see each other. Think, Marie – the only person Harold really wants to see is you!'

And then, before Marie had time to voice an objection, somebody declared: 'And if you can't find the money, we'll buy the ticket for you.'

I was astonished. There was so much warmth and care for each other and a clear appreciation of how important it was for Marie and Harold to meet again. For the first time since she'd joined the group, Marie went home from a session looking relieved. It was as if a huge burden had been lifted from her shoulders.

The more I thought about Harold Haig and the possibility that there were others like him, the more I realized that I needed time and money to investigate. I had talked to many social-work colleagues, all of whom reacted with disbelief. The Civil Servants at the Home Office and the Department of Health didn't seem to know what I was talking about.

I applied to the Winston Churchill Trust for a fellowship to solve this puzzle but was turned down. Finally, I decided to try the British Association of Social Workers and explained my problem.

'Look,' I told the press officer, 'I want to find out how many of these children were sent to Australia and what happened to them. The only way to do that is to go there.'

Even as I spoke, I thought the whole idea sounded fanciful. Who would believe that British children had been shipped to Australia without parents or guardians?

As I expected, the Association couldn't help in a direct way, but the press officer sat down with me and discussed the options. There weren't many. 'Have you thought about going to Fleet Street?' she asked. 'Even if only a few children were shipped out, it sounds awful.'

The very thought of dealing with journalists filled me with horror. Social workers and the media have an uneasy, sometimes downright hostile, relationship, and I worked to a strict code of professional ethics, especially regarding confidentiality. More to the point, I didn't know if I had a story for a newspaper to investigate.

'I have a few journalist contacts,' said the press officer. 'If you like, I can talk to them.'

'But I can't give them names – I can't break the confidences of clients,' I told her.

'Just talk to them in general terms. There's no harm in that. It's the only way.'

I left it in her hands and several days later she rang to say she'd had a tentative discussion with a journalist who worked for the *Observer*.

'She's the health correspondent and I've always trusted her. She wants to meet you.'

Annabel Ferriman was waiting for me when I arrived at the *Observer* offices near Blackfriars Bridge. We had a long talk, but it was clear that I had too few details to convince her editor that there was a possible story.

'There isn't enough,' Annabel said. 'I need more evidence than just two cases to get the paper interested.'

'How do I do that?' I asked.

'Well, what about placing an advertisement in some Australian newspapers asking people to come forward? If you get a positive response, then maybe we can do something.'

Annabel's suggestion was a good one. Regardless of how I got to Australia, I still had to find out if there were others like Harold and Madeleine.

On 10 January 1987, the first ad appeared in the *Melbourne Daily Sun*. It read:

> Would anyone who was sent as a child without parents to Australia from Britain in the 1940s and 1950s, and who was put into a children's home, please contact Margaret Humphreys, a British social worker, who would be interested in researching their past.

A fortnight later, during the morning scramble to get the children to school, the first letter arrived. I sat at the kitchen table, nervous about opening it.

> Dear Margaret,
> I'm writing in answer to your advert in the *Melbourne Daily Sun*. A friend of mine is one of these children sent out to Australia from London on the liner *Asturias* arriving at Sydney on the 13th March, 1950.
> To date I have gathered a lot of information about my friend including a newspaper photograph of these children when they

arrived in Australia. My friend's main reason for this letter is to see if it is possible to trace any of her relatives in England.

Since her arrival in Australia she has spent the greater part of her life in institutions and, as a result of this, she has been able to make few real friends.

If you can help please write to me and I'll pass it on.

During the next week a dozen more letters came through the door, and I grew more and more alarmed. I told Annabel that the response was confirming my worst fears. I couldn't say what was in the letters because of confidentiality, she simply had to trust me that the contents were very disturbing.

At the same time, Merv had managed to unearth some interesting information from the University library and the Public Record Office at Kew in London.

'They were known as child migration schemes,' he told me. 'And they involved most of the major charities. It's not just Australia. Children were sent to Canada, New Zealand and Rhodesia – most before the war but thousands afterwards as well.'

Merv showed me his notes.

Child migration had operated periodically since the seventeenth century. The first shipment involved 100 children sent to colonize Virginia in 1618. Most of them were the equivalent of today's street kids.

The schemes were also popular towards the end of the nineteenth century but, unfortunately, the references were brief and short on detail. We needed more. Merv suggested we look at the histories of several of the charities that appeared to be involved: Dr Barnardo's, the Catholic Church and an organization called the Fairbridge Society.

Annabel Ferriman came to see me in Nottingham and I showed her this background information and gave her a general summary of the letters from Australia. She went back to talk to her editors, and several days later she called me to say that the *Observer* had decided to send her to Australia to research the story.

'We can give you the air fare,' she said. 'We leave in a fortnight.'

Although I still had reservations about working with a journalist, at least I now had the chance to meet Harold and get answers to my questions. The problem was, of course, that Harold was somewhere in the bush and unlikely to break his self-imposed exile for a social worker from England.

I needed Marie. When she heard of my plans, she knew that the challenge had been issued. A week before I was due to leave, the Triangle group had another meeting in the attic room. Marie arrived, looking far more confident than I'd ever seen her.

'I've booked my annual leave,' she said. 'I've paid for my ticket. I'm going.'

7

The Australian Customs Department has an unusual ritual for overseas visitors. After the 747 had touched down, several uniformed men came aboard and began walking down the aisles with an aerosol spray-can in each hand. I coughed into my handkerchief as the fine mist of insect repellent, or some such poison, permeated the aircraft. I was told it was something to do with quarantine regulations, which made me feel as welcome as a dose of foot and mouth disease. I had visions of arriving at the baggage hall and watching my suitcases submerged in sheep dip before they'd allow me through.

It was early in the morning and the immigration hall was crowded. Somebody had sandpapered my eyes. I knew I looked frightful but I was too tired to care. But even lack of sleep could not diminish my first impressions of Sydney. Taking a taxi from the airport, we headed north, passing several golf courses with sprinklers spinning on the fairways. Slowly the red-tiled roofs and houses of suburbia gave way to terrace cottages which reminded me at times of Nottingham – except for the bougainvillaea growing in the gardens, and the beach towels draped from the window sills.

Our driver gave us a running commentary in fluent Australian. I was barely listening as we turned into William Street and first saw the skyscrapers. It reminded me of pictures I'd seen of New York, and Manhattan's impenetrable skyline. Regardless of how much I dislike large cities, I could not help admire such handiwork. There was something dynamic and exciting about it, the pulsing heart of the city.

There wasn't time to waste and I set about contacting people who had responded to the newspaper ad and arranging times when I could see them. Meanwhile, Annabel started her own investigations, calling charities and government departments which might shed some light on the child migration schemes.

Early next morning Annabel and I took a taxi to the nearby Paddington District and knocked on the door of a tall, smartly dressed woman in her forties who held out her hand in greeting.

Sandra Bennett explained how she had lived in the Nazareth Children's Home in Coleshill, near Birmingham, until she was sent to St Joseph's Orphanage at Rockhampton in Queensland when she was eleven years old.

'The culture shock could not have been greater,' she told me. 'In England, we were in a town. We saw people on our way to school; we could go out and buy Granny Smiths – five for a penny. But in Australia we were surrounded by scrub, bushland, the wild. There was just the orphanage in the middle of nowhere. Everything was self-contained. There was the school, the church and the convent. That was considered all that was necessary.'

Sandra sat on the edge of a chair with her hands in her lap, rarely raising her eyes. Now a nurse, she described the conditions of her childhood as 'like something out of Dickens'. 'We wore unbleached calico and ate peas and mince every day,' she said. 'We were allowed potatoes at Christmas. I used to steal roast potatoes from the convent. The nuns had better food.

'We slept in a huge dormitory with thirty-two people. The "wets" – those who wet their beds – slept on the outside and the rest on the inside. We had to clean up the wet beds first thing in the morning and then scrub the floors. We had to draw our own water from the pump, which was full of frogs and snakes. It would have been all right if you had a sense of adventure and had been prepared for it, but we didn't come from that sort of environment. Everything was absolutely and completely different.'

'Did you ever marry?' I asked.

'No. And I think that can be put down to a loveless upbringing. It made me unable to trust anybody.'

Sandra said that to compensate for her loneliness she would like to find out if she had any family remaining in Britain – though she thought that her mother was almost certainly dead. 'I know she was forty-four when she had me.'

'Not having a family makes you feel as if you don't belong to the human race,' she went on. 'I never told anyone about my past until I was forty. I would love to discover that I have a family. It would make me feel I was not alone in the world.'

As I listened, I found myself growing increasingly uncomfortable.

For the first time I was hearing about the conditions and experiences of these British children. Sandra was telling me far more than she could have imagined. For one thing, she remembered that she didn't come on her own. There were other children on the boat. She also recalled coming from an orphanage in the Midlands, which suggested that the local authorities must have organized, or at least known of, her departure.

My mind couldn't grasp this. It seemed totally unreal. I couldn't understand why anybody would send a child from one institution in England to another in Australia.

'Were any of you adopted or fostered?' I asked Sandra. 'Did you ever live with a family? Did anybody tell you why you were being sent to Australia? Did they ask you if you wanted to come? What did you know about Australia?'

Sandra shook her head. She had no answers. In truth, she hoped I would be able to provide them.

Before I said goodbye, I made a commitment to her that if she wanted me to find her family or investigate her background, I'd do this. I would piece together her past and try to give it a meaning.

Syd Stephenson was another who had answered the advertisement. He ran a lawnmower shop in Sydney and remembered being ten years old when he left a children's home in Birmingham and voyaged to Australia. He and his brother were sent to the Fairbridge Farm School, at Molong, near Orange, in western New South Wales.

Unlike Sandra, Syd remembered his childhood with a degree of fondness, calling Molong tough but fair, but he could not forgive

Britain for deserting him. Also unlike Sandra, he knew something about his family. His brother had gone back to Britain and to Manchester where they both remembered spending part of their childhood. He discovered their mother had died of cancer at the age of 54.

Syd didn't blame her for what had happened. She was a single mother trying to feed and clothe two boys. When she couldn't cope, she gave the boys to their father who placed them in the children's home.

'He didn't know we were going to be sent to Australia,' Syd told me. 'They did it without telling anybody. I'll never forgive them for that.'

While I continued the interviews, Annabel dug through newspaper archives and began collating a list of the various charities and agencies that had links with the child migration schemes. Some organizations no longer existed, or had been merged and renamed.

Finally she found somebody who might be able to explain the child migration schemes to us and invited me along to the interview.

Monsignor George Crennan was a former director of the Australian Federal Catholic Immigration Committee, who became involved with immigration schemes in 1949.

When we arrived at his office he immediately asked to see our credentials, and I gave him an introductory letter from the British Association of Social Workers (BASW).

Annabel began asking a series of questions. How many children were brought out to Australia? What was the reasoning? Have you kept in touch with these people? Did they come out with their parents' consent?

I could see Monsignor Crennan suddenly realize that this was no soft interview and that Annabel wasn't about to be fobbed off with waffle and hot air.

In general, the Monsignor said the child migration schemes were a legacy of poverty and overflowing children's homes in Britain. The opportunities for children were thought to be better in Australia.

Annabel explained that we'd talked to some of these migrants who didn't appreciate the 'opportunities' of which he spoke. They had described being very poorly treated and were now desperate to learn about their families.

Monsignor Crennan admitted that he had received enquiries from people trying to trace their families. He normally referred them to the Crusade of Rescue Agency, which had sent them out.

'Do you feel you have a responsibility towards these people?' Annabel asked him bluntly.

I was surprised at her directness but even more surprised at his answer.

'Most certainly not.'

'I'd like to put that to you again,' Annabel said, pen poised over her pad. 'Do you feel you have any responsibility for these people who were brought out here as young children?'

'Certainly not. I don't feel any responsibility for them at all. We didn't arrange for them to come. We were nominated by the Children's Department to find places for them. I have no information about them. On the whole, it was a positive experience for the children. I would venture to suggest that if these people had remained in England, they might not have made such progress. They would have become bell boys and other such things. It was eventually stopped because people felt it was wrong for a country to export its children. Now let me ask you: what kind of country is it that sends its children 12,000 miles away? You want to ask yourselves that.'

Thankfully, not all of the charities we approached felt this way. Annabel and I arranged to see Louise Voight, Executive Director of Barnardo's, Australia, who admitted quite openly that the child migration schemes had led to massive problems. 'These people lost touch with their roots, with their siblings, and their social milieux. There were many human tragedies.'

On my last afternoon in Sydney, I left the hotel and went looking for a place to sit and think by myself. I had no thoughts of sight-seeing; time was too precious, but there was one particular place I had to visit. I began walking through the Botanical Gardens, enjoying the sunshine. I didn't want to talk to anybody, or listen to tour guides, or write postcards. This was my time for peace and reflection.

I walked for a long while, until I came to a rise, and almost unexpectedly I found myself looking across Sydney harbour. My spirits immediately lifted. The Opera House, with its graceful sails, looked ready to break away from the shore and sweep up the harbour in the breeze. This was what I'd come to see. Whether it was the love of music instilled in me by my mother or simply an image from a long-forgotten postcard pinned to my kitchen wall, there was something that had made me want to see the Opera House.

I found my way to the forecourt and walked around it slowly, leaning on the railings above the lapping tide. Then I sat down on the steps and watched the Japanese tourists, laden with cameras, feeding the seagulls. Periodically, green-liveried ferries pulled away from Circular Quay, some of them heading for Manly, others for Mosman and Taronga Park Zoo or for Balmain further up the harbour.

Closing my eyes I imagined that I could hear the great operas and orchestras playing inside. For a while it made me forget. It wasn't long, but it was long enough.

Melbourne reminded me more of England. The parks and gardens were full of deciduous trees and, in places, the architecture was quite Victorian. Perhaps the city founders had been homesick and had sought to create a slice of the familiar in a distant corner of the Empire.

There were more people to see – in particular, Harold Haig who had come in from the wilderness to see Marie. In the meantime, I arranged to see George Wilkins, whose letter had arrived on the day I left England.

George agreed to pick us up from the Travelodge Hotel in Parkville.

'I'll bet George owns a motor bike and sidecar,' joked Annabel, as we waited in reception. 'Or a battered old Land Rover.'

A car pulled up outside.

'Don't look up now,' Annabel said, 'but a Rolls Royce has just arrived.'

I laughed at her. A man alighted and strode into the foyer. He walked straight towards me. 'Are you Margaret Humphreys?'

As Annabel and I climbed into the back of the Rolls, I couldn't look at her or I would have burst out laughing.

George, in his late forties, had become a self-made millionaire from a string of video shops. He was ten when he left Liverpool in 1950 and arrived at the Fairbridge Farm School of Molong, along with his younger brother and sister.

'At Fairbridge you were just a number. I felt there was no love or affection, no friendly arm on your shoulder.'

He was a bright boy and the first among his peers to be sent to the local high school in nearby Orange.

'I will always remember my first day at high school. The headmaster stood on the top of the steps, addressing the students and said, "Who is that boy without a uniform?" I was the only child without one because Fairbridge didn't think it necessary.

'If there were school excursions, like sporting events, the whole school used to go and we had to have maybe 2d for the bus. It was too far to walk. So I would go up to different school kids and say, "I need another ha'penny. I have a penny ha'penny," and sooner or later one would give me a ha'penny and ultimately I'd get a penny and go on until I got my 2d. I always got on that bus, but it wasn't easy.

'For lunch you would sometimes get one baked bean in a sandwich; or you'd have a mutton sandwich and the blowflies had attacked it and it would be full of maggots. But every day at recess I'd eat my lunch as I would be hungry, and the rest of the day there was nothing. I had to wait till I got back.'

After four years at high school, during which he slipped from near top of the class to the bottom, the man in charge at Fairbridge told George that he was going to be apprenticed to a local fitter and turner.

'He told me if I didn't take the job, I would owe Fairbridge two years' farm work because I'd been at high school,' George said. 'I offered to do the farm work, but he told me to remember my sister and if I didn't take this apprenticeship, he would make things difficult for her. That convinced me.'

George did a lot of different jobs over the next twenty-four years – very few of them fulfilling – and then at the age of forty he decided to go to university. He subsequently went into business and became a millionaire. But he refused to give Fairbridge any credit for his success. 'I feel I owe them nothing,' he told me. 'I had to do something to show that despite them I could win.'

George didn't know what had happened to his parents but he thought his sister, Rita, may have returned to the UK. He wanted to find out if he had a family.

During the next three days, I spoke to six more former child migrants. None of them had been sent to Australia to be adopted by families – all had grown up in institutions that did little to prepare them for life outside their walls.

A few consistent strands had begun to emerge from the stories. The former child migrants all told of leaving Britain on a boat and heading for a 'new start'. One woman, who had been in a children's home, described being summoned by the Mother Superior one evening, when she was ten years old.

'She was a strict lady and I thought I was going to be in for some kind of telling off. "Have a seat, my child," she said. Then she started talking about being sent to Australia. Blimey, I thought, have I been that bad to be sent away? Mother Superior said that I had been chosen, that it was a wonderful opportunity, not some kind of punishment. But that night in bed, I cried. I was so frightened of leaving the only home I'd ever had, of leaving my school friends, my sisters, of leaving my best friend Pearl and never seeing any of them again.'

Almost without exception, each person I interviewed in Melbourne insisted that their parents were dead because that's what they'd been told. They were orphans and most, like Madeleine, had no birth certificate or documentation; no letters or photographs. There was nothing to tie them to the past except distant memories.

Marie had arrived in Melbourne the day before me and Harold had met her at the airport.

He knew from Marie's letters that I was a British social worker who wanted to talk to him, but was totally underwhelmed by the prospect. 'Why does this bloody Margaret want to see me? I hope when she gets here she has a good holiday.'

I arranged to meet them for supper at the Travelodge. Marie was absolutely radiant – I could barely recognize her. For the first time I saw her strong, happy and relaxed instead of timid and shy.

Harold had a tremendous presence and when I saw him next to Marie, the physical similarities between them were striking.

That evening we spoke little about the past. It was simply wonderful seeing a brother and sister together after so many years. At times I felt as if I shouldn't be there. Harold and Marie were completely wrapped up in each other.

The next day, on a drive to the Dandenong Ranges, outside the city, I managed to see Harold alone. All morning he'd avoided me, disappearing for a cigarette whenever the conversation touched on a subject that made him feel uncomfortable.

As we walked through a beautiful garden, Harold pointed out the brilliantly coloured galahs that squawked in the trees. He told me that he had no recollection of his mother. He had no photograph or abiding memory to cling to, yet when he was a child, not a day passed when he didn't want to find his mother. Everything in his voice and body language told me that this was still the case.

Harold had married when he was in his early twenties and had three children, a boy and two girls. But not even fatherhood could melt the block of ice inside of him. Ever since his mid-twenties he'd suffered from severe depression.

'My wife, Barbara, was my first and only serious girlfriend. We lived in a flat for a while, and when we were expecting our first baby we bought a three-bedroom weatherboard house in a new housing estate about fifteen miles out of Melbourne. In those days this was akin almost to living in the bush. Trevor was born in 1961 and I was very proud and happy to have started my own family. Fiona, our first daughter, was born in 1965, and Cathie two years later.

'I don't think I was madly in love when I got married. I didn't understand what that word meant, and still have trouble with it now. It's as though this word, this feeling, belongs to other people, but not me. I'm not entitled to feel love.'

Harold started searching for his mother when he was about eighteen. He saw an advertisement in the newspaper – probably a detective agency – that said it could find people. The agency took his money but produced no positive results.

Then, in 1963, Marie found him through the Salvation Army.

'That visit wasn't very successful but it brought feelings and emotions to the surface that I had buried deeply, feelings about my parents, particularly my mother. These feelings had arisen when Trevor was born but I had kept them hidden. While I continued to control them when Fiona and Cathie were born, they kept bubbling away inside.

'I got very depressed and felt alone and empty.'

By 1968, Harold had three lovely children and a happy marriage. He was buying a house and working as a signwriter. To outsiders he may have looked a happy and contented man. Instead, he tried to kill himself. It was a cry for help.

'I thought about my mother a lot, but never talked about her. How can you talk about someone you have been told doesn't exist? It didn't make any sense to me.

'A psychiatrist put me on anti-depressant tablets. I took these and saw him for a while, and slowly they took away my depressions, and so I stopped, and stored up the tablets that he gave me.

'I was all right for a while, and then I started to get depressed again. I kept trying to fight it, thinking it would go away, but it just got worse. I was drinking a lot, trying to obliterate my feelings, but it just made me feel worse.

'The first time I tried to commit suicide I had done it away from home, this time I did it at home. I didn't want to be found in a motel somewhere. I had a few drinks and when Barbara went to bed, I started to drink more rapidly, and then I took the tablets I had stored up. I woke up, or became conscious, a few days later in hospital.'

Harold's marriage broke up in 1970, through no fault of his wife, and they were divorced the following year. He felt guilty about leaving Barbara and the children. He'd always vowed he would never do such a thing.

'I had no idea how to be a father, a dad, I felt so bad about this that I even stopped calling myself Dad when I talked to them. I didn't deserve to be known by that name,' Harold said.

'The only woman I have wanted to find, desperately wanted to find, the one I have always wanted to hold me, and hug me, is my mother. That emptiness has been with me all my life.

'I can't stand Mother's Day. Every year it's a constant reminder, like someone twisting a knife inside me. I always stay inside that day, with my blinds down, and never answer the phone. I've spent years looking at families from a distance, trying to understand what it would be like to be a part of one, my own. To have my own mum and dad.'

In all, Harold attempted suicide three times and became locked in a seemingly endless round of psychotherapy and medication.

He stumbled aimlessly from one crisis to another, with the only constants in his life being alcohol and a yearning to find his mother. The only way he could express himself emotionally was through his art but his paintings were full of disturbing, abstract images of pain and anguish.

Because of his past experiences of counselling, Harold was predisposed not to trust me or have any positive expectations.

I just felt that here was a man who was so lost and lonely, so bereft of feeling, that I had to do something for him.

'Can you take me to the children's home where you grew up?' I asked.

'What for? What good will it do?'

I tried to explain to him that I wasn't just in Australia because of Marie. If I was to search for their mother, both of them had to take the journey with me.

Harold was eleven years old when he arrived at St John's Boys' Home, in Canterbury, a comfortable middle-class suburb of Melbourne. He remembered being told by a welfare officer at Sussex County Council that he was going to live in a land where the sun was always shining and where he would ride to school on horseback. He left England in 1949 from a children's home in East Sussex. They let him keep his name, and packed him off to Australia with only an entry card to prove his existence. It was still the only record that he had of his youth.

The next day Harold took Marie, Annabel and myself to the Boys' Home. We walked along the corridors, into the church and the dormitories, with Harold telling me stories of his youth.

He explained how the large old building was used. The front of the ground floor housed the offices. At the back there was a large kitchen and dining-room on one side, and on the other, a large pantry which the boys would raid whenever possible.

'Joined on to this was the sewing room and laundry, and a large quadrangle. The upstairs was used for the younger children –

bedrooms, bathrooms and so on. The older boys – eleven years and over – had quarters next to the dining-room area. It was a large dormitory with a quadrangle in the middle. From floor to ceiling was half solid walls, and the rest covered by blinds. Great in the summer, a bit bloody cold in the winter.

'It wasn't meant to house migrant children, you know, but I was placed there with state wards from Melbourne.'

'Was life strict?' I asked.

'There were certain rules to be obeyed and if you broke these you were punished,' Harold said.

'What sort of punishment?'

'Strapped on the hands, maybe caned on the backside or given extra work to do. But the housemasters and the Revd Neale Molloy, who was in charge, were always fair. They never handed out punishment unless you had done something wrong; we were never treated brutally, or abused in any way.'

'What was a normal day like?' I asked.

'Regimented, like all institutions. Get up around six-thirty, wash, dress, make your bed, and do whatever inside job you were assigned to – like sweep the dormitory, get the breakfast ready, set tables, make lunches. We would then have a ten-minute service in the chapel, have breakfast, and go to school.

'Sunday mornings we would have Holy Communion after jobs and before breakfast. Two of the boys would be altar boys, so they'd prepare the bread, rolling out thick white slices and cutting them into squares, and prepare the wine. The stuff they used was cheap sherry, and after the service was over, and Mollie Molloy – as we called him – had departed, we would give it a go. Quite liberally sometimes. Perhaps that is where I got my love of red wine.' Harold laughed, but, like his words, this too was tinged with sadness.

'Were you lonely?' I asked.

'Let me put it this way: I had many friends, but I always felt alone. Not lonely. Alone. Particularly on visiting days.

'When I was sent away from England they told me my parents were dead; that I had no family; that I was an orphan. I felt cold and empty. I never talked about these feelings – who could I talk to? Talking about your feelings wasn't encouraged at St John's. Perhaps they felt we didn't have any, perhaps they did not see it as important – and how could I explain my feelings anyway? I didn't understand them.

'Love and affection are what you miss in institutions like St John's. They don't seem to exist. I can't remember anyone putting their arm around me, giving me a cuddle, showing me that they cared.'

Marie stayed close by Harold's side as he spoke, occasionally touching his shoulder.

When we reached the office of the orphanage I told him that I wanted to find out what records and documentation had been kept on him.

The officer in charge of the home invited us into his office and I asked to see the admissions register. He opened a large book on his desk and began flicking back through the pages. Harold's name was there, along with the date he arrived and the name of a Colonel Hale from Hove in East Sussex, who had authorized his admission. Harold thought this might be his godfather or a relative.

That single line of hand-writing was all they could show us, despite the fact that Harold had spent five years at the home.

By the time I left Melbourne I had notes on a dozen interviews in my battered briefcase. I still didn't have any real official confirmation that the child migrants had been sent to Australia with the approval or knowledge of the Australian or British governments. Annabel, too, realized that she needed more evidence before she could turn shocking personal stories into an issue that deserved wider public attention.

The Australia House official in London had told me that all the records for children sent unaccompanied to Australia were now held in Canberra. That was our next stop.

Australia's capital is like a lego city. Custom-built, halfway between Sydney and Melbourne, the streets are well planned and inhabited by the public servants who run the city, many of whom disappear every weekend and leave a skeleton population behind.

Annabel and I found the Immigration Department by the colour of its green roof. Once inside, we were directed to a large library which housed the archives.

'Do you have any material on child migrants arriving here from England without their parents?' I asked.

The staff were helpful but generally could find few references that might apply. We had a similar problem when we wanted to find the ships' manifestos to see if Harold's name appeared.

'Are there any records of individual children?' I asked.

'I'm sorry,' said the senior archivist, 'I don't understand.'

I explained what I'd been told at Australia House in London. The archivist shook his head.

'If that material does exist, it would be handled by the individual state archives.'

Finally, after trying various routes with little success, we were allowed access to packages of photographs kept under the category of 'British Migrants Arriving in Australia'. These pictures were mainly of adults and families – the ten-pound Poms – who were given assisted passage to Australia after the Second World War.

But among the faded black-and-white prints, there were pictures of children coming down gangplanks, clutching suitcases and blinking in the bright sunshine. Some of them looked no more than four or five years old.

As Annabel ordered several prints to accompany her articles, I stayed at the desk, staring at the grainy images of boys and girls with bright-eyed, hopeful faces.

8

I had never spent such a long time away from home. I missed Merv, Ben and Rachel terribly, but my joyful home-coming was tempered by the knowledge that I had thirteen or so new cases and very few answers.

I'd made a commitment to this small group of people and I had to keep my promise to discover their family histories, the reasons why they were migrated, and if they had any surviving relatives in Britain.

Just how I was going to manage this while holding down a full-time job as a social worker with the Social Services Department, was another big question mark. I'd taken annual leave to go to Australia. It was considered a personal trip. Although I had informed my immediate bosses, I couldn't expect them to give me any time off. I would have to use more of my precious leave to visit St Catherine's House.

Some colleagues didn't seem particularly interested in what I'd uncovered. That was understandable, they were up to their eyes in their own day-to-day problems – social workers are operating at the edge most of the time and have very little left for anything else. I found myself closing off from them and being torn between people who needed my help at home and those who needed it in Australia.

In the meantime, Annabel continued researching her articles, although publication was delayed when Margaret Thatcher announced a General Election for June.

Within days of returning home, I began to realize that some of the information given to me by the migrants during interviews in Australia wasn't accurate. Time and again, the most basic search for birth certificates drew a blank. Surely, I thought, they must know when they were born?

I went through my notebooks, wondering what I was doing wrong. I checked and rechecked names and spellings. Still nothing. And then, on the train coming home from St Catherine's one evening, I suddenly realized that these people had absolutely no evidence of when they were born, apart from their own childhood recollections.

'Perhaps they don't know,' I thought out loud. 'Perhaps they're celebrating the wrong date.'

If I hadn't been on the late train, I would have immediately turned around and gone back to London and started again. The next morning I was on the six-thirty train from Nottingham and I started checking five years each side of the date they'd given me. Slowly I started to find one after the other, in unexpected quarters, different years and puzzling districts.

One man who thought he'd been born in London was, in fact, born in Newcastle. Another woman was three years younger than she thought and with a slightly different spelling of her surname.

While I tackled the practical side of the searches, Merv had become fascinated by the official reasoning and logic behind the child migration schemes. He wanted to understand the guiding principles and where the idea had originated. He has an enquiring mind, not easily satisfied until every scrap of evidence, however small, has been unearthed and pieced together.

We needed to go forward on both these fronts, because many of the migrants themselves had no idea why they'd been sent away from Britain.

Merv registered at Nottingham University to do a doctorate thesis in the history of child migration, knowing it would give him greater access to archive material. He travelled to London and Oxford to search through public records and libraries.

He returned home one evening and showed me a faded newspaper advertisement he had found in the *Illustrated London News* of 13 November 1954. It showed a cartoon of a young boy standing alone on a grimy cobblestone street, looking up at a vision of Australia with young children playing in the sunshine. The caption read:

> Left behind! His friends have gone.
> Will YOU help him to join them? It costs £30 – a Christmas
> gift that lasts a lifetime!

The advertisement was for the Fairbridge Society and was endorsed by the society's President, the Duke of Gloucester.

By now Merv had discovered that the child migration schemes involved virtually all the major child care agencies and charities in the UK – Dr Barnardo's, the National Children's Home, the Children's Society, the Fairbridge Society, the Salvation Army, Quarrier Homes – and a variety of social welfare agencies operating under the umbrellas of the Catholic Church, the Church of England, the Presbyterian Church and the Church of Scotland. Other groups were involved in a more limited way, like the NSPCC, selecting and referring children to the major agencies.

The National Children's Home! I thought. How bloody ironic – I used to give them half my pocket money every Sunday!

Between 1900 and the Depression of the 1930s, children were primarily sent to Canada, but after the Second World War the charities and agencies began to concentrate on Australia and, to a much lesser extent, Rhodesia and New Zealand. They were joined by a large number of small organizations formed specifically to promote child migration.

Merv had looked at the histories of several of the charities.

'These people enjoy patting themselves on the back,' he said, 'they're proud of what they do. They don't withhold information.'

He was right, of course. When he began collecting back-dated annual reports and brochures, particularly from the 1940s, he found glowing reports of child migration schemes. Children from Britain and Ireland were being 'rescued' from difficult conditions for the greater good of themselves and the Empire.

The reasoning was simple enough. As victims of poverty,

illegitimacy or broken homes, these children were regarded as 'deprived' and considered a burden on society. Similarly, they would grow up to be thieves and hooligans and probably finish up in jail. Already this urban flotsam was filling orphanages and poor houses – taxing the charities, religious orders and government welfare agencies which cared for them. In the last century, local authorities found it was costing them £12 a year to support a child in a parish workhouse, whereas for a single payment of £15 they could send them overseas and be absolved of any further financial responsibility.

Britain's cities, especially London, were overcrowded with poverty-stricken children who might be a danger to society. The colonies, however, had wide-open spaces crying out for more hands to work them. Two birds could be killed with one stone. Children could be rescued from vice and deprivation and be sent to populate the Empire and its dominions, where fresh air, hard work and religious instruction would make them fine, upstanding citizens. On the face of it, it must have appeared quite a good idea.

'But at least it stopped a long time ago,' I said. 'There can't be that many child migrants.'

'You won't believe this, Margaret,' said Merv, shaking his head. 'The last children went out in 1967!'

I looked at him in total disbelief. Twenty years ago! It didn't seem credible. The Sixties were a time of plenty in Britain. The economy was booming and there was no longer post-war poverty or terrible economic hardship. Why on earth would there be even a misconceived need to send a child abroad?

Annabel Ferriman was also shocked by the news. She'd been calling me several times a week, keeping me informed of her investigations. The *Observer* planned to run its story over two weeks in July.

For my part, I was growing increasingly worried about the mountain of work still to be done. I didn't have the time or the money to carry out searches quickly enough. Every day saw the possibility that death would intervene and keep families apart for ever.

David Spicer, a barrister for Nottinghamshire County Council, had been a colleague and friend of mine for many years. He knew I'd been to Australia and felt strongly about children's rights.

Although normally very calm, as I spoke to him I could see his anger rising. His sense of injustice is strong. 'What can you do for these people?' he asked.

'I've met some who think they're orphans but their parents may well be still alive.'

'How can we help them?'

In sheer relief, I let it all flood out. Here was somebody who believed me. More importantly, he believed the migrants' stories.

'They can't be rejected again,' I said. 'There must be some way we can help them understand their past and repair some of the damage. We can't have the articles go out and not have something in place for these people. Even if only a dozen more cases come forward, it will be a dozen too many.'

David thought for a moment, standing at the window of his County Hall office, looking out over the River Trent. 'This is going to upset a lot of people. I'm not just talking about the charities. The average man or woman in the street is going to be outraged that we could have done this to our children. I think you should declare a charitable trust straightaway.'

'What do I have to do exactly?' I asked.

'Just tell me what you aim to do and exactly how you'd spend any donations. I'll draw up a trust deed, and you'll have to appoint trustees.'

'Can it be completed before the *Observer* articles?' I asked.

'It will have to be.'

Over the next few days we met several times to prepare the trust deed and when it was almost completed David said, 'OK, what are you going to call this charity?'

'I don't like the word charity,' I said. 'Some of these people have already suffered at the hands of charity. We need a word like "trust". And there are lots of children's charities but this one is about adults; adults whose childhood was taken from them.'

David and I thought in silence, occasionally suggesting a name.

'I've got it!' I announced. 'We'll call it the Child Migrants Trust.'

Only days before the *Observer* articles went out, the Trust was registered. David agreed to be one trustee and the other was Philip Bean, a senior lecturer in criminology at Nottingham University. Philip had spent time lecturing in Australia, and he and David had co-operated before on a project about homeless teenagers.

The three of us started to organize ourselves, often meeting at a pub in the evening.

On Sunday, 21 July, I woke early, got dressed and walked around the corner to my local newsagent. Loose change jangled in my purse. Before I reached the door, I noticed a poster behind a metal frame propped up against the shop window. There was an *Observer* banner and beneath it a large black-and-white photograph of a group of young children, with the girls in cotton dresses. The hairstyles and clothes told me they were children of my generation.

I couldn't open the newspaper until I got home. I carried it under my arm until I was inside the house and then spread it over the kitchen table. There was a small article on the front page pointing to a two-page feature inside which bore the headline, 'Lost Children of the Empire'.

'In 1954,' Annabel wrote, 'thirty-eight orphaned and abandoned children set sail on the *SS Esperance Bay* from Southampton to Sydney, Australia. No-one had asked them whether they wanted to go; they had simply been told they were going. No-one had told them why they were going; they were assured they would love it when they got there. No-one had told them what they would find in Australia; they were just shown pictures of kangaroos, and Aborigines with painted faces and long spears.

'These child migrants were wrenched from all that was familiar, all that was homely, all that they knew, to be sent half a world away to fill the homes and orphanages of the British Commonwealth.

'Although they did not realize it, they were the tail end of Britain's child migration movement. For a century or more, Dr Barnardo's, the Salvation Army and other Christian organizations had been sending children, plucked from poverty and deprivation, to children's homes abroad . . .

'Unlike previous generations who are no longer alive to tell the tale, the children who were sent after the Second World War are still very much with us and have chilling tales to tell. Many are bitter that Britain could have pursued such a callous policy so late into the twentieth century . . .

'Unlike the convicts who formed the first white populations in

Australia, these children had committed no crime beyond being born without hope. For this, their reward was exile.'

It was a powerful article – far more aggressive and accusatory than I had envisaged. Annabel had obviously put a lot of thought into it. At the end, she announced the creation of the Child Migrants Trust.

The following morning when I arrived at my office at nine o'clock, I had no idea what awaited me. There were press photographers on the pavement, and journalists had been calling all morning, jamming the switchboard. By mid-morning the calls were also coming from Australia, and County Hall had taken more than a hundred enquiries. It seemed that every newspaper, radio and TV station in the country wanted to interview me.

Fortunately, I had pre-warned the Director of Social Services about the articles, but the overwhelming reaction was still embarrassing. I had my own work to do but this was proving to be impossible.

To minimize disruption to the department, I had to get journalists away from my office. I went home and the circus simply followed. With only one telephone, it was chaos. Some journalists took hours to get through, growing angry and frustrated, and others simply arrived on the doorstep.

Annabel, too, seemed to be under intense pressure. She had identified many of the agencies that had sent children abroad, not only the Christian organizations but also the local authorities. A follow-up story was planned for the next issue and had been trailed in the first feature. According to Annabel, Barnardo's had contacted the *Observer*, asking to see an advance copy. The editor refused.

It was obvious that the charities were besieged by the media. The *Observer*'s revelations must have hit them like a bombshell. After all these years, out of the blue, their past practices had been exposed. They must have been thinking, Why now?

During the following week the national newspapers were full of letters and comments. These were a mixture of outraged responses from readers and attempts by the charities to defend themselves.

Stephen Carden, Chairman of the Fairbridge Society, wrote in the *Observer*:

'If an advertisement of the kind shown in the article is put in a

Sydney newspaper by a social worker responses are likely to be mainly from malcontents. The article has been based on those responses completely ignoring the fact that the vast majority of the 2,500 children sent to Australia by this society will be eternally grateful for the opportunity they were given . . .

'As regards the allegations made about life at the farm school at Molong, it is of course impossible to confirm or deny them after all these years. It is, however, fair to point out that there is a danger of such occurrences in any institution for young people, and the vast majority of those who were brought up there have made no such allegations . . .'

Meanwhile, Australian correspondents in London had wired the story to their home newspapers and the *Observer* article was republished in full by papers in Sydney and Melbourne. Within a week mail was being delivered by the sackload, much of it postmarked from Australia.

The tone was set in the first few words of each:

'I am an orphan, could you please help me find my mother. I don't really know where to start, I'm so nervous. I don't have a birth certificate. I don't have anything . . .'

Another began: 'I'm shaking, shaking as I write this letter. This is the first time I've allowed myself to think about some of these things again . . .

'I'm so angry with the agency that sent me out. I've written to them from the age of twenty and got no satisfactory reply, ever. They've just swept me under the carpet. And that hurts. I mean, they haven't told me anything. If I ever get to England, I would go to them and say, "Look what you've done to me." '

I struggled to read and answer all these letters, but it was becoming more and more difficult to find the time. It was clear that the Child Migrants Trust was a full-time concern.

Not everybody in my department understood the issue. The Director of Nottinghamshire Social Services said it was all very fascinating but it happened a long time ago and didn't really concern Nottinghamshire.

However, the politicians felt differently. Having read the articles, Joan Taylor, the Chairperson of the Social Services Committee rang me.

'It's dreadful, absolutely dreadful. And to think you used your annual leave to investigate this. It's not right. Write me a report for the committee about your Australian trip.'

Seven weeks later I delivered my first report to Joan and her committee. It was rare for a social worker to address the politicians directly and I was nervous about getting the message across.

I told them of the desperate need for a professional social-work service to help the former child migrants.

'Many of them have struggled for several decades to have some information concerning their backgrounds, and the reasons why they were sent across the world. Their letters reflect both a desperation and a despondency.'

When I finished, Joan Taylor asked me what I wanted to do for these people.

'I need time,' I said.

'How long?'

'I don't know. What about a year?'

'What about two?'

'Oh,' I said, very surprised.

'Would you like a secondment? Would you like to just go away and get on with it?'

'Yes, I'd like that very much.'

'I'll approach the committee,' replied Joan.

At the end of November, I cleared my desk and left the department where I'd worked for fifteen years. At home I'd turned one of the bedrooms into a small office. The following morning after I packed the children off to school and Mervyn went to work, I sat in an empty house and wondered, Is this it?

I had no typewriter and the only telephone was in the hall. There were sacks of mail waiting to be answered. I made a cup of coffee and sat down staring at the desk and filing cabinet. Where do I start? I wondered.

My salary and some travel expenses were being paid and the *Observer* article had generated several hundred pounds in donations, but this wouldn't last long when I started trying to trace the families of child migrants.

I also knew that at some stage I would have to approach each of the charities involved with child migration and try to establish the full extent of their role. I hoped they would accept their responsibilities; that they would help the trust both financially and by giving us access to their archives.

The latter issue was vital. I knew the charities and orphanages must have kept files on individual children. And these would contain precious details about who placed the child in care; the names and addresses of parents or guardians, birthdates and correspondence.

If I could get access to these files, the task of finding families and filling in the missing years would be far easier. Time was my enemy.

The initial signs, however, weren't promising. When I had first asked after Madeleine's files, the children's home had insisted the information no longer existed; and, similarly, the major charities had shown no interest in opening up their archives to someone who had revealed their past activities in such an unfavourable light.

I had also interviewed several child migrants who had requested access to their files and either this had been denied or they had been told such information no longer existed or had never been kept.

My standing with the charities was made very clear when I was invited to speak at a professional conference in London on adoption issues attended by social workers from charities and local authorities. I could feel the frost when I arrived. You always know that your views are considered 'different' at a conference when you break for coffee and finish up standing on your own. I knew I was being ostracized because no-one, but no-one, would come any-where near me.

The problem was that I'd broken a taboo and spoken out against the charities. Everybody at that conference either knew people who were working for the agencies or were themselves working for them – for Barnardo's, the Church of England, or whoever. I was criticizing their employers, or potential employers, and it wouldn't advance their career prospects to be seen talking to the likes of me.

As I was getting ready to leave a woman came up to me who apparently worked for a Catholic charity.

'So you're Margaret Humphreys, are you? You're *the* Margaret Humphreys?'

'Yes, that's right,' I said. 'There's only one of me.'

She said: 'Well, I thought I would come up to you before I leave this conference and say something to your face. I want you to know that because of you, Monsignor Crennan in Sydney has been very ill. Those dreadful articles in the *Observer* weren't truthful and they upset him deeply. He's now a very sad man and it's all down to you.'

She was obviously upset and I didn't want to make things worse. I simply told her that I too knew a lot of sad people in Australia.

Although daily media interest in the Child Migrants Trust slowly waned, I found myself fielding calls from documentary – and film – makers who sensed an opportunity to bring some real-life drama to the screen.

I was still wary of any publicity, and concerned that the issue was handled sensitively. There were benefits in publicizing the Trust but not at the expense of hurting the child migrants.

On the other hand, a deep-searching documentary would give them a chance to tell their stories for the first time.

I finally settled on Joanna Mack and Domino Films. Joanna was well known for producing a series called *Breadline Britain*, which gave moving, first-hand accounts of living in poverty in Britain. She had recently started to work as an independent producer, and she struck me as a quiet, thoughtful person who listened attentively to others. Her calm professionalism reassured me.

Joanna and I both agreed that I had to stay close to the production to ensure that the child migrants were given professional counselling and were ready to be interviewed. This meant that Domino Films would pay for me to visit Australia again, as well as Canada and Zimbabwe.

However, we set strict boundaries. Joanna would work on the documentary and I would help her, but Domino Films would not be involved in my own work. My clients were off-limits unless they themselves chose otherwise.

I planned to leave after the New Year and spend a fortnight in Australia but before then I had to find some way of dealing with the sacks of mail arriving each week. The workload was impossible.

Thankfully, it was made a little easier by Yvonne Barlow, a friend who had also been a member of Triangle. She offered to help with the searches at St Catherine's House.

Yvonne knew all about a person's need to discover their roots.

In 1977, while holding her new-born daughter, Lucy, in her arms, Yvonne had suddenly realized that she herself had been adopted. Not surprisingly, it came as an enormous shock.

Because of her own search, she knew her way around St Catherine's House. She also had the patience and total commitment that it took to plough through volume after volume. Yet, from my point of view, she had two even more important qualities – I could trust her and she didn't mind taking IOUs.

With someone to mind the office, I felt happier about going away. I even managed to enjoy the lead-up to Christmas, opening the cards that arrived from child migrants in Australia.

It was so cold on Christmas Eve that we had a log fire blazing in the hall. Rachel and Ben had decorated the tree; the presents were wrapped, and the drinks were flowing. At about 6.00 p.m. there was a knock at the front door.

I opened it and found a half-frozen man standing on the doorstep, holding a torn newspaper cutting in his fingers.

'Are you Margaret Humphreys?' he said in a broad Australian accent.

I owned up immediately.

'You the person in this article?'

'Yes.' I nodded, wondering where on earth this man had come from.

'Well, I just got off a plane from Australia and I haven't been back here since I was five,' he said through chattering teeth. 'I've been all over trying to find you. Here's my birth certificate – I want you to find my mum.'

I looked at him, barely considering it credible and said, 'How about we leave it till Boxing Day?'

9

I had another visitor that Christmas. Harold Haig had flown to England to see Marie and also to work with me in the search for his mother. Full of excitement and fear, he couldn't sit still in Australia.

On a bitterly cold day early in January 1988, I took him on his first trip to St Catherine's House. We caught the 6.00 a.m. train from Nottingham and with us were Yvonne and Paul Harrison, the Australian who'd arrived on my doorstep. On the train, I opened my briefcase and, over coffee from the buffet car, explained how St Catherine's worked and what we had to do that day.

In Harold's case, we had to find a record of the birth of his mother, Elizabeth Ellen Johnson, somewhere between 1904 and 1921. Marie was born in 1937 and I reasoned that their mother would have been no younger than sixteen and more probably eighteen at the time. Similarly, I thought she was unlikely to have been older than her mid-thirties. Seventeen years is a huge time period involving literally millions of births, but we had to start at the beginning and find a certificate.

As the morning wore on I noticed how despondent Harold became at the sheer scale of the task. In his eagerness, he had imagined that we could find his mother immediately; that he would open the first bound volume and 'Elizabeth Ellen Johnson' would be written there, as if waiting to be found.

At lunch-time we went for a walk and had a coffee and a sandwich. I doubted if Harold had the strength or experience to take much more. I was fearful he would throw in the towel and walk away, so I suggested that he spend a while helping Paul Harrison in his search.

Later that afternoon, when he found a relevant entry for Paul, I could see in Harold's face that his happiness was overshadowed by his disappointment at having found nothing about his own mother.

At four-thirty St Catherine's closed and we all trudged to St Pancras Station. Harold looked tired. I wasn't sure if he would be able to cope. Almost all of his life he had been angry and getting nowhere, hitting one wall after another, but at least now a small part of him seemed to be holding tight to the belief that we would finally find his mother. He said, 'I can't run away this time. I understand, in some way, that this is my last chance; the last chance of finding out about myself. I know that if I did run away, I would never come back.'

I told Harold, 'If we're going to do this, we've got to do it all. We can't just take a chunk and leave the rest. It may take days or weeks or much longer, but we have to go through all the twists and turns.'

The search for his mother's birth certificate did indeed take weeks, until we had exhausted every avenue. It was the same story with his father. We could find no record of him being born. Nor was there a marriage certificate for them at any time, anywhere in England, Scotland or Ireland.

This bothered me. I lay awake at night wondering what we had missed. The search had cost a great deal of money in train fares and copies of promising certificates, but we had nothing to show for it. Harold's birth certificate included the names of both mother and father. They should have been relatively easy to find. What had we missed?

There were several possibilities. Perhaps both were born overseas; or neither had used their real name on Harold's birth certificate; or maybe they presented themselves as a married couple but were actually unmarried. It could have been any of these things, it didn't matter. The reality was that it meant more pain and frustration for Harold. If St Catherine's held the answer, we didn't have the key.

Harold returned to Australia in February, totally exhausted and no closer to discovering his mother. I knew I had to look elsewhere so I started trawling the various charities that might have known about his past. In particular, I went looking for the man called Colonel Hale, whose name we had seen in the admissions book at St John's in Melbourne. I had hoped he would be a relative or godparent, but I soon discovered he was the head of the children's committee of a local authority.

This is what amazed me about Harold's story. He wasn't sent abroad by a charity, he was sent by East Sussex County Council. He was in local authority care and ultimately the responsibility of the British government – so much so that the Home Secretary had personally to give his consent before Harold could be sent overseas. This bureaucratic chain of command meant that something had to have been written down. It was policy not accident. So where were the files? Where was the Home Secretary's report?

I contacted an archivist at Sussex County Council and asked him if he could find out if they held a file on Harold Haig, a child who had been in their care many years ago.

He was very co-operative, although I doubt that he appreciated the importance of my questions. At the same time I began putting pressure on the Department of Health to reveal what the Government knew about sending Harold abroad. I needed to know why he was taken into care and who placed him there.

Harold had every right to know these things. He wasn't adopted so parental rights hadn't been severed by law and there was no legislation preventing him finding out about himself.

East Sussex County Council had no details of Harold or his parents, and the Department of Health continued to maintain that it had no records.

What could I tell Harold? It had been almost a year since we started the search and he was living so near to the edge that only blind hope was keeping him from falling. And then, one night, I suddenly remembered the Salvation Army, who had arranged Marie's adoption in 1947. How had it managed, back in 1963, to find Harold when Marie had asked after him?

I rang Harold, waking him at some ungodly hour.

'Listen! How did the Salvation Army find you? How did they know you'd gone to Australia? Write to them. Ask them if they have a file on you. Ask them how they found you.'

'The good old Salvos,' Harold said. 'They won't let us down.'

A fortnight later he received a short note bluntly informing him that no records existed. Nor was there any evidence of the Salvation Army ever having found him for his sister. He could, however, rest assured that they were saying a prayer for him.

When Harold blows, he just blows, and this was like a flame to the fuse. He screamed down the phone to me: 'I'm getting on a plane. They can't do this – not to me, not now. How can they get something this important wrong?'

By the time Harold arrived in England I had decided that he should go to the Salvation Army on his own. I had become a red rag to the charities because of the growing reputation of the Child Migrants Trust. Harold was articulate and could deal with the issues; they would surely see and feel his pain.

Sadly, however, the answer was the same. There were no records at all. Harold recounted the meeting and said that, initially, they denied ever finding him for his sister, but later went on to say, 'Well, if we did – aren't we wonderful?'

'But how did you know I was in Australia?' Harold pleaded. 'You have to have known my mother, because you placed my sister for adoption. Please tell me, what did you do with me? What did you do?'

Later that day, feeling very depressed, Harold told me about a recollection he had carried with him since childhood. He remembered being a small boy and seeing a woman in a Salvation Army uniform walking up a hill holding a little girl's hand. The little girl was Marie being taken away.

It was obvious to Harold that the charities offered nothing – some wouldn't and some couldn't. Because he was sent to Australia as part of a Government scheme – a fact that hurt him deeply – he decided to approach the politicians. He wrote a letter to the Prime Minister, Margaret Thatcher, asking for his files.

Four months later he received a reply from the Community Services Division of the Department of Health and Social Security which stated:

Dear Mr Haig,
Thank you for your letter to the Prime Minister . . . I have made
enquiries with our Records Office and have been advised
that unfortunately there are no longer any individual case files
in existence concerning post-war emigration of children to
Australia. I am sorry that this means I cannot provide you with
any information about the circumstances surrounding your
emigration . . .

Harold later wrote to Kenneth Clarke, the Secretary of State for
Health, and explained to him the horrors of exporting children.
Mr Clarke's reply infuriated Harold. He felt the Minister couldn't
even be bothered to look up a simple detail about one of his
predecessors.

> . . . I am not quite sure which Secretary of State had responsi-
> bility for the [child migration] policy in the 1945 Government.
> If you could obtain from the Child Migrants Trust that infor-
> mation it would make it possible for the successor Department
> to be asked whether records of the kind which you are seeking
> have been kept.
> . . . I know that you will find this deeply disappointing, but
> I would be misleading you if I raised your hopes that Govern-
> ment archives somewhere have the kind of information you are
> looking for.

Sadly, this is just the kind of response that reinforces the view of
many child migrants that they were exported, abandoned and
forgotten.

Harold's emotional ups and downs mirrored our search. I saw
him more or less every day through some really bad times when
he would lock himself away for days on end at the small house he
rented in Nottingham.

Harold celebrated his fiftieth birthday during that time. With his
long grey hair and wild beard, he looked quite striking, although
out of the ordinary.

I made a conscious effort to help him feel part of my family and
when he asked me, on his birthday, if he could take Ben to the
park to play football, I didn't think twice about it.

'And what about his little friend next door?' he asked.

'Fine,' I said. 'If they want to go.'

On the way back from the park, some friendly neighbour had rung the police and said, 'There's a strange bloke with these two kids, holding their hands.'

A police car appeared out of nowhere and pulled up next to Harold and the boys.

'Who are you?' they demanded. 'Are these your little boys?'

'No.'

Harold had not had the world's best experiences with authority, and it was clear to everyone present that the situation was going to escalate. One of the policemen put a hand on Harold's arm and Harold grabbed it.

Suddenly, Ben said, 'This is Harold and he's fifty today. This is my mum's friend from Australia. My mum's working with him, you can't talk to him like that!'

Not many small children would have had the maturity to step in and defuse such a situation but Ben, aged seven, was already learning about the realities of life.

Harold's birth certificate mentioned that he was born in a place called Twyford Lodge in Willesden, London, on 24 February 1938, but his family home was in Acton. It was a large house in which his parents had rented rooms. I wondered if it was possible to find anybody who had lived there in 1938 and 1939. If so, perhaps they would remember Harold's family. It was a very long shot, but I was running out of ideas.

I went to the electoral office for the borough and began making a list of everybody who had lived in the house. There were no new electoral rolls collated for the war year of 1939, which only left 1938.

Eventually I had a short list of people who had lived in the house, including several married couples. Although I knew there was little chance they would still be alive, I concentrated on the couples because I hoped they might have had children who would remember Harold's and Marie's parents.

From marriage certificates I moved to the birth certificates of their children and then the children getting married and eventually having children. It was a search down three generations that stretched me beyond imagination. I took the search as wide as it would take me – even to the other side of the Atlantic.

Finally, after months of work and countless applications for birth, death and marriage certificates, I discovered a woman who had been eleven years old and living with her parents at the house in 1938. I found her address through the London telephone directory and wrote a letter, hoping she would confirm her old address. She rang me at home, terribly excited, one evening.

I was desperate. So much time and effort had gone into finding her, she had to be the right one.

I remember her words: 'Yes, we lived at the house. What's this all about?'

I hardly dared ask. 'Do you remember a Mr and Mrs Haig living there?'

'Oh, you mean Betty and Harold.'

'Did they have any children?'

'Oh, yes – two. A little girl and a little boy. Little Harold and little Betty.'

It was ten o'clock at night and I was jumping up and down excitedly, and wanting everybody to hear the news. At long last I'd found somebody who'd known Harold's family. I'd never tried so hard to find somebody – learning as I went – and I knew that we'd earned this. I opened a bottle of wine and drank a toast.

I arranged to meet Harold the next day. I told him about the new lead and, along with Marie, we arranged to go to London and have lunch with the woman who was the first link to their past.

We sat outside at an Italian restaurant in Hammersmith on a lovely summer's day. Food was the last thing on anybody's mind. The meeting was astonishing – desperately sad in many ways – because this woman could remember Marie and Harold as children. She was nervous at first and I could see that she was taken aback by the desperation in Harold's and Marie's questions. She described how Marie used to sit in a high chair in the kitchen and how she herself used to bounce baby Harold on her knee.

I watched Marie and Harold experience something that most of us just take for granted. They couldn't believe that they'd ever been children. They were totally spellbound, simply frozen to the spot as this woman described them as babies.

'Tell me what my dad looked like?' asked Marie.

'And what was Mum like?' said Harold.

It just went on and on as this woman, who was only eleven when she knew them, tried to pull everything out of herself. Harold, in a way, felt he'd never been born but now he had confirmation that he did have a family. The four of them had lived together – Mum, Dad and two children – with Dad going off to work each day and coming home in the evening like a normal father.

Although in her sixties, the woman had an amazing memory for that time and could say that the family was probably from the North of England. The father sounded Scottish and their mother had a northern accent, but she didn't know what happened to them afterwards. She looked across the table at Harold and Marie and asked quite innocently, 'Where are your mum and dad now?'

'We don't know,' said Marie.

'Well, what happened to you both?'

Marie explained how she was in care and later adopted. Harold didn't mention Australia.

The woman looked horrified and said, 'Oh, no – there must be a mistake. The mother I knew would never have parted with her children. No, no. You've got it wrong. She would have died for her children. Nobody could have taken them away from her.'

10

Of the hundreds of letters the Child Migrants Trust had received from all over the world, there were a surprising number from Perth in Western Australia. Domino Films had been researching the documentary and Joanna Mack decided to tackle the Australian leg first – beginning in Perth and then working our way across to the eastern states.

David Spicer and I discussed the trip and decided well in advance that the workload would be far too much for one person to manage. He offered to take annual leave and come with me. We had worked together before, normally on child protection cases that came to court. Some of the children in those cases had suffered horrendous abuse, but David had shown his toughness and determination. He is very precise and doesn't let go.

'I'm a lawyer, not a counsellor,' he said. 'I wouldn't know how to conduct an interview.'

I told him not to worry. 'You visit the charities and handle the publicity. I'll talk with the child migrants.'

We left England in March 1988 and flew via Hong Kong to Perth.

Landing early in the morning, I was struck by how almost clinically clean the airport was. The staff wore shorts and white, knee-length socks – which looked quite odd until I walked outside and the heat hit me. By mid-morning it was 42° Celsius, 120° Fahrenheit; I'd never felt anything like it.

To save the Trust money on accommodation Philip Bean, a trustee, had contacted former colleagues at the University of Western Australia. They offered to let us stay in the halls of residence. My small room was in a building ironically called St Catherine's College – a large modern building.

The university also offered us a small house in which to work, away from the campus and relatively central. It had a small lounge area with comfortable chairs, a kitchen and an office. Although not air-conditioned, there were large desk fans.

Early next morning, David was interviewed on a local radio station and while he was still on the air, the telephone rang.

It seemed strange to be thousands of miles away from home and to be saying 'Child Migrants Trust'.

A rather angry voice, asked, 'Who sent you?' Before I could answer he continued, 'And what took you so long?'

I smiled, thinking he meant that I'd been slow in answering the phone.

'I want to know why it's taken you so long to come and see us? The British government sent us here years ago. They didn't want us. Just left us here to rot. They don't answer my letters.'

I tried to explain that I wasn't from the Government and, what's more, I felt sure that it wasn't the British people who didn't want him.

'I doubt whether anybody even realizes you're here,' I said kindly.

My caller, Bill, became very tearful and distressed.

'I'm almost seventy-five years old,' he said. 'I've never been home but I'm still British. I've been here more than sixty years.'

I tried to explain why I was in Perth, but Bill wasn't listening. He was too upset and I could hear his wife in the background trying to calm him down.

There was a knock at the door and I asked Bill to hold the line for a moment.

David was still talking on the radio – answering callers' questions. I was expecting him back to help me but he had become an instant talkback star.

I opened the door. A woman asked me, 'Are you the lady from England?'

'Yes, I think so.' I smiled.

'You must be with that pale complexion. So what's the weather like in the old country?'

'The old country?' I asked.

'Much colder than here,' she said. 'Oh, it was cold when I left.'

'And when was that?' I asked.

'November 1950. We had gloves and scarves.'

'We? How many were you?'

'Oh, there were about sixty of us on the boat. We were collected from all over England. And there were kids from Scotland and Ireland. It was very hot when we arrived here. A bit like today.'

Outside it was already forty plus.

'You'd better keep out of the sun,' she said. 'My God, we burnt. Our arms were burnt raw within days.'

I told her to come inside. Bill was still on the phone and I made arrangements for him to come and see me later that day. Then I began arranging furniture in the sitting-room for the first interview.

There was another knock on the door. This time a man stood there.

'Is this the place the man spoke of on the radio? I've had a hell of a time finding you.'

Graham was in his late forties. 'I'm an orphan from England. God, it's taken years. Have they forgotten about us?'

Before I could answer him, the door rattled again.

'Good morning,' I smiled at the six people who were now standing in front of me. 'I think we'd better get organized here.'

By the time David arrived back from the radio station there must have been more than twenty people waiting. The veranda and garden were full with people, sitting, standing, talking, smoking and waiting their turn. Some were on their own, others with husbands and wives. Some recognized each other from long ago.

David made cups of tea and cold drinks in between answering the phone. He was making appointments for later in the day or the following day, but many said they'd wait, regardless of how long it took.

'I'll wait all day if necessary. I've waited all my life,' said one woman.

The desk fans were humming but offered little respite. Perspiration trickled off me.

I arranged a settee and two armchairs in the sitting-room and began the first interview by trying to explain what I was doing.

'I've come to Perth to talk with people who were child migrants; people who arrived in Australia without their parents.'

'You mean you've come all this way to see us?' the first woman asked.

'Yes, I've come to see you.'

As soon as I said it I could see the physical relief on her face. She asked, 'Can I hold your hand?'

I was taken aback but went over and sat beside her on the settee. She took my hand.

'Where do you want to start?' I asked.

'Do you think I've got any family? Cousins, anybody? I'm not fussy. Anybody. They told me that my parents were dead. Do you think that's true?'

'I don't know, but I can find out. I'll need your help.'

'How can I possibly help you? I don't know anything about myself.'

'Well, let's start with your name.'

'Ann Theresa.'

'Are you married?'

'Yes.'

'Do you have a family?'

'Two children. They're teenagers now.'

'When did you marry?'

'Getting married was very painful for me. I couldn't tell people who I was. I didn't have a birth certificate. I felt ashamed.'

The tears just flowed down her face.

'What did we do wrong?' she asked. 'Can you find out why they sent me? What did I do wrong?'

'You did nothing wrong, Ann.'

She looked at me as if I was being kind to her.

'Do you know how old you were when you came to Australia?'

'Eight.'

'What could an eight-year-old possibly have done that was so bad?'

She smiled a little.

'Can you remember when your own children were eight years old?' I asked.

'I remember them at every age.' She paused and squeezed my hand.

As she wiped away tears, I explained to her, 'We have to view this like a journey. You have to help me understand, somehow, the milestones of your life so far, and from there we will take another journey. Neither of us knows where it's going to lead. I know it's going to be painful but you have to help me.'

Ann nodded her head.

I asked, 'What are your earliest memories? What can you remember about England?'

'I can remember a lady visiting me. I was in a room and this lady came with a man who used to put me on his shoulders. Sometimes they took me for bike rides.'

'Was she elderly or young?'

'I think she was young. She used to sit me on her knee.'

'Who do you think this lady was?'

'I think she was my mother.'

'Why do you think that?'

'She had a fur collar on her coat and I used to like to put my cheek on it. And then she would put her hand on my bottom and give me a nice pat. Only mothers do that to their children, don't they?'

Ann was describing an intimacy. She didn't know where or why, but it was the physical closeness that she remembered.

'Did you like those times?' I asked.

'Yes. But I've never had them since. Do you think it was my mother?'

It was hard to answer. 'It's not important what I think, Ann. Only what you think.'

'I think it was my mother,' she said.

'Why do you think you came to Australia?' I asked.

'It must have been that nobody wanted us in England. I've never forgotten England. It's my home. It's my birthplace, but they just didn't want me.'

It had been two hours since we began talking and Ann's voice was beginning to show the strain. Gently, I managed to discover a few more important details – the name of her children's home in

Liverpool, the boat on which she arrived and her date of birth.

'I'm going to go back to England and this is what I'm going to do: I will visit the children's home where you used to live, and the school. If they're still there, I'll take photographs and post them to you. I shall get you a full copy of your birth certificate which will have the names of your parents or at least your mother.'

'And you'll try to find my family?'

'Yes, that's what I'm going to do.'

When Ann got up to leave she threw her arms around me and gave me a hug. She said, 'Are you going to come back and see me?'

'Yes, of course I will.'

'When?'

'I don't know. But I will come back.'

As I watched her leave I couldn't help noticing the look of relief on her face.

David was in the office still taking phone calls and handing out cold drinks. He was desperate for me to finish.

All those waiting looked up at me.

'If all these interviews are going to take two hours, we'll be here for days,' I told David. 'We'll have to send these people home and make appointments for them to come back.'

'The day diary is already full,' he said. 'I've been making plans to see people in the evening at their homes.'

My shoulders drooped a little further. 'It's going to take a lot longer than I imagined.'

'I thought as much. Are you going to be OK?'

'Yes, but it's a bit daunting.'

By four-thirty that afternoon I'd managed to interview three more child migrants. Their stories were remarkably similar as was the painful process of extracting from them even the most basic details which I needed to begin the search for their families. I was finding it difficult to take notes while they talked. I wanted to maintain eye contact to show that I was concentrating fully. Often I waited until they'd finished and left before filling several pages of my notebook.

David interrupted me as I was writing my notes.

'There's somebody outside who wants to see you. It'll only take you a moment.'

Ann was waiting in the entrance hall. She'd gone home and

returned with her husband. 'I'm sorry,' she said. 'But I had to come back. I wanted my husband to meet you. I wanted to make sure this was all real.'

After she'd gone, David took me aside. 'I know it's getting late but there's somebody else who I think you have to see today. He's been waiting since this morning and he's very distressed. He's full of so much anger. I tried to arrange for him to come tomorrow but he insisted on waiting. If we don't see him, I think he'll wait outside all night.'

When Graham came into the sitting-room, I sensed immediately what David meant. He was a powerful looking man in his mid-fifties. He had fair skin but the Australian sun had etched deep wrinkles around his eyes and across his forehead.

'And who sent you?' he said, quite sceptically, before he even sat down. 'What are you here for? Because if you want to know what happened here at Boys' Town, Bindoon,' he almost spat the name out, 'then I'm the right bloke to tell you.'

Before I could answer him, he asked, 'What do you know about Boys' Town, Bindoon?'

'Sorry, but I've never heard of it. The only Boys' Town I've heard of was in an old Hollywood film that I saw years ago.'

'And what do you know about the Christian Brothers?'

'I'm sorry, but I've never heard of the Christian Brothers.'

A mischievous smile flitted across his face. 'Well, the brothers are going to love you.'

He was very aggressive, pacing around the room. I couldn't make eye contact with him or get him to sit down.

'What I want to know is, why the British government sent us out here to Australia to be used as slave labour? And I'm talking about the Forties, Fifties and Sixties, not the nineteenth century.'

He paused, and in an instant his shoulders sagged and the swagger disappeared. He turned to me, looking directly into my eyes for the first time, and said, 'We were just innocent little boys. Some of us only four or five years old.'

This man didn't want to hear why I was there or what I was trying to do. He only wanted to talk about what had happened to him.

'We built that bloody place. We built it with our bare hands.'

'What place?'

'Bindoon. We built Bindoon. We mixed so much cement the dust burned our feet and the sores on our knees and hands. We were slave labourers. Have you been there? Have you seen it?'

'No.'

'After we did the buildings, we built the Stations of the Cross. They're made of stone. The boys built them. They represent what we lost – all of us. But who was crucified?'

After half an hour of this, I was so shell-shocked by his anger and pain I almost felt that I was responsible for sending him to Australia. That it was somehow my fault.

I didn't know how to reach him – to convince him that I believed him, I didn't doubt for a minute what he was saying, but he had to calm down and explain things from the beginning.

Finally he paused for a moment, staring at his hands. I quickly asked, 'Have you any family?'

The effect was astounding. The fight went out of him.

'I suppose somebody gave birth to me.'

'What can you remember about England?' I asked.

He told me his recollections were sparse but he could remember the war and being evacuated from London to the countryside. He was in a children's home and had been there ever since he could remember. There were no memories of a mother or father visiting him or of birthdays and Christmases.

'We were just innocent little kids. We didn't know why they sent us here. We had no idea.'

Graham was about ten when somebody came to the children's home and asked him if he wanted to go somewhere where the sun shone all the time and they would get pocket money every week. The place was called Australia and Graham had no idea where it was or how long it would take to get there.

'I left my friends behind. I remember being so sad about leaving them. I still think of them – they don't know how lucky they were. At least in England we had warm beds and regular meals.

'There were other kids on the boat – they came from Ireland and Scotland and all over England. I made new friends but they too were taken away from me. When we arrived in Fremantle, just south of here, we were split up. Some stayed on the boat and went further east.'

'They fingerprinted us at the dock as we left the ship. They treated us like bloody criminals. We were innocent little boys.'

Graham had used the word 'innocent' five or six times since we began and it was spoken with such conviction that I sensed there was some deeper reason for choosing to repeat it time and again. I wanted to ask him why, but let him continue.

'The Christian Brothers put us on trucks – some going to Perth and others to Bindoon about 60 miles north of here. The heat was unbearable—'

There was a commotion outside and I heard loud voices – one of them belonged to David.

'Is this where you come about the kidnapped kids?' a man shouted. He was furious and extremely agitated.

I went out, thinking this man had come to the wrong place. He probably wanted the local police station.

'Was it you on the radio?' he screamed at David. 'I've got a mate who was brought over on a boat and just dumped here by your lot – by the British. I want you to see my friend. I want you to help him.'

'OK, all right. I'll see your friend,' I said, trying to calm him down. David took his details and I went back to Graham who was sitting quietly on the settee.

He continued telling me about the voyage.

'Before we left Southampton, they gave us a set of new clothes. It was the first time I'd ever had new things. I got trousers and shiny shoes. But when we arrived at Bindoon they took the clothes away. They left us without underwear. It was degrading.

'I remember standing on the tray top of the truck, before jumping down. I looked up and for as far as I could see there were fields and trees and not a single other building. And I thought, How the hell is anyone going to find me here?

'Bindoon was like a building site. There was rubble and rock everywhere. We had no shoes. We worked in our bare feet. Every day. Winter and summer. We built that bloody place for them. We ate brick dust with our breakfast.

'I was ten years old and I used to wet the bed most nights. I was so afraid of wetting the bed that I wet it even more. We used to sleep on mattresses that were stained and soaked with urine.' Graham looked at me, imploring me to understand.

I told him that I'd be more surprised if he hadn't wet his bed.

'We used to live in fear of the beatings. In fear of being noticed or singled out. They used to beat us with belts, thick leather ones with heavy buckles. They'd beat us in front of the other boys. They'd pull down our trousers in front of everyone and give us a hiding. It was so bloody humiliating.'

Graham looked at me. 'You believe me, don't you?' he asked.

'No-one could disbelieve your distress,' I told him.

'It's not the worst of it, Margaret,' he said, using my name for the first time.

'What do you mean?'

'The beatings weren't the worst of it. They were paedophiles and sadists. Some of the brothers got their kicks out of beating us and others got their kicks in other ways. Margaret, you don't know what it's like to see little boys woken up in their sleep and taken from their beds. We'd hear a brother coming – his footsteps on the wooden floor – and we'd pray he wouldn't stop beside our bed. I'd lie there on a wet mattress, praying it wouldn't happen to me. And then somebody else would be woken and carried from the dormitory to a brother's room.'

Graham was looking at me. I believe he wanted to see if I was shocked. He wanted to know if I still felt the same way about him; if anything had changed.

Of course it had, but I couldn't let him see any emotion other than sadness. I was sad for the child and sad for the man. Among the emotions that filled my mind, one of the things that concerned me most was, What will his mother say?

I expected feelings of abandonment and rejection but what I met here were feelings of total alienation and degradation. It was one thing to be talking about governments failing children and families, but Graham was talking about the Christian Church with all its emphasis on caring and compassion and family life. He was talking about men of God brutalizing and violating young boys. The implications were more frightening and far reaching than I'd ever imagined.

I sensed Graham had been abused, although he didn't say as much. He didn't have to. I had to make a decision. These were serious allegations, but was it my job to investigate? I was a visitor in a foreign country. Or should I remain the therapist and try to bring some healing into his life? I had only one way of reaching him. I had to piece together what was broken. It wasn't enough to listen – that was only the start.

'What is it you want me to do?' I asked. 'I want to help. There's a lot I can do. But you have to help me.'

'I think I've got a brother. I remember him being younger than me. I'm not sure if he came on the boat with me or I left him in England.'

'Why do you think he's your brother?'

'There was another boy at the children's home and we had the same name. People said we looked alike. And what about my mother? Do you think I have a mother?'

'We all have mothers, Graham, but I can't tell you if she's still alive.'

He grew angry again. 'What were you lot doing while we were being abused? What were you doing when we were working like slaves?'

I could still hear these questions, long after he'd gone. I didn't have the answers. It seemed everybody had failed this man, the Government, the Christian Brothers, welfare workers. Through his entire life every single person had failed him. I was determined not to be another one.

At ten o'clock that night David and I were finally alone. We hadn't eaten all day and the darkness had brought no respite from the heat. Locking up the house, we drove through the empty streets trying to find a restaurant that was still open.

We found a small Italian place and sat outside in the courtyard, thankful for the breeze and the almost empty tables. As I sat down, I suddenly thought how ordinary the scene must have looked. There was a sense of unreality because everything around us remained the same. The world was the same but I was looking at it differently.

Eating for the sake of eating, I couldn't stop thinking about what had happened to the child migrants. This is the place where children had arrived from another country. Perth held no beauty for me. There were palm trees, white beaches and happy faces, but underneath all of it lay a terrible secret.

'Are you OK?' David asked.

I nodded slowly.

'They were crying. These people were so grateful to see us. It was as if they were waiting for us. I can't believe it.'

'It's going to get worse,' David said. 'I've been sitting and talking with them all day. Some of the stories are terrible.'

I nodded. 'It's not just about being sent away any more. It's much worse. Some of these children were violated. They say they were abused and exploited by men who preached compassion and caring.' I shook my head, trying to make the thoughts disappear.

David said, 'Just because someone is a member of a religious order does not mean they are not child abusers.'

'But these were young children,' I murmured. 'They were alone. They had no-one to run home to when things went wrong. They were so vulnerable.'

David looked up at the darkened sky. The lawyer in him was already hard at work mulling over the implications. 'Who the hell is liable?' he asked.

'I can picture them as kids,' I said. 'Whenever they started talking about what happened, I didn't see them as adults any more, I pictured them as children. I saw them getting on the boats. I saw them in the back of trucks. It was terrible.'

'But why has it taken so long for this to come out? Why didn't they say something earlier?'

There were so many questions that troubled me, but there were no answers that night.

11

For the next eight days, the crush continued unabated. David and I arrived at the house at six each morning to get ready for the first of the migrants to arrive. The sprinklers were already spinning on front lawns, and paperboys weaved through the streets on their pushbikes.

It was the only time of day when the temperature seemed bearable and I was surprised that more people weren't up and working.

Despite the heat, David continued to wear a suit and tie. I joked to him, 'I knew when you took your waistcoat off that we must have crossed the Equator.'

Each day was similar to the last. Stories of cruelty and abuse now filled dozens of notebooks, and the pain and misery were relentless. Time and again the name Bindoon was spoken with a mixture of anger and sadness. Every ounce of self-esteem and self-confidence had been taken or beaten from the boys who went there – they felt nothing. The most repeated line in all the interviews was, 'I'm nobody.'

Men spoke of being flogged with strips of leather, fan belts and axe handles; one told of being made to walk past the crush-ed body of a young migrant who had died under the wheels of a truck.

They ate thin porridge for breakfast, mixed with bran from the chicken feed, and constant hunger drove them to forage for food.

One man hadn't shed a tear as he described being raped, but broke down and sobbed inconsolably when he recounted getting on trucks and going to a neighbouring private boarding-school. 'Margaret, we used to empty their bins. And we used to eat it. We ate their slops.'

That hurt him far more than being violated sexually. What did it tell him about himself, about his worth?

One particular name was repeated with enormous bitterness. Brother Francis Paul Keaney, the former head of Bindoon Boys' Town, was portrayed as a brutal, sadistic man whose obsession with building projects overrode any sense of caring for the young arrivals from Britain.

Irish-born Keaney, who died in 1954, was so celebrated by the Christian Brothers that the Boys' Town was renamed Keaney College in his honour.

'He had this thick knobby stick and he would crack it over our heads,' said one former migrant. 'If a skull was split and bleeding, Keaney didn't care. He just kept hitting. He was the cruellest bastard God ever put on this earth.'

Another described how Keaney would belittle and publicly humiliate boys by having them strip naked and stand on tables.

But the brutality wasn't confined to Bindoon. Similar stories of varying degrees of cruelty were told by men who went to Clontarf, Castledare and Tardun – all orphanages run by the Catholic Church.

When I set out, I had expected to work with people who felt rejected by their families, but here we were talking about people whose genuine pain and hurt came from having been abandoned by their country. I'd never experienced a hurt so profound. I had begun something that I didn't know how to stop or control.

Each day we worked at the house until late afternoon and then in the evening went on home visits. Meals were grabbed whenever we could. Clean clothes were in short supply but there was no time to wash them or buy more.

We were already on a tight schedule, but as each day passed nothing became easier. 'We'll have to skip Melbourne,' said David.

'We can do Adelaide and Sydney, but not Melbourne – not in the time we've got left.'

Joanna Mack was due to arrive that Sunday. I was already feeling anxious for her. We were to spend two days with her before leaving her in Perth to fly to Adelaide. I wondered how she would cope by herself.

David and I had relied a lot on each other. What had happened in Perth was so unimaginable that we needed each other to validate the experience. Joanna wouldn't have that kind of support. She was due to do research interviews for the documentary and I'd told many of the child migrants that she was coming. I was surprised at how many wanted to see her. They wanted to tell their stories.

When we met her off the plane, I didn't tell Joanna about Bindoon and the Christian Brothers. If the child migrants she interviewed wanted to reveal what happened it was their decision.

We now had a list of some of the charities and the orphanages which had accepted child migrants. David and I decided to make contact with those that still existed. These included the Fairbridge Society, the State government and the Catholic Migrant Centre. The latter is a Catholic welfare organization that deals with all migrants to Western Australia, young and old.

Our main aim was to inform the charities of the existence of the Child Migrants Trust to ensure that as many child migrants as possible knew that a trust had been established specifically to meet their needs.

It was an introductory approach. David didn't go in asking questions or voicing accusations. Instead, his main purpose was to make sure that everybody who needed our help knew how to get in touch with us.

David also went to see the Community Services Department – the Australian equivalent of our Social Services – and was surprised to find that no-one he spoke to had more than a limited knowledge of the child migration schemes.

One of the officials said, 'You mean the orphans who came from England?'

'Yes,' said David.

'I remember hearing a story about a child migrant who'd been asking for his records for years,' the official said. 'He made lots of threats, including one against the Royal family. Eventually he set fire to the Catholic Migrant Centre and finished up in prison.'

Meanwhile, I continued with the interviews.

Over and over, people said to me, 'We've been waiting for you all our lives, where have you been?'

One man said, 'I waited and I waited, and thought surely someday, someone would come and ask, and today's our day.'

Among the handful of people who'd written to me from Perth before I left England was Maureen Briggs, a forty-five-year-old who was sent to Australia in 1953. She arrived on the *SS Australia* with a 'large group of parentless children'. Maureen, along with many others, was sent to a Catholic orphanage in Geraldton, a coastal town five hours' drive north of Perth.

I took her letter with me, rereading it several times in the days leading up to our meeting.

Maureen stayed with the nuns at Nazareth House in Geraldton for five years.

She wrote: 'At the age of sixteen I was put on a bus and sent to work as a domestic on a farm in Western Australia for two pounds plus keep. What a dreadful experience it was after spending so many years in the care of the nuns and having so many other children around me. Then I woke up one morning early to find that I was completely on my own. I had no idea where I was going, or to whom I was going, and worst of all, not knowing who I was.

'I clearly remember being made to sign a wage book. Upon seeing my name, I asked, "Whose name is that? I don't know that name."

' "Don't you know your own name?" I was asked.

' "I've never heard that one."

' "Goodness, fancy not knowing who you are!"

'I ran to my room and cried and cried. It was at that moment that I decided to find out who I am. I'm forty-five years old, with two children of my own, and still I have no identity.'

'I have a dream that maybe one of these days I will be able to ring my sons and say, "Your mum has found herself. She has an identity after all." '

When I finally spoke to Maureen I realized that her letter couldn't possibly begin to convey her tremendous longing to find her mother. As soon as I began asking questions, she fell to pieces. Sadly, the mother whom she couldn't picture or remember had never left her; she was always in her thoughts.

'There are others like me,' she said. 'There are hundreds of us here.'

'Is it possible for me to meet any of them?' I asked.

'Of course. I'll arrange it.'

Later that day, Maureen called and said she'd spoken to her friends and a group wanted to meet me at one of their homes in the suburbs of Perth.

David and I got lost twice trying to find the modern brick house. We arrived late, at 7.30 p.m., and found seven or eight women sitting around a large dining-room table.

They were all about the same age and had spent their childhoods in Nazareth House at Geraldton. From the moment we sat down I was struck by how relaxed these women were with each other. They were like a large family, chiding each other and laughing. The bonds were incredibly strong – sealed in their childhood.

I noticed, not for the first time, that the word 'orphan' was being used over and over. The women would say, 'I'm an orphan, do you think I have a mother?' 'We're orphans, we were told we had no-one.'

It was a contradiction in terms. On the one hand, they'd been told they were orphans and their parents were dead. But on the other, they had this dream that one day they would find their parents.

Their stories were similar to Maureen's. Each had been sent from England when they were aged between five and eleven. One woman described how she knew she'd never see England again: 'Because we'd been on the ship for so long, we knew it would take a long time to get back. What chance did we have of going back? None.'

Another talked of life at Nazareth House. 'What I missed most was a bit of love. You had no-one, you had the girls you came out with but they were in the same boat as you. Some of the nuns were nice, but still they didn't give you the love you needed. I think when someone's sick or going through an emotional time they should be shown a bit of love, but we weren't. I think to bring up a child you've got to give them love so they have the security to go out into the world.'

Adjusting to life in an outback orphanage was traumatic for all the girls because they were still bewildered by their journey. It was a feeling that stayed with them all their lives because nobody had been able to explain to them why they were sent.

I didn't know whether they were truly orphans. I was fearful of raising their expectations. But I made a commitment that evening to each and every one of them that I'd do my utmost to trace their families.

David, Joanna and I felt humbled and privileged, but at the same time we found it hard to contain our disbelief. Having arrived with only three or four possible contacts in Perth, we were suddenly swamped with people who believed we were their last hope – their only hope.

As each day passed, David grew more outraged.

'Other people had to know about all this. A conspiracy of silence has existed over many years. Where were the police, the doctors, the welfare officers? Why didn't they know? Someone had to have known what was happening.'

David couldn't hold his anger back. He would tell the child migrants that they shouldn't have been treated this way.

It wasn't just the enormity of it that hit me but also the complexities raised by the allegations of physical and sexual abuse. It was an area I'd worked in for a long time – always with children. But these people were adults – adult survivors of institutional abuse – not by parents or friends, but by a religious organization. This was a totally different kind of abuse and I had little experience of how to deal with it.

They had stripped these tiny children of their identity by continually telling them they were nobody, that they were worthless. It was desperately difficult for these men to come to me and I admired them for doing it. Throughout their lives they had known no mother figure; there was never anyone to offer them maternal care. They grew up in an essentially all-male environment, believing that the one mother they might have known had supposedly abandoned them, or that, as far as they knew, she was dead. Nobody wanted them.

One night I went into David's interviewing room when the last migrant had gone and found him sitting with his head in his hands. He was struggling to come to terms with what he'd heard.

The difference between adults and children had been brought

home to us. Adults are articulate; they can tell you everything that happened, down to the last, heartbreaking detail.

When it came time to leave Perth my feelings were mixed. I knew that these people needed my help but their stories were so overwhelming that I had to step back for a while.

As David and I sat at the airport waiting to leave on the flight to Adelaide, I became aware of a noisy group coming towards us.

'Who are all those people?' I asked David.

'I think you probably know them,' he said.

The women I'd met from Nazareth House in Geraldton had come to wave us off. It became very emotional when one of them presented me with a beautiful hand-embroidered tablecloth.

I found it hard to speak. I thought it was terrible that these people should feel grateful. I turned to David and sighed, 'You must make sure this never happens to me ever again. No-one should be grateful for our services. It should be theirs by right.' Their friendship and hospitality overwhelmed both of us. But I knew that I would be returning to meet with them again.

12

When we left Perth, I wished we were on a plane home. Aside from what we'd been through, David and I were both homesick. Tiredness seemed to be almost constant.

It was difficult to adjust to such a long period away from home – from Mervyn, Ben and Rachel. Although I'd tried to send them postcards every second day, when I sat down to write I didn't know what to say. In the end it was always a simple 'Miss you' and 'love you all'.

On the journey from England, we had stopped over in Hong Kong for a day and David presented me with a Mother's Day card that Rachel and Ben had asked him to give me. Since then, I'd propped it open beside my bed and it was the first thing I saw when I woke each morning.

It made me even more homesick, but I was also conscious that I was working with people who must have found every Mother's Day extremely painful.

Before leaving Perth, David had contacted the Community Services Department in Adelaide and asked if they could help. They kindly paid for our accommodation and provided us with an office. It wasn't ideal but we were thankful for any help given. Situated in the suburbs, it was opposite a large hospital, which meant that we could buy coffee and sandwiches from the cafeteria. Again we struggled to cope with the heat.

Even before we left Perth a TV station in Adelaide, Channel Nine, called me and said that about fifty women had come forward following publicity about the Child Migrants Trust. A number of them wanted to welcome me to Adelaide.

I was given directions to the home of one of the child migrants. When I arrived at the door a bunch of flowers was presented to me and a TV camera was about four feet from my face.

Fifteen or so women were waiting with beaming smiles and warm handshakes. What struck me most was the question: 'Why were you in Perth?'

'I was interviewing child migrants,' I said.

'Were there others?'

'What do you mean?'

'Well, we thought we were the only ones.'

Over the next three days, I interviewed each of them. They had been sent to an orphanage called Goodwood in Adelaide, an institution which was also home for many Australian girls.

There seemed to be an anti-British policy at the orphanage. At every opportunity the girls were told to forget Britain and any thoughts of going 'home'. They were punished if they sang 'God Bless England', instead of 'God Bless Australia'.

None had been prepared for their new life in Australia. Being uprooted and separated from their schools, their friends and all that was familiar had traumatized them.

I noticed when I visited their homes and walked into their sitting-rooms that I could have been anywhere in England. Whether consciously or not, they had decorated their houses and gardens in a particularly English style.

At Goodwood, the new arrivals slept in dormitories. Many wet their beds and these girls were singled out and made to sleep elsewhere. One woman remembered being terrified of going to sleep in case she wet the bed but each morning the sheet and mattress were soaked.

'And if you wet your bed you were made to stand up in front of the class with the wet sheet over you. It makes me feel sick, remembering it.'

The children were not allowed pillows and had only two thin blankets for cold winter nights.

Punishment at Goodwood was swift and sometimes brutal. I was told stories of girls being caned for having a hole in their socks, a stain on their dress or getting prayers wrong. These beatings were often public and girls would have to pull their pants down and lie across their beds.

'The Reverend Mother came up with this huge strap and whacked me one right through the sheet. Then she ripped my nightie off, and there I was in the raw, trying to cover myself up. She kept hitting me until I was covered in welts.'

It seemed hard to imagine, listening to these articulate, well-dressed, middle-aged mothers and wives, that any of them could have done something to warrant such a beating.

Their days seemed very regimented and revolved between chores, classes and more chores. They were woken at six every morning and had to dress for mass in the chapel. After mass they changed to do their chores and have breakfast. After school and on weekends there were more chores.

'On Saturdays we did the washing. There was a massive laundry with industrial machines and it took two of us to manage each machine. In England, we would have been outside in the sunshine enjoying ourselves. But not at Goodwood,' one woman recalled angrily.

Another complained at having to wear the same underwear for a week regardless of whether it was soiled. 'When one girl's first period started, she had no idea what the blood was and hid her pants behind the door.'

One by one, I interviewed these women and I asked each if there was a single moment which stood out about their childhoods?

Almost all recounted the same event – a story that troubled them deeply.

There was a very young child migrant, no more than five years old, who arrived from England. She was very upset and couldn't stop crying. The little girl had long curly blond hair and was very pretty.

After being at Goodwood a few days, she packed all her possessions in a bag and ran off down the drive in her nightie. The nuns followed her and dragged her back. The next morning, all the girls were made to line up in the yard and watch her being punished.

Although each of them gave a slightly different account of what happened next, the details were the same. Two of the nuns held the little girl down, while another started cutting off her hair with garden shears.

Her struggles and cries went unheard. When they had finished, there was just an inch or two of hair left on her head. 'God wants her punished more than that,' one of the nuns said, and she produced a pair of secateurs. She started cutting again and didn't stop until the young girl's hair was gone completely and her scalp was bloody with cuts.

All those I interviewed who witnessed this event remained traumatized by it, even decades later.

Among them was Pamela Smedley, who arrived at our makeshift office on a Tuesday afternoon, accompanied by a friend. She was very nervous and David had to reassure her.

All her life, Pamela told me, she'd been searching for the truth: 'At the back of my mind is the fact that I'm a nobody. I've got no roots.'

Pamela could only ever remember growing up in institutions. She had no memory of a mother or father and had been told that her mother abandoned her in hospital as a newborn baby.

At the children's home in Middlesborough she and a group of other girls were informed that they were being sent to Australia to be adopted by families.

When the six-week voyage ended in another institution, the realization was devastating.

'I couldn't believe it. We sat on the iron steps at the home and cried. We sat there and cried for three days. We just wanted to get on a ship and go home to England.

'I thought, How am I ever going to see England again? How am I going to find anybody all the way out here?'

When I asked Pamela about conditions at Goodwood, her description wasn't as harsh or uncaring as others had recounted. Pamela accepted the punishment and regime as part of institutional life. She didn't blame anybody, least of all the nuns, for what had happened to her.

Pamela was fifteen when she was sent out to a shearing station some five hours' drive from Adelaide, in bone-dry countryside where temperatures in the summer rose to well over one hundred degrees. It was an isolated farm, miles from anywhere.

'It could have been Mars! It was so different from England,' she said. 'I was being sent away again, you know, even further away. Talk about being punished for something you didn't do.

'I hated it. I cried myself to sleep every night. I was cut off from all the friends I ever had.'

'What did you do on the farm?' I asked.

'I cooked for seven shearers. I had to be up before dawn to cook them breakfast and then make them morning tea, then lunch and then dinner. It was a big old place with wood floors and great huge wooden tables. I would have to light the stove early to heat the water.'

'What was the owner like?'

'The woman that I worked for often made out she was having a heart attack, to frighten me. I thought she was going to drop dead on me and I'd get the blame, so I would work twice as hard. I was that used to getting the blame for things that I didn't do.

'I had to wash and clean for all of them. They had seven children. I got one weekend off in six and worked every day in between. It's a hard life on a farm, I accept that, but it didn't have to be cruel.

'They paid me £1.2s.6d. a week and I had to buy clothes and everything out of that. But when I got my first wages I went and bought a little miniature made in England. I never bought anything that was made in Australia if I could help it. It took all my money. It was a tiny little English house.'

Pamela paused and buried her hands deep in her lap. Tears hung gently in the corners of her eyes.

'How long did you stay on the farm?' I asked her.

'Not long, really. Something happened and I had to leave.'

'What happened?'

'The farmer had a seventeen-year-old son. He was much bigger than me. I was a thin slip of a girl. One night I left my bedroom to go to the toilet, which was outside, a little way from the house. He met me coming back and pulled me into his room.

'I didn't know anything about sex but I knew that he was trying to rape me. He was forcing my legs apart and had his hand over my mouth. I just crossed my legs and put my hands between them. I knew that I shouldn't let him touch me, so I kept my legs crossed.

'He became very angry. He was very strong and kept me in his room for two hours. I was too scared to cry out. I knew I'd get the blame. I kept pleading to him: "Please don't touch me, don't hurt me, don't do anything wrong," begging him to let me go back to bed.

'The next morning at the breakfast table, his mother said to me, "Where were you last night?" She had looked in my room. "In bed," I said, but she knew that wasn't true. "You were not. You were with the shearers, weren't you?"

'I tried to tell her no. I looked at her son but he smirked and said, "I don't know how she could do it, how she could go, the trollop."

'After that he tried to get me whenever he got the chance. I'd go in to make his bed, and he'd sneak in very quietly, come up behind me and pick me up. He'd throw me on the bed, but I was always quicker and crossed my legs. He wasn't going to have me.

'But I was so scared. He was so strong and I thought he would simply hit me until I couldn't fight back.'

Pamela was too scared to tell a priest about the son and his attempts to rape her. She feared that, yet again, somebody would blame her and claim she had tried to seduce him. But after a year of cruelty and frequent attacks she told a girlfriend in Adelaide.

'She told me that I should leave the farm and find a job in the city but I knew it wasn't that easy. I had no rights. I wasn't free. I was sixteen years old and like a slave.'

When Pamela finally talked to the Catholic welfare agency who had placed her on the farm, she was told that she had to stay. She phoned twice more.

'They threatened me with everything. They told me I was ungrateful and couldn't leave. I was crying and begging. Eventually they gave in and said yes, I could come back to Adelaide.

'We were supposed to consider ourselves very lucky that they had found us a job and a roof over our heads; a home where we could become part of a family. Only, these people didn't love me, they treated me like dirt, like a slave. They weren't my family.'

'Do you think you have a family?' I asked.

'There must be someone,' she said, imploringly. 'I must be related to someone, even if it's an aunt or an uncle. I feel I'm a nobody, a nothing, without any roots at all. I used to lie in my bed on the farm, clutching my miniature English house, and dream of having a proper family. In my whole life, I've never called anybody Mother.'

I spent a long while sitting with Pamela, explaining what I was doing and trying to help her understand that she wasn't to blame for what happened to her in her childhood. Yet as she began to understand this, her anger grew.

'I still resent the fact that someone could walk into a classroom in England, pluck you out, take you to Australia, with no prospect of ever coming back,' she said. 'You do that to animals – you sell them off and cart them away – but not children. You don't do that to children.

'I've always wanted to go back to England; to be there in April when the flowers come up and the leaves return. I remember so little. My childhood was taken away from me . . .'

I saw two other people that day. They were sisters, both in their late forties, and one, the older, was very much in charge of her sister.

They had been sent out to Australia together, and I asked them the same question that I asked everybody: 'Does anything particular stand out in your mind about your childhood?'

'Yes,' one of them said. 'My sister here had all her hair shaved off. She ran away and the nuns dragged her back. It scarred her emotionally. It scarred us all.'

I had found her: the angel with the blond curly hair. She had never recovered from the ordeal and neither had her older sister, who had witnessed the attack.

There were not enough hours each day to get the work done. David's appearances on TV and radio had triggered another astonishing response. Our diary was overflowing and we had to catch a flight to Sydney on Thursday. It was inevitable that we couldn't see everybody and I promised many that I'd come back later.

On the day we left Adelaide I had ten meetings with child

migrants and a magazine interview, while David answered thirty-nine telephone calls and did three radio interviews. As we closed the office door and dashed for the airport, the telephone was still ringing.

13

Although I was concerned at having to by-pass Melbourne, there was still much to do in Sydney. The *Observer* articles had been reprinted in the *Sydney Morning Herald* and had generated many letters.

We stayed the first night in an inner-city hotel and the next morning David visited Sydney's Community Services. They offered us accommodation in an old reform school that had been turned into a training centre for social workers. The office and accommodation were under one roof and close to public transport.

One of the letters I had received was from Eric Baldwin, who arrived in Australia in 1939, at the age of eleven.

I had sent Eric a reply and he wrote another short note that arrived in Nottingham after I'd left for Australia.

'You might be unaware that over the weekend of the 26–27 March, the Old Fairbridgians and their friends will be celebrating their fiftieth anniversary. We would very much appreciate your presence there at that time, both for your own advantage in the pursuit of your worthy task, and to give some of us the opportunity to personally thank you for your efforts on our behalf.'

I remember sighing when Merv read this to me over the telephone. The thought that I would be a welcomed guest at a

Fairbridge fiftieth reunion made me both smile and shudder. I doubted if Eric had any idea what he was doing.

My involvement with the Fairbridge Society had been very limited, but I could recite by rote exactly what Stephen Carden, their UK Chairman, had written in the *Observer* in response to the first articles about the child migrants.

'If an advertisement of the kind shown in the article is put in a Sydney newspaper by a social worker responses are likely to be mainly from malcontents . . .'

I knew that the reunion would be an emotional time for the Old Fairbridgians and I felt that my presence might be unnecessarily provocative. I'd made up my mind by the time we reached Sydney.

'I'm not going,' I told David. 'What purpose would it serve? I'd only antagonize the Fairbridge Society. This is supposed to be a celebration. I can't go.'

David disagreed. 'There are people there who need our help. They need the Trust. This is a wonderful chance to meet a large group of migrants. They are scattered across different states but are coming together for this weekend. And anyway, you've been invited. It's not as if you're gate-crashing.'

'But I feel that I'm not really welcome.'

Finally David convinced me, but not before I'd called George Wilkins in Melbourne.

'Eric Baldwin has invited me to the fiftieth reunion of the Fairbridge Society,' I said, 'Do you ever go to these things?'

'No, never.'

'Oh God!' I said, 'Then I won't have any friends there at all.'

'No worries, Margaret,' George said at once. 'I'll be there. We'll drive up and meet you in Orange. I'll book you into a hotel.'

In the months since the Trust was founded, Mervyn had been spending his spare time researching the child migration schemes for his doctorate thesis. He'd unearthed quite a bit about Kingsley Fairbridge, the founder of the Fairbridge Society. A Rhodes scholar, Fairbridge had a dream of sending the poor and deprived slum children of Britain to the rural idyll of Australia, Canada and Rhodesia.

He was the ultimate empire builder who wanted to populate all corners of the Commonwealth with good, white British stock.

In Australia, the society had established 'farm schools', one in
Pinjarra, Western Australia, in 1912, and the other at Molong,
near Orange, New South Wales (NSW), in 1938.

Orange is a quiet rural town west of Sydney. David hired a car
and we drove six hours to get there on Saturday afternoon.

As a courtesy, I informed the Community Services Department
of NSW that we were going to attend the reunion, because I knew
it was a sensitive issue. They, too, decided to send somebody along
to 'monitor' events. Child migration had obviously created more
waves than I expected, especially in NSW.

The reunion involved a weekend of events including golf, tennis
and a 'Nostalgic Tour' by bus to the farm school and local
landmarks. The Reunion Dinner was in the auditorium of the
Orange Ex-Services Club. Drinks at 7.00, dinner at 8.00 and
dancing until 2.00 a.m.

I had hardly got inside the main reception area when a woman
came rushing up.

'Are you the terrible woman who wrote all those things?' she
said. 'You are! You are! Well, you aren't coming in here. We're
not having journalists in here. No, no, no!'

A man standing near by, hearing the fuss, leaned over and said,
'It might have happened to Catholic migrants, but not to us. We're
Fairbridgians!'

Others began to take an unhealthy interest in the proceedings
and I started to feel uncomfortable. I was standing there trying to
smile and wondering what to say, when George steered me into
the auditorium.

Among the guests of honour was Miss Judy Hutchinson from
the Fairbridge Society in England who had flown to Australia to
be at the reunion. She was dressed formally and, by comparison,
I felt under-dressed. My fairly plain navy blue silk dress had been
in a suitcase for a fortnight and even without the creases wouldn't
have been my first choice for such an occasion.

Miss Hutchinson was inside the door and approached me as
George and I entered. She shook my hand. 'Now, dear, we must
have a little word. You must realize that everything that was in
those *Observer* articles was untrue and you must acknowledge
now, before you go any further, that it was all untrue.

'You're going to see this evening what happy people they are. If you'd been on the bus this afternoon you would have seen their faces. They are so grateful for the opportunities offered and the farm holds such fond memories for them.'

Miss Hutchinson seemed to be almost imploring me to agree with her. I told her, very directly, 'That's not right. I can't agree with you.'

'But you must, you must . . .' she said, growing flustered.

'I am sorry, but I can't,' I said adamantly, quite prepared to walk out then and go back to Sydney.

David sensed the tension and intervened. 'This isn't the time or the place to talk about this. What we should do is put some time aside for the three of us to talk together. Miss Hutchinson, I don't think you're aware of some of the things child migrants have suffered.'

David changed the subject and began asking about her flight and if she was enjoying her stay in Australia.

I was surprised by how many people were in the auditorium. From what George had told me, the farm school at Molong had taken about 330 children over the twenty-five years from 1938. It seemed that a large percentage had come to the reunion.

George and his wife had organized a table for us and I was relieved to sit down. There were two bottles of champagne on the table. He set one of them in front of me and whispered, 'It's really water: you can't afford to take a drink.'

'You're right,' I smiled, 'but I'd love a gin and tonic.'

Tables were arranged around the room, some seating more than others, but at the end of the auditorium was a top table with a Union Jack hanging from the front. Miss Hutchinson was sitting near the President of the Old Fairbridgians, Dennis Silver, who was master of ceremonies for the evening. Dignitaries from the Australian Fairbridge Foundation were also at the table.

Before the meal was served, Dennis Silver stood up and said, 'We've got some very honoured guests here this evening,' and went through a roll call.

'We're also very pleased to have with us this evening Margaret Humphreys, a director of the Child Migrants Trust, and David Spicer, a trustee. I wonder if they would care to stand up?'

In a stroke, we were identified to everyone in the room.

Dennis Silver then asked those assembled to rise and sing 'God Save the Queen', followed by the Fairbridge song, 'Follow the Founder' . . .

We are Fairbridge folk, all as good as e'er,
English, Welsh and Scottish, we have come from everywhere;
Boys to be farmers and girls for farmers' wives,
We follow Fairbridge, the Founder.

As I listened to the words and looked around me, I could see that there was tremendous joy and pride on their faces, but beneath it I could almost touch the pain and denial in some of these people.

Our table was quiet during dinner. We swapped small talk and didn't comment on what was happening around us. I found it difficult to eat.

After the main course arrived, I saw a woman get up from a neighbouring table and walk towards me.

'Are you the Margaret Humphreys?' she snapped, full of anger.

'Yes.'

'Look at this then,' she said, slamming the palm of her hand on the table so the plates jumped. Beneath her hand was a photograph. 'You want to look at this. This man is a professor and he's an Old Fairbridgian. Look at how well we've done for ourselves. Why didn't you write about him?'

'I haven't written about anybody,' I explained, trying to be as gentle as possible.

'Yes, you have.'

I wasn't going to argue. She had a right to her view. When she left, all of us just looked at each other.

We carried on eating and when the meal was nearly over, Miss Hutchinson was asked to deliver a congratulatory address on behalf of the Fairbridge Society in London.

'It's so wonderful to be invited here and to see so many happy faces on this special occasion. I have a surprise – a gift from the London office to mark your fiftieth anniversary. When Kingsley Fairbridge first . . .'

I wasn't listening any more. It's the files! I thought. She's brought them their files. I knew what that would mean. Ever since these children were sent abroad, Fairbridge had kept a file on each of them. Each had his or her past locked in a filing cabinet 12,000 miles away.

Surely she must have brought the files, I thought. What else could it be?

Finally, as Miss Hutchinson finished her speech, she said, 'Yes, I've brought some photographs. We'll put them up on the walls and when we've finished eating, we can all go and have a look at them. I think you'll find there will be some wonderful surprises. They are photographs of all of you as children. I'm sure your families will want to look at them too.'

We stayed at the table and later, as the plates were cleared and the band set up their instruments, I noticed people starting to get up and gather around the rear of the auditorium. I heard whispering at first, which grew louder.

David went to investigate.

'What's happening?' I asked him, sensing his disquiet.

'People are crying,' he said. 'It's amazing. They're looking at themselves as children and breaking down.'

I suddenly realized what was wrong. Many of these people had never seen themselves as children. They were gazing at small black-and-white images of youngsters gathered on the docks and on railway platforms in England. There were other pictures of them on the farm, sitting on the steps or in the shade of trees. This was part of their past and for the last five decades it had been locked away.

Fairbridge's gesture appeared to be backfiring.

I had no way of knowing why Fairbridge had decided to open its archives and show the photographs. Perhaps it was always planned as a nice gesture on the fiftieth anniversary; or was triggered, at least in part, by the *Observer* articles.

'I think you'd better go over there,' said David.

The photographs were pinned to a wall. Men and women were leaning close, pointing out faces to their wives, husbands and children.

'Look. Look. This is me,' they exclaimed, voices choked with emotion.

To anybody else they were just ordinary snapshots, but to some of these people, the photographs represented a rare and precious link with the past. They wanted copies, but Miss Hutchinson told them that she didn't have the negatives.

Men and women began coming over to me. Others approached David. We were surrounded by people asking us about the Child Migrants Trust and what it did. For the next hour we answered their questions.

Many wanted to meet me privately and David reassured them that I wasn't rushing straight back to Sydney and would join them the following day at the reunion barbecue.

Next morning, I interviewed several migrants at our hotel before returning to the reunion. By the time we arrived at the barbecue the tables were set up and hot-plates were being stoked with wood.

It was a picturesque setting, in a large field surrounded by pine trees.

A small girl in a sundress came up and presented me with three pine cones. 'I want you to have these,' she said. 'I want you to take them back to England.'

'Oh, they're lovely,' I told her. 'Why are you giving them to me?'

'Because you're going to help my grandad find his family.'

I recognized many of the faces from the previous evening. People seemed more relaxed in casual clothes. I certainly felt more comfortable.

'Where am I going to interview people?' I asked David. 'I can't sit in the middle of a field.'

'Never fear,' he chuckled.

Sure enough, he produced a table and chair and pointed me towards what looked like a sports pavilion.

You must be joking, I thought, but obediently settled into the room.

Meanwhile, David began mingling with the migrants letting them know that I would see them. People started queuing up.

From the very first interview, I sensed that the Fairbridgians were in a dilemma; caught between a wish to be loyal to Fairbridge and a need to know about the past. They wanted to see me but the reunion was a celebration of their time at the farm school, not an examination of past wrongs. I tried to answer their questions as best I could.

During one interview with a husband and wife, Miss Hutchinson walked in. She saw there was no spare seat and disappeared, only to return within minutes with a chair under her arm. Without being invited she sat down next to me.

'How could you bloody well do it?' the wife rounded on her. 'How could you have done it?'

Miss Hutchinson was shocked. Her whole demeanour changed. I picked up my chair, moved myself to the other side of the room and left her sitting there, totally silent.

'My husband had nothing, nothing at all,' I heard the wife continue. 'Nothing to give his children. How could you have done it? Where are the records?'

There were tears streaming down her husband's face.

As she held his hand, the woman said quietly, 'Last night he saw photographs of himself as a little boy for the first time in his life. We cried all night.'

Miss Hutchinson was dumbfounded. She could obviously sense that these people were suddenly turning on her and the Fairbridge Society. She couldn't understand their anger. 'Times have changed, now,' she said. 'It wasn't like this years ago.'

The woman replied, 'My husband wants to find his family. He doesn't know if he has a family. He should have been able to do this years ago.'

I felt Miss Hutchinson was fighting a losing battle. She softened when she saw the tears. Finally she told the couple, 'When I get back to England, we're going to do everything we can to co-operate with Mrs Humphreys and get you access to the files.'

By late afternoon the queue of people waiting to see me had dwindled but I now knew so much more about the experiences of child migrants at Molong. I was starting to doubt that any of these children had been orphans when they left Britain.

Some could actually remember parents, and a few, in the early days, had received letters from people who they thought were relatives.

Although I recognized the efforts that the Fairbridge Society had made for the migrants, I could also see that each had lost a part of their lives – it was a loss which, for many, had permeated the years since their departure from Britain.

David and I still had a long drive ahead of us, back to Sydney, and I had notes to write up. While I had been conducting interviews, David had talked to the migrants waiting outside. Among them was the woman who had stormed up to our table the previous night and slammed down the photograph in front of me.

As we packed the car to leave, she approached me. Her demeanour had changed totally.

'I've been talking to David,' she said. 'Do you think it would be all right if I wrote a letter to you when you get back to England?'

'Of course. I'd love to hear from you.'

As we drove out of Orange at dusk, trees were silhouetted across the horizon. I thought of something George had shown me the previous day when we drove along a dusty road towards the farm school.

'You see that tree?' he had asked, pointing out a lone gum-tree set back from the road.

I nodded.

'Well, Margaret, I wanted to show you that tree . . .'

'Why's that then?'

'I wanted you to see that tree because that's where I used to sit every day at four o'clock, thinking about my home in Liverpool. That was my childhood in that tree. And I used to walk down this road and think, Oh, please knock me over. I want a car to knock me over. Don't kill me, just break my legs so I'll go in hospital. Because then somebody will pick me up . . . then somebody will hold me.'

14

I boarded the plane back to England very tired, very sad and not a little angry. The final four days in Sydney had been tough going. David did more than a dozen radio and press interviews and I had many migrants to see, including one living in Wollongong on the south coast.

Joanna, David and I sat together on the flight home.

Joanna was clearly exhausted, emotionally as well as physically. She had been working on her own for most of the time; we'd been going on ahead of her, doing the interviews and arranging for her to follow some of them up. The stress of listening to the migrants and then travelling thousands of miles alone, without the consolation of someone with whom to share her reactions, had taken its toll.

David's face looked almost haunted, and I could sense his anger. It was beyond his comprehension that anyone could treat children in such a way. That anybody could physically and sexually abuse such vulnerable human beings. Occasionally his fury would surface and he'd say things like: 'There's never been anything like this. Never. The abuse of these children is on a scale that is totally unknown. The perpetrators have got to be brought to account. They can't get away with this.'

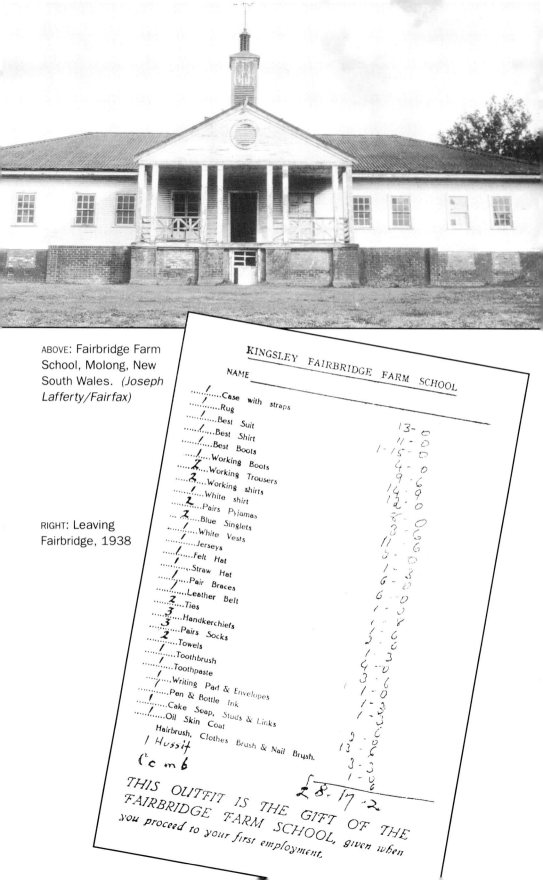

ABOVE: Fairbridge Farm School, Molong, New South Wales. *(Joseph Lafferty/Fairfax)*

RIGHT: Leaving Fairbridge, 1938

KINGSLEY FAIRBRIDGE FARM SCHOOL

NAME

1....Case with straps
1....Rug
1....Best Suit
1....Best Shirt
1....Best Boots
1....Working Boots
2....Working Trousers
2....Working shirts
1....White shirt
2....Pairs Pyjamas
2....Blue Singlets
1....White Vests
1....Jerseys
1....Felt Hat
1....Straw Hat
1....Pair Braces
2....Leather Belt
2....Ties
3....Handkerchiefs
3....Pairs Socks
2....Towels
1....Toothbrush
1....Toothpaste
1....Writing Pad & Envelopes
1....Pen & Bottle Ink
1....Cake Soap, Studs & Links
1....Oil Skin Coat
....Hairbrush, Clothes Brush & Nail Brush.

1 Hussif

C c m b

13- 0
11 - 0
1 - 15 - 0
4 - 0
9 - 6
14 - 9
12 - 0
3 - 0
3 -
11 -
9 - 6
1 - 3
6 - 3
6 - 0
1 - 0
1 -
3 -
1 - 0
4 -
1 - 0
3 -
1 -
1 -
1 -
13 -
3 -
3 - 3
1 - 6

£8. 17. 2

THIS OUTFIT IS THE GIFT OF THE
FAIRBRIDGE FARM SCHOOL, given when
you proceed to your first employment.

ABOVE: Desmond at Clontarf.

LEFT: 'The portals through which 2451 Orphan Youth have passed to become worthy citizens of Our State.'

ABOVE: Boys camping out at Clontarf. *(West Australian Newspapers)*

LEFT: War hero Douglas Bader with survivors of the Clontarf bus crash. *(West Australian Newspapers)*

ABOVE: Charles Devonport at the graveside of his mother whom he found too late. *(Ron Duggins)*

CENTRE: Pamela Smedley as a child.

RIGHT: Pam, who was reunited with her mother in 1989.

ABOVE: Me with Marie and Harold. *(T. Bailey Forman Newspapers)*

LEFT: Harold Haig, Melbourne, 1993. *(Penny Myles)*

ABOVE: CMT team who staffed telephone help-lines following the ABC transmission of *Lost Children of the Empire*, Sydney, November 1989.

BELOW: Help-lines in Nottingham after the BBC showing of *The Leaving of Liverpool*, July 1993. *(T. Bailey Forman Newspapers)*

ABOVE: CMT office, Nottingham. Child migrant Bernard Murphy returning home at last, with Yvonne and Beverly.

CENTRE: Child migrants celebrating the announcement of the Order of Australia Medal in March 1993, Dalkeith Road, Perth.

BELOW: 10 December 1993, CMT office in Melbourne. Open house with child migrants from all over Australia. The Hon. Joan Taylor of Nottinghamshire County Council is on my left.

ABOVE: At Bindoon Boys' Town, 1993. *(Select/Tony Ashby)*

LEFT: The investiture of the Order of Australia Medal at Government House, Canberra, with His Excellency the Governor-General Bill Hayden, 13 December 1993. *(Penny Myles)*

I, too, was shattered – both by what I'd heard and by the scale of the task that lay ahead. I kept thinking to myself, How am I going to do this? I had a small study in my house, one phone, no fax, a part-time researcher and a mountain to climb.

Above my head and beneath my feet were six bags full of notebooks and migrants' documentation. David and I had had to argue for permission to carry them on as hand luggage but I was adamant. I wasn't letting them out of my sight because they represented all that some people had of their past lives.

'We've got to tell the Government, haven't we? We've got to tell the charities.'

'Yes,' said David. 'They've got to be told. They have to know that it went dreadfully wrong for so many.'

'What about the files? We need to get access to them. It could help us find their families.'

I had a terrible sense of foreboding as we landed at Heathrow. And when I reached up to unload the bags from the overhead lockers, I turned to David and said, 'I'm in trouble, aren't I?'

He just looked at me and said, 'Yes.'

It was Good Friday but we had no sense of it being Easter. The tulips and daffodils were blooming but they brought little joy. Philip Bean picked us up from the airport and from the moment I saw a familiar face I knew that I couldn't talk. He was full of questions, but I couldn't answer. I was too shocked by what I had learned. It would take a long while before I could share the experience in Australia.

'Where's the rest of you, Margaret?' Merv asked. 'Your clothes are falling off you.'

'I've lost a bit of weight.'

The house was spotless and there were flowers everywhere. Welcome-home cards decorated the hall and the mantelpiece. Rachel and Ben had made a little banner which was pinned across the front door saying 'Welcome Home'.

They were very excited to see me, full of hugs and kisses. Ben was eight. He wouldn't let me out of his sight. He trailed me through the house and upstairs when I went to bed. He lay on the bed beside me and prised my eyes open when I tried to sleep, saying, 'Don't sleep now, talk to me. Talk to me, Mummy.'

It was difficult. They kept asking me questions about what I'd seen and who I'd met. They wanted to know all about Australia. What could I say? I'd seen hotels and airports.

A week later, when the children were back at school, a teacher took me aside when I arrived to pick Ben up from the local primary school.

'Ben's been terribly upset while you've been away,' the teacher said. 'I saw him sitting in class one day with his eyes shut and when I asked him what he was doing he said, "I'm trying to see my Mummy's face." '

Swallowing the lump in my throat, I explained to the teacher that I was due to go away again within a few months. 'We've tried to cushion it. Is there anything else we can do?' I asked.

'What about putting a photograph of you in his satchel?' she said. 'Ben knows you're coming back, but three weeks seems like forever to an eight-year-old.'

For a long while I couldn't talk about Australia. There was a barrier around me and I didn't laugh as much. My assumptions and long-held beliefs, all those things a person relies upon, had been turned upside down. The world itself looked slightly different when I looked out the window at ordinary scenes like families going off to church.

I thought, These people are OK. They don't know about the thousands of children sent overseas who could have been their friends and their neighbours. They have no idea how lucky they are.

'Where do we begin?' I asked Yvonne, as we sat in the upstairs office staring at the unpacked bags.

My main priority, I decided, was to be able to return to Australia in six months' time, having made at least some progress with everybody I'd seen. In most cases this might mean only having found them a birth certificate.

I knew that Joanna was in London with a full team working on the documentary. Her priorities were different from mine but understandably she wanted to be able to finish the programme on a positive note. She wanted the reunion of a child migrant with his or her family.

This wasn't my concern but if my research eventually created the possibility and all parties agreed then I knew it would be the opportunity to show the world that the child migrants had been outrageously deceived. They weren't orphans. They did have families.

So what name did I start with? The first? The most recent? The most unusual?

The Australian trip had generated about 300 requests for help and over the next two months Yvonne and I began research on all of them. As with most searches, the results were mixed. The birth certificates for some child migrants were easy to find, others took far longer. I knew from experience that often names had been changed, and that dates of birth could be incorrect. Some had no idea if they were born in England, Scotland, Ireland, or Wales.

The letters kept arriving, many simply expressing thanks and wishing me success. The child migrants were embarrassingly grateful.

Among them was a letter from Christine, the woman who had stormed up to me at the Fairbridge reunion and accused me of having misrepresented the lives of the child migrants.

> Dear Margaret,
> After my talk with you and David I have done some deep thinking and soul-searching and, yes, you were right, I do want and need to know who I am and what my roots are.
>
> I have always wondered why I had no-one – brothers, sisters, aunts, uncles, cousins, mother or father. It has never seemed logical that there should be no-one at all. I've often wondered why and who sent me to Fairbridge? What was wrong with me that no-one wanted me?
>
> Margaret, even as I write, the memories of the loneliness and rejection come flooding back and I am weeping for the lost years; the years of not belonging to anyone, not knowing anything . . .
>
> When I asked about my family, the people at Fairbridge told me that my parents were killed in a car accident, but I think they told me that to give me something to hang on to; to give me a background of sorts . . .
>
> It is a very emotional thing to start and peel back the years and face the feelings and emotions that have been buried over

a lifetime. I thought it didn't matter any more but it does. And perhaps more now that I'm in the latter half of my lifespan.

Please try to find out who I am. Where do I come from? Is there anyone I belong to? Do I have any family?'

It was an important letter, for Christine and for me, because it showed that regardless of how proudly the Old Fairbridgians had presented themselves at the reunion, some still had profound feelings of rejection.

I was putting a lot of faith in the documentary, hoping that it would raise public awareness, that people would realize what had happened, for the first time.

At the end of May I flew to Harare in Zimbabwe to begin investigating its child migrant schemes. I had never been to Africa and tried to keep an open mind about my expectations.

15

It was a scorching Sunday afternoon and the only breeze came from the slipstream of the cars and trucks that hurled themselves through the streets at breakneck speed. The taxi ride from Harare airport passed in a blur of loud horns and petrol fumes. Near the hotel, traffic came to a complete stop as a congregation marched past singing hymns and carrying banners.

I had already seen the work of Kingsley Fairbridge in Australia and now hoped to see if the schemes had been any different in the former Rhodesia, where child migration had begun after the Second World War.

Kingsley Fairbridge had spent his teenage years in Rhodesia in the late 1890s where a vision came to him one summer's day which he described in his autobiography:

> When you close your eyes on a hot day you may see things that have remained half hidden at the back of your brain. That day I saw a street in the East End of London. It was a street crowded with children – dirty children, yet lovable, exhausted with the heat. No decent air, not enough food. The waste of it all! Children's lives wasting while the Empire cried out for more.

In 1909 Fairbridge gave an impassioned speech to the Colonial Club at Oxford University describing his vision. Such was the power of his oratory, all fifty of those present enrolled as members of the 'Society for the Furtherance of Child Emigration to the Colonies'.

On my first day in Harare, I visited the State Archives, hoping to find records about the children sent to Rhodesia and also details of the policy that underpinned the scheme. It gave me my first taste of dealing with the local bureaucracy, a nerve-racking experience, particularly when the keepers of the State Archives told me that I must refer to them as 'comrade'.

One of my new 'comrades' showed me a brochure which publicized the 1946 opening of Fairbridge Memorial College, situated in the bush outside Bulawayo. As I read the brochure, my eyes fell on several important sentences.

It revealed that in Southern Rhodesia most of the manual tasks on farms were performed by Africans. At Fairbridge, the white immigrant children were not expected to perform the farm work or other chores, as they had been in Australia. The inference was that they were the élite and had been brought from England to join the next generation of professionals and politicians that would run Rhodesia.

I felt quite vulnerable in the archives. I was making enquiries about a very sensitive area of the country's history and I feared that not everybody would welcome me.

Joy Melville, a writer from England, had come with me to Zimbabwe to begin researching a book to accompany the TV documentary. The following day we took a taxi to the Fairbridge college at Bulawayo. I expected to see a rather grand-looking campus but instead found what looked like a row of Nissen huts. The actual college had once been an RAF base and Fairbridge had converted the building. The ground was dusty and dry; it must have seemed like another planet to the boys and girls who began arriving in 1946.

The college had since been turned into a primary school for local black children, and the headmaster showed us around the class-rooms.

Before I left England, an ad was placed in a local newspaper in Harare, stating that a researcher was arriving who wanted to interview former child migrants from Britain. There were nine responses.

When I arrived I rang all of them and arranged interviews. On the second morning I had a very different visitor waiting in the lobby, a young African boy with a typewritten letter from Dame Molly Gibbs, the wife of the former Governor-General of Rhodesia, Sir Humphrey Gibbs.

> Dear Mrs Humphreys,
> In case you are out when we call, I am writing this note to say that in seeing the item about the Fairbridge scheme in the paper this morning, it occurred to me that you might be interested to meet me and my husband because we used to have some of the Fairbridge boys to stay on our farm outside Bulawayo from time to time.

The Gibbs' residence was something from Empire days, as if time had been frozen and the sun had never set on a small corner of England. I was struck by the beautiful gardens being tended by African gardeners. Inside the house there were more African servants, each impeccably dressed.

Sir Humphrey took us into the house which was decorated with photographs of children and grandchildren, and Dame Molly, dressed informally in a skirt and blouse, poured tea in the sitting-room.

I still wasn't sure why they wanted to see me, although I had my suspicions. Sir Humphrey began by asking exactly why I was in Zimbabwe, and I explained about the Child Migrants Trust.

'Do you understand the politics of Zimbabwe?' he asked. 'Things have changed quite a bit over the years.'

He seemed to understand my work, and that many child migrants whom I'd seen in Australia wanted to find their families.

He said, 'My understanding is that the children who came to Fairbridge Memorial College were all sent with their parents' permission. They weren't orphans. I can't tell you how many there were but it didn't involve thousands.'

I listened intently, fascinated by the prospect that child migrants might actually have been sent by their families rather than the authorities. If true, this raised a whole new issue. Why would parents consent to their children being sent to Africa? And why was this consent never sought for the children sent to Australia?

'This could all become very embarrassing,' said Sir Humphrey. 'If there is a big fuss you won't be doing these people any favours. Most of them are very happy here. They've done very well for themselves.'

The inference I drew was that Sir Humphrey was asking me to be careful. Perhaps he was worried that the new regime in Zimbabwe would learn that white children had once been brought to Rhodesia and educated in the hope that they would help sustain white rule.

Sir Humphrey kindly drove me back to the hotel and told me about the difficulties of being a white in Zimbabwe. Warning me not to walk in certain areas of the city, he shook my hand and said, 'Times have changed.'

I thought I understood what he meant. Times had changed for people like Sir Humphrey and the whites of Zimbabwe. But they had changed for everyone.

Walking back from the bank at midday the following day, I was attacked in the main street. A thief snatched at my bag, but the strap was crossed over my shoulder and unless he cut it, there was no way he could get it from me. I was determined not to let go. It contained all my interview notes, which were more important than any amount of money.

My attacker grew more and more desperate as I fought back, and he kicked me to the ground. I was lying in the gutter and he kept kicking me in the back, almost rolling me along the street with each blow. I kept trying to stand up but couldn't.

Eventually, I think he realized he would have to kill me to get the bag, and decided to run. I slowly stood up, bruised and bleeding. My lip was split and my knuckles grazed. I looked around. The street was crowded with Europeans, but not a single person helped me in any way.

I staggered back to the hotel, aching all over but feeling incredibly calm. It wasn't until I reached the sanctuary of my room that I collapsed.

Joy thought I should go to hospital but I declined. Merv wanted me to get on the first plane home. I was bruised but OK. The shock was the worst thing, but it didn't seem to be a political or racist attack. A thief simply wanted my money and thieves are the same the world over.

I didn't leave my room again without somebody with me. The next day, the pain was worse but bearable. I wanted to discover more about Sir Humphrey's belief that children had been sent abroad with their parents' permission. As I reread the letters from Zimbabwean migrants who wanted to see me, I noticed that they used surprisingly different language than I had expected.

'I was privileged to be selected as one of the first eighteen underprivileged children to be sent to the Rhodesia Fairbridge Memorial College in 1946 . . .' one wrote. 'The selection process was most rigid and only those of a higher IQ were selected.'

I finally met Tom, an engineer for a mining company, at his home in Harare. It was a beautiful house with large gardens enclosed behind high walls. The guard dogs were locked up for my arrival.

We sat in the living-room and I began by asking him what he could remember about England, and how he had arrived in Rhodesia.

He was raised by his grandparents in the East End of London. 'We were living in a Victorian terrace house and were poor, poor as church mice. I was a boy scout with the local troop, and it was the scout master who told me about the Fairbridge scheme. I asked him how to apply.'

'How old were you?' I asked.

'I was ten.'

'Why did you want to leave England?'

'I was happy but I could be a real naughty little bugger, playing in the streets. I was forever standing outside the pub asking for packets of crisps. I used to get into strife.

'I jumped at the chance to go to Rhodesia and was most persistent. My grandparents signed the form. My grandfather took me up for the medical and the IQ tests. I think they encouraged me.

'It was like a great adventure, I'd never even ridden in a motor car; but I know I wasn't aware of the implications. I remember wearing grey short trousers and a hat with 'F' for Fairbridge on it. I was in a group of eighteen, aged from seven to fourteen. We left Southampton dock on board the *Caernarvon Castle* which was still rigged out as a troop ship. We had a splendid sea voyage and then a three-day train journey.'

'What was your first reaction when you arrived?' I asked.

'It was summer and I really fell in love with the place. I had a cockney accent and several of the others were Scots, so we had difficulty making ourselves understood. My grandparents used to write to me and I replied up until they died in the Fifties.'

As Tom spoke and referred to his childhood in such glowing terms, I was struck by how different his experience was to those of the migrants in Australia. Then I realized that to him, going to Rhodesia had been a little like being sent away to boarding-school. He had maintained contact with his family and, more importantly, had had a part in the decision to leave his country and his family.

So far, none of the child migrants that I'd met in Australia had been given a choice. The decision had been made for them.

Tom continued. 'After I left the college, my first job was on a farm and then I followed my own career. Scholarships were very scarce. I think initially it was envisaged that most of us would become farmers but only a few ended up going onto the land.

'There would have been no future for me in post-war Britain. I hate to think what would have happened to me when my grand-parents died.

'Needless to say I've never set foot in England since my departure.'

For all Tom's pride and sense of achievement, as I looked around at his lovely house, I sensed that he was trying to justify his life. There was a need inside him and eventually he asked me if I could help him find any surviving relatives in London.

Over the next ten days, I met other migrants who presented a similar picture of how they had arrived in Rhodesia. There were no stories of sexual abuse or brutality here. Nevertheless, they had lost a part of their lives and wanted it back.

Among them was a man who recalled living with an aunt and uncle in England until he was nine years old. 'One day my uncle said to me. "How would you like to go to Rhodesia? At least if you arrange a picnic there it won't rain."

'I was cross at the time so I said yes. Many years later when I looked at my own son who was nine I couldn't believe my decision.'

Another spoke to Joy and told her how he and his brother had been living in a children's home when their father applied to the Fairbridge scheme because he wanted to give his sons a better start in life.

'There were some children who came with us who were very homesick and had problems. But children of that age are very resilient and are not going to be upset for very long.

'With hindsight, I think they were probably sending us out here to be part of the élite. We were brought up like any other ordinary kids, but the schooling was strictly for white children.'

His description of leaving school and getting married indicated how much control Fairbridge had over his life. When he failed at his first job he returned to the college and slept in a building nicknamed 'Rejects Cottage'. There was a particular table in the dining-room where such boys had to eat.

And he described turning twenty-one, when he was handed his birth certificate and documentation by Fairbridge. He called it a 'big stage in my life'.

Rhodesia must have looked beautiful in the brochures – and long after my visit, I still had an image of fine, sunny weather and bright flowers against a very clear blue sky. But I couldn't help thinking what a contrast it must have been for those from the inner cities of Liverpool or London.

Among the last migrants that Joy and I visited was a lawyer who also recounted how he'd been given an IQ test before leaving England. He had been told that he was privileged to be sent to Rhodesia. My impression was that he still felt that he was one of the chosen few.

He lived in a huge house in an attractive suburb of Harare and was concerned and embarrassed about my mugging. He told me how terrible it was that everything had changed; but he couldn't leave Zimbabwe now without sacrificing his wealth. He would have to leave the house, the cars, his job, everything.

I said to him, 'Go. Get out. Leave with what you stand up in then.'

But of course he wouldn't.

He shook his head and said, 'I love this country. I couldn't live anywhere else.'

I spent all day with him and his wife, and Joy joined us for supper. I didn't expect anything formal but was again given an insight into how these people lived. We sat in the dining-room being served by Charles the waiter, dressed all in black and white.

I didn't know how to deal with this. When the third course arrived, I asked the lawyer where Charles lived.

'He lives at the end of the garden.'

'And is he married?'

'Oh yes – and he's got children.'

'Does his wife live here?'

'No, we let him go and see her once a year.'

These people were right. Their lives would have been very different if they'd stayed in England. For the most part they were not orphans or abandoned children; their families had actually agreed to their passage. The children had also played a role in the decision. They were destined to become leaders and to keep the Union Jack flying high over Rhodesia.

But though their experiences were very different from the Australian migrants, many needed to deal with their unresolved pasts.

16

When I arrived back in England, I was still badly bruised from the attack in Harare and wondered if I'd damaged my liver or kidneys. I went to my doctor in Nottingham who said I should consider myself lucky.

Yvonne and I worked frantically to trace families, aware that within a month I had to leave again to visit Canada, where our list of names was certain to grow even longer. There would be no holidays, or even relaxing weekends off for the foreseeable future.

Joy Melville had gone directly to South Africa from Zimbabwe to interview child migrants who had moved there after growing up in Rhodesia. She telephoned me on her return to Britain and told me about her research.

Among the people she'd found was Mrs Robinson, the wife of the longest serving headmaster at the Fairbridge College in Rhodesia.

'Margaret, I asked her about the files because I know it's important for you,' Joy said. 'The news isn't good. Mrs Robinson said her husband had been told by the committee in London to destroy all the records when the school closed.'

I couldn't answer. Totally astonished, I wondered why anybody would do such a thing. It was just another inexplicable incident.

*   *   *

What would Canada hold? I knew little about it save for having read one or two novels by Margaret Atwood and having watched several Canadian films. Its fashion and food were a mystery to me.

Joy Melville joined me on the flight to Toronto on Saturday 18 June. By the time our taxi pulled up outside the hotel I was exhausted. I was surprised to see armed policemen on the rooftops and helicopters buzzing overhead.

'Security sure is tight,' the taxi-driver explained. 'There's somebody very important in town.'

As I stepped on to the pavement a small crowd near the hotel became quite animated. Someone shouted, 'It's Margaret! She's here, she's arrived!'

Joy shot me a disbelieving glance. I raised an eyebrow back at her, but I was so tired by now that anything would have made sense. As I gripped my suitcase and staggered towards the hotel doors I realized that the eyes of the crowd were not on my taxi but on another vehicle, a long limousine, that had pulled up outside a hotel near by.

I watched as Margaret Thatcher climbed out and waved to the crowd. Minutes later Ronald Reagan, the American President, arrived. I'd quite forgotten that Toronto was hosting the World Economic Summit.

It was quite ironic that Mrs Thatcher should be in town. I was in Canada to investigate what was fast becoming a terrible blight on Britain's history and one which successive governments ought to have known about.

I knew from Merv's research that Canada had accepted more British child migrants than any other country. From 1880 to the Great Depression 100,000 were shipped across the Atlantic by a variety of charities and agencies. Over a quarter of this total had been sent by Barnardo's.

Instead of being cared for in institutions, these children were put in distribution centres where they were allotted to farmers and householders – boys worked on the land and girls were trained as domestic servants.

Very few children were emigrated to Canada after 1930 – hence most of the surviving child migrants were well beyond retirement age. They were also spread over a wide area.

Before I arrived, advertisements were published in the major Canadian newspapers and these brought an amazing response. I spent until midnight on the first night, telephoning migrants and arranging to see them. Because they lived so far apart, I had to start immediately. So the next day I took a train from Toronto to London, Ontario, to see a lady who was in a nursing home.

It was a three-mile walk from the station and we arrived in time for a late afternoon tea. It was a far better welcome than this particular child migrant had received when she arrived as a child.

Florence Aulph was eighty-seven years old and had arrived in Canada in 1913 when she was twelve and a half.

I sat on a chair beside her bed and poured the tea as Florence told me that she was one of seven children from a mining family in Newcastle, and had been born with a deformed leg. When she was four years old she remembers being picked up by her mother and taken to a place called 'Babies Castle', a Dr Barnardo's home for children with physical handicaps.

'She told me that if I was a good girl they would straighten out my leg and I'd be able to walk proper. I never saw her again.'

When her father died of TB, Florence was sent to Canada. She wasn't asked if she wanted to go. The boat docked at Quebec and she was taken to a children's home at Peterborough with hundreds of other boys and girls.

'They had our names all down in a book and they would take a couple of us into the room at a time and ask us, "Where would you like to live, in the city or out on a farm?" And stupid me said, "On a farm." '

She was taken to a foster home and went to school for a year. But the British children were treated differently from the local children. They were considered to be second-class citizens.

'You don't know what that does to you,' Florence said. 'I have never got over it; even now.'

Later, Florence worked as a nanny and housemaid with a nice family, but after three years she was moved to a town called Fergus. Her new boss was a brutal man who beat her regularly and paid her only a few dollars a month. She was given the family's discarded clothes which she would mend and sew together at night.

Finally, thanks to a friend who had been on the same boat to

Canada, Florence escaped to the city and found a good job as a housemaid for a woman who treated her kindly and bought her new clothes. She had a day off every week and could go to the cinema.

At the age of twenty-two she married but her life got no easier. Her husband was very poor and they worked their hearts out to get by, keeping chickens and packing eggs every day. She raised three children and remembers the hardship with fondness because their small wood cabin was full of love.

'My mother wasn't educated and couldn't write but I kept in contact with my family in England until she died. I just have one sister left and she's been to Canada to visit me. We weren't sisters, we were strangers. There was no feeling of family or kinship, there couldn't be.'

I spent the following day at the University of Toronto researching the background to child migration. There were very few details but what I found was horrifying. I stumbled upon a newspaper report from the *Evening Telegraph* in St John's Newfoundland on 10 January 1924.

'Farmer Censured,' was the headline. 'Harsh and Cowardly Treatment of Immigrant Boy.'

> Holding that there was no legal responsibility to provide medical attendance and care, Judge Maclean, sitting at Moosomin Assizes, Manitoba, Canada, acquitted George Ford, a farmer of Broadview, who was charged with the manslaughter of a British immigrant boy named John Bayns. In ordering Ford's discharge, his lordship severely censured him for his harsh and cowardly treatment. The case excited great interest and feeling, and more so because of recent criticisms of the immigration system as affecting the placing of lads from the home country. Bayns was alleged to have been neglected and ill-treated, and to have received no medical attendance when suffering from the double pneumonia which was the cause of his death.

Joy and I took an early flight to Ottawa and arrived shaking after a mid-air emergency threw the plane into a steep dive. Passengers screamed and coffee cups were hurled into the air as the jet dropped like a stone.

Mercifully, the plane levelled out, but for those few seconds I thought my worst nightmare – being in a serious accident away from my family – had come true.

Joy and I had an appointment to see a former child migrant who was now a proud grandparent. He very much wanted to tell us his story of being sent to Canada as a fourteen-year-old. He felt a considerable degree of satisfaction in having overcome a range of hardships and obstacles, especially his lack of formal education.

'There was hardly any furniture, just bare boards and benches,' he said. 'No tables. We ate outside in the woodshed. We were there until they found a place for us. The younger ones were snatched up within a day or two. Up to fourteen, you see, employers didn't have to pay wages. They went to school but they had to work for their keep. Any of us over fourteen did not go to school. I remember us sitting and crying after the little ones left. Even us bigger lads were very homesick.'

The luck of the draw of the migrants' arrival and placement was echoed by another man who described being put on a train alone and unsure of his destination. The conductor was to tell him where to get off. Confused, scared and homesick, he watched station after station pass, not knowing what the future held.

'I thought the conductor had forgotten me and I'd missed my stop,' he said. 'But eventually I was put off the train and this old farmer pinched my arms, seeing if I was strong enough.

'He told me if I worked hard and behaved myself, I would have a good home. It was OK eventually. I got food and clothes. I was better off than some of the boys.'

Another migrant, a seventy-two-year-old man, described how, at the age of ten, he arrived at a huge distribution centre for child migrants where the farmers came to inspect and choose children to take back to their farms. They looked him over, and said, 'Nah, we won't take him, 'cos he won't last the winter.'

He was crying as he spoke and I kept thinking, Why has nobody asked him these questions before? Why isn't there one single office in the whole of Canada that deals with child migration? Why doesn't Barnardo's have an office? Why doesn't the Catholic Church?

*   *   *

I wasn't prepared for the immense distances that had to be covered in Canada. Travel had become a logistical nightmare of plane schedules and train timetables. From Ottawa we flew to Calgary on the western edge of the Canadian prairies near the American border and the Rocky Mountains. Sadly, I had no time to appreciate the scenery.

John Jones lived in the outskirts of Calgary but his first sight of Canada, fifty years earlier, had been from the deck of a ship, the *Duchess of Atholl*, that arrived in Halifax in 1937. John was seven years old at the time. He recounted how he and about twenty other children were put on a train that took three or four days to reach Vancouver on the west coast. After a ferry ride to nearby Vancouver Island, the children were bussed to the Fairbridge Farm School at Duncan. This was the Fairbridge presence in Canada, built in 1935 following a public appeal for funds in Britain which was endorsed by the Prince of Wales.

John was part of the second wave of child migrants sent to Canada between 1935 and 1948. They were fewer in number and had an entirely different upbringing from the children who preceded them. Instead of being sent to isolated farms, they grew up in an institution. Fairbridge operated a series of cottages each housing about twenty-five children under the care of a cottage mother.

'We were segregated, the girls at one end of the school and the boys at the other; and until we were twelve we wore short blue pants and horrible sweaters. You would get up in the morning and go to this gigantic dining-room and have your breakfast. Then you went to school. It was a whole self-contained community: the school was there, the farm was there.

'There was no time to ourselves. After farming work, there was the cottage mother to contend with and what she wanted us to do. The seniors picked on us worse than anybody else. And they used to make us fight each other. There was bullying from the old kids to the new kids.

'There was always total authority around you at all times. One time, they said everyone had to have their tonsils out and the whole school was sent off.

'The cottages were like army huts and the daily routine of eating, washing and working was like a prison regime.

'The cottage mother would beat you if you did something wrong. It was a way of life. I had to rake the yard one day and I did not finish it, maybe I was slow, and that was enough to get the strap in the morning. Your cottage mother had complete control over you, she answered to nobody, she was our keeper.'

John was still bitter about the experience. Halfway through the interview he looked up at me and asked, 'Why am I here?'

He knew I didn't have an answer.

'I've tried hard not to be bitter,' he said. 'I didn't want to let it ruin my life. Survival was the most important thing.'

Family life was a mystery to John. His only experience of it came from the infrequent trips outside the farm when he'd see families together. He told the story of one Christmas when he was over-heard telling other kids that Santa Claus didn't exist.

'There was a catalogue and you had to pick your gift prior to Christmas. You could have one up to three dollars. When I got down on Christmas morning, I got a piece of coal and that was it. All the other kids got oranges and nuts. I cried that day, but I started believing in Santa.'

John left the farm school when he was fifteen and got a job on a chicken farm. Later he worked for the Canadian Pacific Railway and joined the Army. 'There were times when I was down-and-out, living in the seediest parts of Vancouver. Most people have a family to go to when things get rough but I had no-one. Fairbridge was my only home.

'My birth certificate, the short version, just arrived in an envelope on my twenty-first birthday almost to the day. I was always told my birthday was 24 June and then I found it was 7 June. Fairbridge must have had some records, but we were not privy to them at all. They were a closely guarded secret.'

John told me that Vancouver was a beautiful city with a natural harbour ringed by gardens. I soon discovered he was right when Joy and I flew to the west coast to interview more child migrants.

These were a mixed group. Most were like John and had been sent out during the inter-war years.

I didn't get to meet Charles Devonport, but he wrote his story down and sent it to me, describing his childhood and the sad search for his mother. It came as a shock to learn that Charles had been sent from my home town, Nottingham, which was involved in one of the smallest of the early schemes, sending mostly teenagers from youth clubs to Nova Scotia.

Charles had been living in a workhouse for a year because of bronchitis and an intestinal problem caused by malnutrition. Then the Child Welfare Society took him away from his mother who couldn't look after him and placed him in a foster home.

'Just outside Nottingham there were orchards, but they were surrounded by iron railings, and we would gaze at the lovely apples. One evening we jacked the railings apart and got in and this big chap with leather leggings on and two dogs caught us. Then this huge bobby came on his bicycle and I wound up in front of the magistrate. I was sentenced to one year probation and had to go to a branch of the Nottingham Boys' Brigade two days a week for a year in lieu of going to reform school.'

At the club, twelve boys were asked to volunteer to go to Canada. Forty applied and Charles was one of those chosen.

'Two weeks later, we were given instructions to pack our clothing and be on the railway platform of the London and Midland Railway. I was sitting there on my little suitcase and I heard footsteps and my mother was walking along the platform towards me – she spotted me right away. I was sitting there with my head in my hands and she said, "You're leaving me!" I said, "Yes, Mother, I'm going to Canada." So she says, "I've brought you something," and I stood up, of course, and my mother gave me a five-pound note and a box camera. She told me to save my money and be a good boy and write to her, and then she kissed me again and started to cry. She wrote me one letter. I answered that letter faithfully and I wrote another one later on to the same address. She replied once and after that there were no more letters, ever.'

Charles spent forty years trying to find his mother. Unlike other child migrants, he knew he wasn't an orphan. 'I always told myself that I'd go back and find her. Even when I joined the Army during the Second World War, I thought that it was a chance to get to England and look for her.'

It was a long, unrewarding search, involving great disappointment and soul-searching. Genealogists were hired, neighbours and former workmates were found. There were seven Nellie Devonports born in 1888 – and each had to be researched.

Charles eventually found his mother but it was too late to meet her. Nellie had died six years earlier. 'I knew she'd be very old, but I never stopped hoping that I'd find her alive.'

Having organized a gravestone and a memorial service, Charles made the painful journey back to England and visited the cemetery. Kneeling beside her grave he said, 'Mother, I wish I'd found you were living. We could have exchanged views. I could have told you what I've been doing and we could have got to know each other; and you could have told me who I am – that's important to me, to know who I am.'

It has been estimated that there are about a million Canadians descended from the child migrants – an astonishing figure that I've never heard disputed.

The children transported before 1920 were collectively known as the 'Home Children' – a label which they now associate with feelings of stigma, inferiority and being second-class citizens.

'The first winter I was there,' one elderly woman said, 'I wore my summer coat and straw hat until the end of January. The temperatures were below freezing, but I had to wait for the January sales before she bought me a winter coat and hat. I remember wearing that straw hat in an open sleigh for nine miles. I remember that trip so well as I had to stable the horse at the hotel and the man who was helping her said, "Who is that you have standing there?" And she said, "That's just the girl from the Home." And he said, "They're pretty poor trash, ain't they?" And she said, "Yes, they are." '

Another former child migrant summed up her bitterness in a letter to me.

> I was one of the so-called Home Girls who, in the space of one morning, was torn away from my school, my home and all my playmates at the age of eleven.
>
> A man came and took me and my sister away in a bus to a children's home. It was nothing short of a prison – nothing short of a disgrace to the name of England.
>
> There were many girls there and about two months after we

arrived, we were told we were going to Canada and shown slides that created a picture of this wonderful land waiting for us across the water.

On an April day in 1912 or 1913, we were marched crying to the port and put on a boat. It took us two weeks to cross the ocean and most of us were seasick. We couldn't keep our food down, but the meals were so disgusting it was a blessing.

We finished up in Montreal. My sister and I were separated on that first day and I didn't see her for many years after that. I was sent out with a man and wife to a farm. They had two children and another on the way. I'd never been on a farm.

The wife was always angry, insulting and scolding me. She would continually tell me that the English were no good; that we'd never been any good. I ate too much, I was slow and lazy. Nothing I did was right.

I spent six years putting up with this before I told them I wanted to go back to the Home in Montreal. I left the farm with ten dollars and a few old clothes.

I have never forgiven England for sending me away. How can a country have no rooms or food or shelter for its helpless children? Oh the shame!

When my eldest son was of age, they called him to fight for them. This country that had no room for us. I tried to explain to him that I'd already lost my father and four of his brothers in the first Great War and look what they'd fought for – a country that sent its children into slavery.'

In all, I interviewed about forty people throughout Canada. The heat was tremendous; the distances were enormous; and it was a merry-go-round of trains, planes and buses.

The child migrants were very welcoming and hospitable, inviting Joy and me into their homes. Many had survived periods of enormous hardship with their integrity and their sense of humour intact.

They would ask me questions about Britain, wanting to know about everything from pub opening hours to the prices of food. Others wondered whether I'd ever been to their places of birth, naming cities and villages across the whole of Britain.

Like their Australian counterparts, these people had no

documentation, save for perhaps a short birth certificate. Some had been told their parents had died and others simply assumed that the decades in between had ensured that they were truly orphans. Not surprisingly, all wondered why Britain had sent them abroad with so few effective safeguards.

But most of the children sent to Canada were now in their seventies and eighties. Age increased their longing to find their families, but it also robbed them of any chance that their mothers and fathers were still alive.

Their own children – the next generation – now adults themselves, would ask me about their parents. 'You know, the one thing Dad would never give us was information about his childhood . . .'

The longing and pain and hurt had never gone away, even though they were grandparents now. How sad to be seventy years old and not know who you really are. And how desperate, because they knew that their mothers and fathers had gone for ever.

One man said to me, 'You know what you can do to help?'

I said, 'No. What can I do?'

'Just help me to die knowing who I am. Let me have a birth certificate.'

Canada was immensely sad for me because it represented a generation of people I knew I could do little to help; it was far too late for them. I'd do what I could, of course, by finding their birth certificates and locating where their parents were buried.

However, I had a difficult decision to make. Thankfully, the former child migrants of Canada helped make it for me. I told them about what had happened in Australia after the Second World War and how many children were involved.

Many Canadians replied, 'Margaret, do something for them, because it's too late for us. Make sure they get to know their families.'

These people touched my heart, and helped me make the decision. Events in Australia were so recent and appalling, and my resources were so limited, that I decided I would immediately focus my attention there.

On the Saturday before I flew back to England, I caught the car ferry to Vancouver Island and drove to Duncan looking for the Fairbridge Farm School. There was a wild beauty to the landscape.

The architects of Britain's child migration movement had been very determined and dedicated individuals. Despite many setbacks and difficulties they had persisted and established the machinery for sending many thousands of children overseas.

The Fairbridge farm at Duncan was a perfect example. The fundraising that built the institution was a tribute to the society's ability to sign up the great and the good in support. Nearly every patron was either a lord, an earl, a marquess or a countess. The Prince of Wales had donated one thousand pounds towards the target of one hundred thousand pounds sterling when he launched his appeal in 1934 with a full page of *The Times*, featuring pictures of children from British slums enjoying their new and happier life abroad.

I wondered how many earls, countesses and sirs would support my appeal. How many would give money to the Trust to help find a birth certificate for these former child migrants, or trace their families?

There was nobody at the farm when I arrived. In truth, I could see little except a small wooden chapel surrounded by trees.

Before I wandered inside I noticed the foundation stone. The inscription was attributed to the Lieutenant-Governor of British Columbia. It read:

To the Glory of God and the Children of the Empire.

17

Yvonne had continued working on the family searches while I was away. Some yielded results quickly while others, I knew, would take longer. Already it was beginning to look as if many of the Australian child migrants were not, as they believed, orphans.

The search was beginning to make sense for one of them, Pamela Smedley from Adelaide.

Pamela turned out to be an only child, as her mother had been. There wasn't a huge family tree, but the search was made more difficult by the fact that her mother had lived for a time overseas.

The final piece of evidence fell into place only ten days before I was due to return to Australia for the filming of the documentary. It meant that I had very little time to uncover Pamela's history.

St Catherine's had yielded her birth certificate and a marriage certificate for her mother. Then after a long trawl through the electoral registers and phone books I had managed to find somebody in Hastings who I thought might be this woman.

I wrote her a small card:

> I am a social worker based in Nottingham. I would like to discuss something with you of a rather delicate and confidential nature. I'd like to travel to Hastings on Monday arriving at

about eleven o'clock. Would it be possible to meet you at your home? If not, I'd be prepared to meet with you anywhere.

I gave her my home telephone number and stayed close to the phone all weekend. When she didn't ring, I kept wondering, Have I got the right lady? Has she got the letter? Perhaps she's on holiday?

Finally, on the Monday, with a great degree of apprehension I got on the train in Nottingham at six in the morning.

When the train pulled into Hastings, I was quite anxious. I took a taxi and told the driver to park at the end of the road. It was a quiet street in a beautiful area, full of large trees and well-kept bungalows.

As I walked to the door, I still had nagging doubts.

I knocked and the door opened immediately.

'Hello, come in,' said an elegant, well-spoken lady, smiling warmly. She looked much younger than I expected. I knew from the marriage certificate that Pamela's mother was in her seventies.

I was a little taken aback. I wanted to establish my credentials and show her my identity card on the doorstep but she was insisting: 'Come in, come in. You've come a long way, haven't you? Haven't you come a long way from Nottingham? Are you in a car, dear? Come on in.'

She introduced herself and I met her husband. We all sat down and had tea in china cups. We talked about the weather, the trains and about everything except the business at hand.

How am I going to stop this? I thought.

'Would you like more tea, dear?' Betty asked. 'Would you like to stay here tonight?'

Finally I managed to say, 'Did you receive my letter?'

'Oh yes, dear. Yes, I got your letter. Why has it taken you so long?'

She was looking at me all the time, studying my face. Suddenly it hit me: She thinks I'm Pam. She thinks I'm her daughter.

I glanced awkwardly at her husband.

'Is there anywhere we can go and talk together?' I asked Betty.

'Don't worry about that, dear,' she said. 'I told my husband everything last night.'

They sat there smiling.

'You see, your letter came on Saturday morning while I was in bed and he brought it up to bed with my cup of tea. I looked at this letter with the strange handwriting and I thought, This is about my baby. I don't know why. I just looked at it. I looked at it for ages and ages and then my husband said to me, "What is it?"

'I don't have any letters that come just for me, you see. He said, "It's not your birthday." Because it looked like a birthday card, you see. "It's not your birthday, and who do you know in Nottingham?"

'I wouldn't tell him. And I read your card and kept it to myself all day, but I told him last night. "I've got something to tell you," I said. I explained to him that before we married I had a baby and my mother had intervened and my little girl had been adopted.'

Betty still thought I was Pamela and I had to stop her talking for long enough to gently explain that I was a social worker from Nottingham who worked with adults who had been adopted as children. Betty couldn't hide her disappointment – she wanted so much for me to be her daughter. As I explained, she nodded occasionally, beginning to understand that I had news for her but had to be sure she was the right woman.

She said, 'Ever since adopted people have been able to find their families, I've been waiting for this. My daughter was adopted, as you probably know. Where is she? When can I meet her? Is she with you?'

I took Pamela's birth certificate from my case and handed it to Betty.

'Is this your daughter?'

'Yes, it is.'

I knew it was going to be difficult to break the news about Pamela's childhood. It had to be handled carefully. I had to let Betty set the pace; let her ask the questions.

'Have you met her? Do you know her?'

'Yes, we've met. You look very much alike.'

She smiled broadly and said, 'Well, where is she?'

'Pamela is living in Australia.'

'Why did you call her Pamela? Her name is Elizabeth.'

I wasn't ready to explain the details – more importantly, Betty wasn't ready to hear them.

'How did she get to Australia?' Betty asked.

'Pamela has been in Australia since she was very young.'

'Well, when did she go there?'

'As a child.'

Betty's look of astonishment turned to sadness. 'I saw something on the news the other day. It was about children going out to Australia on boats. It was awful . . .' She paused and simply looked at me. 'Please tell me it's not that.'

The next few minutes were very emotional, and very personal.

Betty needed time to absorb what had happened and gather her thoughts. Her husband disappeared into the kitchen, preparing lunch and setting the table.

Betty took a deep breath and began explaining what had happened to her as a nineteen-year-old, living in London. She had been educated abroad and graduated from a finishing school. When she became pregnant, her mother was horrified and didn't approve of her boyfriend, despite the fact that he wanted to marry Betty. Instead, they decided they would bring the child up together – mother and grandmother.

'But that became very difficult, and when the baby was only a few months old my mother announced, "I'm going to take this baby to the nuns." '

Betty was told that her daughter would be adopted by a loving couple, who would raise her as their own.

When I left Hastings, late that afternoon, I was thrilled to have found Pamela's mother, yet terribly sad. Here was proof of a case where a mother had not given consent for her child to be migrated. She had placed her daughter for adoption in England. Of this I had no doubt.

That day my fear and apprehension had been for Betty, now I felt the same emotions when I thought of Pamela, at home in Adelaide. How was I going to tell her?

I flew to Australia on 25 November. The last person I spoke to before leaving was Betty who had sent me a letter for Pamela, along with some photographs and a small gift.

Apart from these, I was loaded down with family details for thirty child migrants. In some of these cases, Yvonne and I had also managed to find and visit their families. I was bringing with me photographs, letters and family mementos.

The production crew from Domino Films was due to meet me in Sydney, several days after I arrived. They had already been filming in Canada and Zimbabwe.

As I cleared customs and emerged into the arrivals hall at Sydney Airport, I saw a familiar face which was totally out of place.

'Harold!' I said. 'What on earth are you doing here? You live in Melbourne!'

'Well, I've come from Melbourne to meet you.'

'When did you fly in?'

'I haven't flown.'

'How did you get here?'

'I've still got my old banger.'

I wouldn't have trusted that car to go to the end of the road and back, and he had driven it over 500 miles, through the night, to meet me.

'That's lovely, Harold,' I said, 'but why have you done it?'

'I've come to give you a lift.'

'Where to?'

'To your hotel.'

'How long are you staying?'

'Just for a cup of tea.'

'Then you're going back?'

'Yeah.'

So Harold chauffeured me to the Sheraton and saw me to my room. We had a cup of tea and dinner, and later that evening he climbed back into his van.

'Why did you do it?' I asked. 'This is awful.'

He said, 'Well if you can come 12,000 miles to help us, surely I can come from Melbourne to bloody Sydney to pick you up?'

The following day I began meeting child migrants and telling them of the search for their families. I was painfully aware of the sensitivity of the subject. These people had spent decades with nothing and I couldn't simply drop information on them. It had to be done with great care and many would possibly need counselling for a long time before and afterwards. I had just a few weeks before going home again – a situation that was totally unsatisfactory.

When Joanna arrived with her film crew, I had another dilemma to sort out. Her first question was, 'Have you found anybody's mother?'

'Yes, I have,' I replied, watching her face light up. 'But it's not that simple.'

Joanna wanted a reunion to complete her documentary but I had reservations about exposing families and former child migrants to the camera. A reunion was such an emotional time that I felt it was a gross intrusion to film such a private moment. I explained to Joanna that it was up to the parties concerned to make the decision whether they wanted it filmed.

'Is it anything to do with Pam?' she persisted. 'We're going to spend a long time with her next week, filming in her house, talking about her childhood. Should we at least tell her you're coming to see her?'

'You can tell her that much. Also ask her to sign a contract with you. I want you to promise that if she wishes anything at all to be withdrawn from the film, you'll comply.'

I arrived in Adelaide two and a half weeks later. The roses in Pamela's front garden were glorious – and so English. Inside the house the film crew were helping Pamela put up her Christmas decorations. They were obviously getting on well.

'It's lovely to see you again,' Pamela said, 'but I'm sure you've got other people to see who are more important than me. Anyway, come and have a cup of tea.'

Much of what happened next was captured in the documentary. I started by getting Pamela to describe again some of her feelings about being a child migrant.

'I've always felt that I'm less than other people who can talk about at least an auntie or an uncle,' she said. 'I can never say that. There's always an emptiness for me, and it never really goes away. I love my children but they don't completely fill that gap. I felt as if I was robbed, not having anybody that I was related to. Deep down I've always thought, maybe one day I might be able to find out something, but nobody seemed to care. They'd say, it's awful but there are people worse off than you – and there are.

'If I only had a sister or an auntie or an uncle . . . but it's such a long time ago . . . and there were millions of people killed in the war. I'm sure mine were amongst them.'

When Pamela stopped talking, I finally felt it was time. 'I'm going to tell you another story now,' I said gently. 'In some ways it's similar to yours.'

I handed Pamela a birth certificate. As she put on her glasses I noticed that her hands were shaking.

'You've been able to find out about her?' she said.

'I have.'

'You haven't? Oh!'

She was on the verge of tears.

'You can see that this lady was born in 1916,' I went on. 'She could only have been a young girl when she was having a baby, and her mother would not let her marry the father of the baby.'

'How can mothers do that? But they do, don't they? How could she do it?'

'Very difficult days in London, they didn't have proper accommodation, they had to find jobs, they had to keep themselves, they had to survive, they were on their own, and this baby was going to be born. This baby was born in hospital and this young mother wanted to keep her baby, so she took the baby home to a flat with very little furniture, hardly any money, and the mother said to her daughter, "This isn't the way I want my granddaughter brought up." War was impending "I'll take this baby to the convent where we'll ask the nuns if they'll look after her for a short time." '

Pamela interrupted. 'Fancy telling me that I was left in the hospital. Why would they tell me that?' Pamela asked. 'The nuns said my mother walked out of the hospital, leaving me there. I was told that, so I believed it. That poor woman.'

'That poor child,' I said.

'Who was responsible for this?' she asked. 'Was it the nuns? Nuns don't make these decisions? Who did these things?'

'Perhaps we'll never know.'

I continued my story. 'Pamela, while you were growing up in Australia and getting married and having a family, there was a woman on the other side of the world who has never stopped thinking about you. You were the great loss in her life.'

Pamela's jaw dropped.

'Is she still alive?'

'She is.'

'I can't believe it! I couldn't be that lucky! What's she like?'

'She's lovely.'

'I've got a mother!'
There was a long silence, and then I heard a sound behind me.
'What's that?' I said, turning around.
The film crew was in tears.
So was Pamela. We had to stop filming.

Later that evening, Pamela took me to one side and showed me the letter that Betty had given me to carry out to Australia. It was very moving.

Dear Pamela,
Can you ever forgive me for causing you so much unhappiness in your life? Even now I cannot make it up to you as we are so far apart. But you have always been in my thoughts.

Betty ended the letter:

You would like Hastings. It is on the South Coast and we live not far from the sea. I can tell you much more after I hear from you, which I hope will be soon.
In fact, I can hardly wait for you to get in touch, and thank you, Pamela, for trying so hard all these years.
With love from your Mum.

18

I was dreading going back to Perth. The memories of my last visit were still too vivid and came flooding back as I drove from the airport into the city. I felt physically sick.

When I arrived at the hotel and walked into my room there was already a pile of telephone messages stapled together like a book and bunches of flowers still in cellophane wrapping. More were being delivered all the time.

I was tired. No, I was exhausted. There were literally dozens more child migrants who wanted to see me and this time I didn't have David to support me. I was on my own.

I rang Merv to tell him I'd arrived safely but found myself saying, 'I want to come home. It's chaos. I can't get any sleep.'

Over the next two days I began a new round of interviews with former child migrants, many of whom had been brought to Australia by the Christian Brothers and had gone to one of four orphanages run by the Order.

Men described how, instead of going to school, they had been made to load trucks with rocks as they cleared paddocks at Bindoon. The bricks were made by hand, as were the terrazzo slabs.

One boy who tried to escape had his head dipped in a forty-four-gallon drum of liquid lime. This seemed difficult to accept, but it was not for me to investigate. Another told of getting half a mile down the road when he was picked up by a brother on horseback. 'I was put into a cold shower and flogged for hours,' he said.

During each interview, I would ask the men, 'Wasn't there anybody you could tell?'

They would shake their heads.

A middle-aged man described how he went to confession at Bindoon and told the priest about being sexually abused.

'The priest asked me who did it, and I told him the brother's name. But a few days later this brother found me and beat me. He obviously knew what I'd confessed. You know what upset me most?' he asked.

I shook my head.

'It wasn't the beating. No, that father broke the sacred seal of the confessional. There was no-one left to trust, ever.'

I was pleased when Joanna arrived, if only for the moral support. But there was little she could do to lessen the constant barrage of pain and hurt I was facing.

Unbeknown to me, the film crew had made a decision to film at Bindoon. Joanna had decided that this wasn't going to take place until I'd left Australia. Even if I had known, I wouldn't have gone with them. There were too many dreadful stories about Bindoon and it was the last place in the world that I wanted to see.

The day before I left Perth, Merv phoned and said that a social worker had called the house about a client of hers who was in hospital. This man had been telling his doctor for a year that he was put on a boat as a child and sent to Australia, then allegedly deported back to Britain at the age of fifteen. Nobody would believe his story.

However, he heard David Spicer talking about the Child Migrants Trust on radio and his social worker rang to talk to me.

'Can you try and find his family?' Merv asked. 'He thinks he might have sisters still in Australia.'

'You must be joking,' I said. 'You can't imagine what it's like here. The phone hasn't stopped ringing. I can't look for anybody now. I'm getting on a plane tomorrow.'

'All right, all right,' he said. 'I'll write it all up and wait till you get back.'

I put the telephone down and it rang again. It was reception.

'There is a lady down here; she hasn't got an appointment, but she's desperate to see you,' the girl said. 'She won't take no.'

I found this woman pacing the foyer. 'My brother's been missing for years! Bloody years!'

'I'm very sorry,' I said, 'I can't see you now. Come back this afternoon and we'll have a cup of tea, is that OK? What's your brother's name, by the way?'

She told me. I thought somebody was playing a joke on me.

She repeated the name.

'Right, sit there!' I said. 'Don't move!'

I ran straight to my room and looked at the notes of the details Merv had given me. It was the same name. I called Merv to make sure.

It was ten days before Christmas and here was this woman who for all these years had been parted from her brother and suddenly she seeks help and within minutes somebody tells her exactly where her brother is and how to contact him. I thought to myself: They'll think I'm a bloody miracle worker.

When I told her the news, she asked, 'What should I do?'

'Well, if it was me, I'd go out and buy him a Christmas card! I'll make sure he gets it.'

As she left and I returned to my room, I kept thinking of a saying my mother liked to use whenever something unexpected and pleasing happened. She would tell me, 'Margaret, God moves in mysterious ways.'

The next morning – my last in Perth – I was packing and arranging for the flowers in my room to be sent to a local hospital, when the telephone rang.

A man's voice said, 'You're not welcome in Perth and you'd better not come back.'

It was difficult to know if it was an Australian voice; I've always had difficulty with accents. But the person was quite well spoken. The voice was calm, not angry. There wasn't a hint of agitation.

He hung up after making this one bold statement.

I was shocked rather than frightened. It was just so unexpected. Yet something broke deep inside of me.

It was nine days before Christmas – a day that seemed to

epitomize 'family', and I knew that thousands of former child migrants had never had a true family Christmas. They had everything taken from them: their toys, their names, their birthdays, their brothers and sisters, their identities, their childhood, their innocence. Everything. The more I thought about it, the emptier I felt. It came to the point where I didn't know how I was going to relate to anybody. How could I tell them what had happened to these children? How could I begin to describe it – even to Mervyn?

19

I slept for twenty-four hours and woke up at about seven o'clock on the night of 18 December.

Wandering downstairs, I slumped in a lounge chair in the sitting-room and Merv offered to make me a cup of tea. The television was on but the programme was interrupted by a news flash.

A grim-faced announcer said a 747 had crashed over Scotland. They were searching for survivors.

'Where is it?' asked Merv, coming in near the end.

'Near Lockerbie,' I said, feeling numb and disorientated.

Somehow, on top of everything else, it was just too much.

I sat for a long while staring at the television until Merv put his arm around me, worried that I was too quiet.

'It's the lights,' I said. 'The Christmas lights.'

'What about them?' he asked.

'Can we turn them off?'

'But why? What's the matter? It's Christmas.'

'I can't cope with Christmas this year.'

It all seemed so trivial to me. It was sad, really, because normally Christmas was such an important time when the whole family was together. We'd almost hibernate for a week, performing the annual rituals and over-indulging.

In the hallway, the Christmas lights were brightly lit and I thought, I can't take this.

Merv turned them off and I could sense him wondering, How do I tell the children that Christmas has been cancelled?

I think he expected that in an hour or two the lights would be turned back on and everything would be back to normal. But as I sat in the hallway, staring blankly into the darkness, I think he realized that I was shaken and absolutely exhausted.

Tears were streaming down my face. I just couldn't stop them.

Ben arrived home from a neighbour's house and walked into the hall. He saw me and looked up at Merv. 'Daddy, why is Mummy crying? Why is she sad?'

I heard Merv tell him, 'Mummy's upset about some of the friends she's left in Australia.'

'Why?' Ben asked.

Merv was at a loss. Finally he explained that some of them, as children, had not had happy Christmas Days with their families.

The festivities did go ahead, for the children's sake, but for me the season passed in a slow-motion haze. Little things would trigger the tears. Often, when I looked at Rachel and Ben, opening presents, or sitting on Merv's knee, the tears would just flow. Small details became magnified in my thoughts. I thought of the tremendous loss and misery caused by the terrorist bomb on the Pan-Am flight. And also the loss and misery that I'd witnessed throughout that year in Australia, Canada and Zimbabwe.

I didn't want to be with people. Apart from Merv and the kids I didn't even want to be with members of the family. Above all, I couldn't bear anybody to touch me. People would come and put their arms around me and I'd freeze, but I couldn't tell them why. I didn't know.

The local vicar lived just across the road from us and every year he and his wife invited all the neighbours for carols around the piano. The kids would make up their own songs or read a piece of poetry they'd written specially for the occasion. The whole road went along and it was all very wonderful. This year, however, I sat in the kitchen thinking, I can't go across the road!

'Don't let the children go, Merv!' I said.

Merv looked at me hard. 'Listen,' he said, 'while you've been away they've been writing their Christmas poetry and Rachel is going to play the piano.'

'No, no! They can't go.'

'But you don't have to be there. If you like, I won't go with them – they can go on their own.'

It was totally illogical, but in my mind I wanted to blame this lovely, kind-hearted vicar for all the sins of the Church and the role it played in sending innocent, vulnerable young children to the far side of the world and then failing them, time and time again. The discovery that children had been abused by members of the clergy shook my spiritual foundations for a long while afterwards.

The children did join our friends and neighbours, and I stood in my bedroom, in the pitch black, and watched them singing in the vicar's front room. All my neighbours were congregated there, around the piano, celebrating Christmas Eve. And I thought to myself, they are all nice Christian families, leading good Christian lives. If only they knew.

Merv came up to comfort me and I said to him, 'I'll never speak to anyone on this road again!'

'Why not?'

'I don't know why not!'

Merv shook his head. 'What happened to those people is disgraceful, Margaret, but you can't blame the whole world for it.'

I knew what he was saying was true, but my feelings were so raw and open. There was nothing rational about them; very little in the past few months had seemed rational.

The next day I was getting in my car and my next-door neighbour came up with a broad smile as he shouted, 'Did you have a good holiday?'

Did you have a good holiday!

I stared at him in disbelief and said, 'Yes, bloody wonderful!'

He thought he'd misheard me somehow.

'I hear they've got good beaches in Australia?' he persisted.

'How the hell would I know?'

Merv came out and saved the situation.

It was a terrible few weeks. I showered many times a day. I'd go up for a shower, get changed and I'd be all right. Then half an hour later, I'd go up and have another shower.

Eventually, Mervyn arranged for me to see a professor of psychology at Nottingham University. I wanted an explanation for my desperation and anger.

There is a growing realization that professionals need skilled debriefing after being involved in traumatic events. I was no exception.

The professor told me that some of my feelings were similar to those of a rape victim. I had been exposed to so much emotional pain and suffering, that it had traumatized me. He was also concerned that I had gone through this experience primarily on my own.

It took time before I could accept my experiences in Australia and let them become part of me. Eventually I could laugh at my own extreme reaction – and hoped my neighbours would understand.

One of my first priorities was to organize official approaches to the various charities and government agencies that were responsible for the child migration schemes. I wanted to keep them informed of exactly what I'd discovered in Australia, Canada and Zimbabwe.

Surely, I thought, they couldn't possibly know how drastically wrong their schemes had gone for so many.

I was confident that when I showed them my evidence they, too, would be outraged and immediately swing into action. I expected that the files of individual child migrants would be made available to the Trust to help find families and that we would get desperately needed funds to expand our work.

This sense of urgency was heightened by a distraught phone call and then a letter from Christine, the Old Fairbridgian that David and I had met at the reunion in Molong.

Judy Hutchinson had kept her promise regarding the Fairbridge files, as it appeared that Christine had indeed been sent a copy of her file.

This horrified me. All along I'd tried to stress to the charities that these files contained very sensitive information which needed to be imparted with some forethought and common sense. Child migrants were going to need counselling before, during and after being given information which had been deliberately kept from them for so long.

Sadly, this advice was ignored by the Fairbridge Society, and Christine experienced the consequences. She was simply sent her file through the post.

Christine knew that she'd been adopted; I had managed to discover this, and had broken the news to her when I was last in Australia. But now she learned that her adoptive parents had rejected her – a shocking realization for anybody, let alone a child migrant whose feelings of abandonment are already so profound.

The file also revealed that Christine had been IQ tested at the age of eight in the UK and was found to be extremely intelligent; so bright, in fact, that it was recommended that she be fostered in England and not be sent abroad.

Unfortunately, that recommendation came too late. Christine had already been earmarked for Canada. When she missed that boat, they found her passage on another – this one to Australia.

I now faced a bizarre situation where some charities refused to release files or acknowledge they even existed and others were handing them out with little thought to the consequences.

David Spicer, as a trustee of the Child Migrants Trust, wrote letters to all the major charities and agencies, including the Department of Health. I wanted to make sure that no other child migrant received their file in such a way. It was also time that the various organizations involved began to accept their responsibilities to the children they sent overseas.

We were greeted with almost total silence. I found it difficult to understand.

Eventually we heard from the Catholic Church which said that it was unwilling to share its confidential records with any other organization working on behalf of former child migrants.

Despite this lone response, I still didn't want to criticize the charities and agencies involved with child migration. I knew that these organizations hadn't purposely got together and said, 'Let's ruin the lives of thousands of children.' I simply believed that very little thought had been given to the long-term implications. Perhaps they genuinely believed they were giving the children a new start, and that the end therefore justified the means.

Whatever their motives, time was running out for everyone concerned. Already former child migrants had missed meeting their mothers by only a few years. They were too late, death had intervened, and with each passing day, more opportunities for reunions were being missed.

Pamela Smedley had lived in Australia since she was eleven years old, but had no documentation to prove it. To visit her mother in England she needed a passport. Not a difficult document for the ordinary citizen to organize, but then, ordinary citizens have birth certificates and all the other bits and pieces of paper that define who they are and where they belong.

We managed to get Pamela a birth certificate and finally a passport.

In February, I met her at Heathrow airport and we travelled by train to Hastings. She and her mother had been speaking on the telephone and writing letters, but both were extremely nervous.

As we got out of the cab, Pamela said, 'Margaret, you'll have to hold me up. I can't get to the door.'

She was almost paralysed and needed a comforting arm.

It was such a private moment, I didn't want to be there. I felt I was intruding. I decided that when we got inside I would disappear into the kitchen, out of the way.

Betty had been waiting at the window for the cab to arrive. As we came up the drive I caught a glimpse of her at the curtain. Betty's expression told me that she'd been waiting for more than a morning; a lifetime.

The door opened and I disappeared, along with her husband, and left mother and daughter together. I put the kettle on and chatted to Betty's husband. We both knew we were surplus to requirements.

When I took the tea into the sitting-room, Pamela and Betty were side by side on the settee holding hands. They were totally absorbed with each other.

Betty took Pamela's hand and led her to the window.

'Is this your daughter, Betty?' I asked.

'Oh yes,' she said. 'Oh yes.'

'How do you know?'

Betty studied Pamela's face the way a parent looks at a newborn baby – that intense, enraptured look as if marvelling at all creation.

During lunch, I thought of how quickly things had happened. Only weeks earlier I had told Pamela that her mother was alive and here she was sitting down and having her first meal at her mother's table.

By mid-afternoon, the long journey and intense emotion began to show on Pamela's face. She was tired and needed to sleep.

'Your bed's through there, Pam,' Betty smiled. 'You'll like it – there's lots of lovely teddies and toys. Go on in, get yourself all ready.'

She glanced at me, then called out, 'Look, I'm going to call you Elizabeth, do you mind? Or Lizzie – do you mind Lizzie? Just give me a shout when you're ready, because I'm going to come in and tuck you in.'

Betty brought me another cup of tea and said, 'I won't be a minute. I'm just going to go and tuck my Lizzie in.'

Domino Films decided to call the documentary, *Lost Children of the Empire*. It was due to go out at 10.30 p.m. on 9 May 1989.

A fortnight beforehand, the Granada publicity machine cranked into action. Press releases were sent out and I was expected to do a series of radio, TV and press interviews to publicize the programme.

I went from one studio to the next, explaining the importance of the documentary. A couple of nights before *Lost Children* went out, I was booked to appear on the *Wogan* show and Granada were thrilled with their publicity *coup*.

Terry Wogan was on holiday and Sue Lawley was fronting the show in his absence. She was fascinated by the subject and even wanted to read an advance copy of the book that accompanied the documentary.

It was all arranged, but at the eleventh hour my appearance was cancelled and later I discovered that my replacement was Shirley Temple, who was in town publicizing her autobiography. Sadly, she was considered more newsworthy than the plight of the thousands of child migrants. Their stories had been sunk by the good ship Lollipop.

I felt even more disappointed when several days later I saw the BBC were broadcasting a half-hour programme on the history of Barnardo's and the efforts of the charity to get away from their old-fashioned, nineteenth-century image.

The programme made absolutely no mention of the child

migration schemes. That part of Barnardo's history was strangely missing.

Lost Children of the Empire was a powerful and balanced documentary. I felt it would generate tremendous anger and disbelief in the general public. Some would need counselling; others might come forward to provide vital information – teachers, nursery staff and child care officers who remembered the child migrants leaving Britain.

I talked to Granada and they immediately arranged to provide phone-in lines at its Manchester studios. These were staffed by experienced counsellors who had volunteered to help the Child Migrants Trust.

At midday all the phones were in place and a technician threw the switch to test them. Every phone rang. Granada had been trailing *Lost Children* all week, and the numbers had been published in the *TV Times*. Already people were trying to get through.

Fifteen of us sat watching the programme that evening, including George Wilkins and Harold Haig. As the end credits rolled, every telephone rang and we ran to our seats.

The response was incredible. People were distraught. There was anger and outrage at the way British children had been treated, resentment at the involvement of charities with household names, and guilt that this could have happened in the twentieth century.

Many ex-servicemen called, incensed that they had fought a bloody war only to see children treated like this in peacetime. Other callers demanded to know who was responsible for sending them. Who allowed them to be treated like this?

Mothers wanted reassurance that their children had not been sent overseas. Teachers said they remembered children going missing from their classrooms. Former child care workers said they had been assured the children were going to good homes in Australia and felt betrayed. People who spent their youth in children's homes remembered their friends being taken away. One man said the only reason he wasn't taken was that he had chicken pox.

We finally turned the help-lines off at about three in the morning. I felt shattered. Nothing could have prepared me for such a response. *Lost Children* had pricked the conscience of a nation.

I also felt immense relief. I had worried all along that people wouldn't believe me; that they would doubt that this tragedy had happened.

I remember asking migrants, 'Why didn't you tell somebody about this?'

And often they'd look directly at me and say, 'Who would believe us?'

Now the world did know. The world did believe them. The burden had been shared, along with the responsibility. Surely no government committed to family values could turn its back on these people. Nor could the charities deny their needs.

I was wrong.

Five weeks later, I finally sat down at a table with the major organizations involved in child migration and asked for their help. The Trust had written regularly to each of the charities, keeping them informed of our work, but it was obviously the documentary that spurred them into action. A director of Barnardo's invited me to attend a meeting at the Commonwealth Institute in Kensington, London.

The charities represented included the Salvation Army, Barnardo's, the Fairbridge Society, the Children's Society, National Children's Homes and representatives from the Church of England and Roman Catholic Church. An observer from the Department of Health also attended.

The 16 June meeting began in the morning, but David and I had been invited to join them in the afternoon. This didn't fill me with confidence. I wondered why it was necessary to exclude us from the morning's discussion. Instead of feeling welcome, I felt as if I was about to be given a dressing down for having blotted their copybooks.

It seemed bizarre really. These charities are all about 'families'. They promote themselves on a Christian family model. They should be delighted that child migrants were finding their families after so many years. They should have been thanking the Child Migrants Trust for pointing out this tragedy.

But as David and I travelled down to London on the train, I felt this would not be the case.

'I feel like a lamb going to the slaughter,' I said to him.

When we arrived, everybody present was sitting down around

a large conference table. There was a studied avoidance of eye contact and much shuffling of papers.

Mike Jarman of Barnardo's was chairman and as he showed us to our seats he tried to introduce a note of joviality into the proceedings.

'We've been talking about you,' he said with a tone of mock reproach.

I sat and stared at them, my face expressionless. I didn't say a word.

After an interminable silence, Mr Jarman began the meeting by telling me that there were people around the table who felt very hurt. He looked at me and there was silence. I looked around the table at each face in turn. At the two representatives from the Church of England. At the Monsignor from the Catholic Church. At Lady Dodds-Parker and Miss Judy Hutchinson from the Fairbridge Society. At the Colonel from the Salvation Army and the director of the Children's Society. All of them.

I said nothing.

David ended the silence. He began to give a report on the enormity of the problems we'd discovered.

Afterwards, I briefly tried to give them a sense of the desperation and isolation that the former child migrants were feeling. They needed help to find their families; they needed a professional post-migration service. But – and it was a very big but – this service had to be neutral and totally independent of the charities and agencies that had sent them away.

I felt the shudder around the table. Yet those present who were professionals should have fully understood and endorsed the position of neutrality. They knew, just as I did, that you do not send abused children back to their abusers for help.

I felt there was no acknowledgement or support for my stand.

It was not a formal meeting and, one by one, those around the table began putting in their tuppence worth, telling me exactly what they thought of the Child Migrants Trust.

The Children's Society representative was keen to indicate that his agency had only sent a small number of children and should not be confused with schemes run by the Church of England.

Fairbridge seemed dismissive of any need for a service at all. When David pressed the point about funding, the Fairbridge response was that there was nothing they could do to help because the properties in Australia had been sold and the proceeds put in trust. The terms of the trust dictated that any income could only be spent on children – and the former child migrants were now all of adult age.

David continued his questions. He wanted to know first of all whether the charities had records on individual child migrants, what the files contained, and whether they would be made available to the Trust.

'I'm sure you all appreciate,' he said, 'that this information is very sensitive. These migrants have no knowledge of who their parents are, or if their parents were married, or how they themselves came to be separated from their families. Many need counselling before, during and after they are given this information which has been kept from them for so long.'

The Salvation Army representative responded: 'We've been at this for over one hundred years now. We know what we're doing, we have the most experienced people.'

I wasn't convinced, as I had scores of letters from people who had tried to use the Salvation Army's tracing bureau, only to have their applications turned down and their money returned.

The meeting broke up after two hours without reaching any satisfactory conclusions.

I was disappointed. It was time for everyone to pull together and ensure that the Trust had the funds to carry out its primary goal, but instead people were arguing about the past.

As I was about to leave, the Salvation Army colonel approached and said that she could see I was a well-meaning person, but it was unfortunate that I had talked to the press. She told me to let the whole matter drop. I would never get the Child Migrants Trust off the ground.

'Go back home to your family, dear, and leave it alone.'

Then Mike Jarman took me to one side and asked for a word in private. We went into another room while David was politely saying goodbye to the others.

'Barnardo's would be prepared to give your trust a small amount of money,' he said, 'but in return for that we would want trusteeships. I could be one of them. It is a way to add funding to the Trust.'

'It would also be a way for you to control it, which could potentially compromise the Trust's neutrality,' I replied.

I agreed to consider the proposal but knew that I could never accept it on such grounds. Barnardo's may genuinely have wanted to help, but I felt it also sought control. How would the child migrants view an offer with strings attached?

The workload was horrendous. Yvonne and I battled through in the little office upstairs in my house, with no promises of funds and the mounting expense of each certificate we ordered.

We needed help and it arrived on my doorstop in a very unexpected way.

John Myles had seen an article about *Lost Children* in his dentist's waiting-room.

'I couldn't get out of there quick enough when I realized that you lived in West Bridgford!' he told me, waving the magazine. 'I want to help. It would be too easy to write a cheque – I really want to do something.'

John was very persistent. He explained that he had trained as a lawyer and had experience in tracing family trees. His girlfriend, Penny, was also skilled and both wanted to work for the Child Migrants Trust.

'I can't pay you,' I said, but money wasn't the issue. I really had to be sure that both of them had the understanding and the expertise to tackle the work. As it turned out, they both had these qualities in abundance.

John and Penny spent their days at St Catherine's House, while I prepared families to meet their sons and daughters for the first time, and Yvonne held the fort answering phones and letters.

We still had serious worries about funds. Without the support of the charities I was relying on the public donations triggered by *Lost Children of the Empire* and the newspaper articles.

But if the Trust was to find these families quickly, it needed far more resources than this.

Something had to be done so I turned to the grant-giving charities, of which there are several thousand in Britain. I submitted applications to those charitable trusts with a long history of funding welfare programmes, giving them precise details about our work.

Naïvely, I thought they'd say, 'Wonderful! Here's £10,000. It's a worthy humanitarian project.'

But each time the response was the same. They wrote back saying, 'No! No! No!'

I was surprised that they did not consider this to be a worthwhile humanitarian project. Perhaps most grant-giving charities believed it was the responsibility of the Government.

Early in January I'd applied for funding from the Department of Health but there was confusion over who should deal with the request. Finally, in August, a meeting was arranged in London at which the Department said it would meet with some of the interested voluntary organizations to 'facilitate a working and possible financial relationship'.

To add to my problems, I also knew that *Lost Children of the Empire* was due to be shown in Australia later in the year. If the impact in Britain was anything to go by, then it would be dynamite over there. I had to be there for that broadcast, but had no idea how we'd find the money.

I've had many surprises turn up on my doorstep, but rarely have they been so unexpected and so welcome as the couple who knocked on my door one night late in September.

'We've read the articles about your work, but missed the documentary because we've been away. Can you lend us a video of it?' the man said.

I gave them my only copy, which they agreed to return.

A few weeks later the man turned up again.

'May I come in?' he said. 'I'd like to talk to you about this terrible business.'

We exchanged a few pleasantries, and as I handed him a cup of tea, he said, 'Mrs Humphreys, I'll come straight to the point. There's not really anything to discuss, because my mind is made up. I've seen the articles and the documentary.

'Next week, you will be receiving a cheque from me for a hundred thousand pounds. It will be anonymous and I must ask you please to keep it that way. It is a gift, and the only condition attached to it is that no-one has a say about its use but you – and you must use it totally to do this work.'

I will take the secret of this man's identity with me to the grave. He had no direct link with the child migrants, but could certainly identify with their feelings of loss.

'Start to think about how you'll spend this money,' he said as he stood to leave. 'My advice is to get yourself a proper office. You can't keep working upstairs.'

20

Joanna Mack managed to give me a month's notice that *Lost Children of the Empire* was being broadcast in Australia. Thanks to the Trust's anonymous benefactor, I flew into Perth two weeks beforehand.

I wanted to be early because I had news for many of the people that I had met in Perth the previous year: birth certificates for some, for others whole families. I was going to be able to tell quite a few of the Nazareth House girls that I'd found their mothers, brothers and sisters, and was carrying letters and photos for some of them.

Penny and John had booked a holiday abroad, but they cancelled it just before I left England.

'Why?' I asked.

'Because we're coming to Australia,' said John. 'Thought we might be useful. If not, we'll work on our suntans.'

My past experiences of Perth filled me with a sense of foreboding but at least this time I had some good news for people. Perhaps it would ease the burden.

The last person I expected to hear from on my second day there was Brother Gerald Faulkner, the provincialate of the Christian Brothers in Western Australia. I knew who he was but had never

161

had any dealings with him. Nor had I dealt directly with the Christian Brothers.

Brother Faulkner phoned my hotel and invited me to meet him. I could hardly say no, and I was intrigued.

Penny commented to me, 'This could be a difficult meeting, Margaret.'

I nodded. 'Yes, but it could also be constructive. I think you'd better come with me to take notes.'

It was a fiercely hot day but we decided to walk. The head office of the Christian Brothers, on Hay Street, was only a few minutes from our hotel.

It was a large building, in a high-rent area of the city centre. We arrived at midday and were ushered into a large room. Sitting on straight-backed chairs around a table were a gathering of brothers and priests. Some of them were very elderly and most wore the clergical 'uniform' of black suit, black socks and black shoes. They sat quietly throughout the meeting.

I anticipated that they had probably seen the documentary. A copy may have been sent from England. I approached the meeting with a very formal attitude and asked Brother Faulkner how long the meeting would last, who was the Chair, and whether I could have a written copy of the agenda. I don't believe Brother Faulkner appreciated my formality.

'What agenda?' he said. 'You've been invited to come here for a discussion.'

For some reason, it sounded like I had called the meeting. I hadn't asked to come. I sat there, wondering what would happen next.

There was a long pause, then Brother Faulkner broke the silence.

'We wanted you to come here to tell you, in our view, that these outrageous claims of physical and sexual abuse are unfounded. It is all grossly exaggerated. There are many students who are very grateful for the time they spent here. This has been blown up out of all proportion.'

I had a familiar feeling that I was being brought to account. His tone of voice was belligerent, but, unless I was very much mistaken, I detected an underlying defensiveness. I sensed that the men present, perhaps because of the lives they'd chosen, did not know how to relate easily to women. They had spent their lives in a closed, predominantly male environment. In my view this was part of the problem. The Christian Brothers should never have been allowed to look after child migrants because the schemes they ran lacked the full and active involvement of women.

Brother Faulkner continued. 'This television programme is not balanced, you know. It's been sensationalized.'

I felt at this point that the meeting was more about shooting the messenger than addressing the issues that the documentary raised.

We were then joined by two professional workers from the Catholic Migrant Centre, and our conversation shifted from abuse to the important issue of the child migrants' records. I was assured that the Migrant Centre had little information on the child migrants; I was told categorically that records did not accompany the children from the UK. Some files had been burnt, and the remaining files had little useful information about the migrants' families. Finally, I was told that the brothers had dedicated their lives to looking after these boys under difficult conditions.

I was not asked for my opinions, I therefore said nothing. Indeed, there were times when I felt I was there to be seen but not heard. This was not the constructive discussion I had hoped for.

At one o'clock a tray of sandwiches and drinks arrived and was offered around. Penny gave me an enquiring glance.

'Brother Faulkner,' I said, 'I have come here to meet with you because you asked me to, but I didn't expect to have lunch. If the discussion has finished I have important work to do elsewhere.'

Outside in the fresh air I turned to Penny and said, 'Well, what do you make of that?'

She smiled. 'Margaret, I think they call it the Inquisition.'

I was surprised by what I believed to be a basic lack of the compassion that I automatically expect from someone in Brother Faulkner's position. Even if he could not accept the allegations of physical and sexual abuse, he must surely realize that these men had suffered a great injustice. I thought, Here is a man who is blinded by denial and whose ears don't hear. He had asked me why the child migrants were revealing these things now after all these years. I was saddened that the question was spoken in such a disbelieving tone.

Unfortunately, Brother Faulkner did not seem to be familiar with the idea of long-term trauma. He gave me the impression that he believed the years of silence suggested that the abuse had never happened, whereas I, on the other hand, wasn't surprised at all that it had taken so long for victims to speak out.

This kind of sexual abuse leaves the victim with the guilt and the shame, not the perpetrator. It seemed to me that, regrettably, the Christian Brothers were going to suffer a great deal of pain and soul-searching before they accepted the accounts of the child migrants.

As Herbert Agar said, The truth which makes men free is, for the most part, the truth which men prefer not to hear.

Back at the hotel, John asked me if I'd heard of someone called Peter Couchman.

'No, why?'

'Because you're the special guest on his television show. It's just been advertised on the TV.'

'That's news to me,' I said.

By the time *Lost Children* was released in Australia, it had won a gold medal in New York and been nominated for a Bafta award. Joanna was very excited. Again, the publicity barrage was launched.

Couchman was recorded the day before the show and went out immediately afterwards. It was to be recorded in front of a specially invited audience. Peter Couchman forewarned me that there would be a large number of Old Fairbridgians in attendance.

Despite my visit to their reunion, there were still some child migrants from Molong who resented any criticisms of their beloved founder and were angry at some of the media reports.

I was told the Couchman show was a debate-style programme, sometimes quite confrontational. The last thing I wanted was for the tragedy of child migration to become a bitter, point-scoring argument.

The Fairbridgians were, indeed, well represented. So many turned up, that not all were allowed into the main studio. They watched from a special ante-room. Couchman wasn't impressed. He had wanted the audience to be representative of all the migration schemes, some Catholic, some Fairbridge, some Church of England.

Harold and Pamela were there, and I recognized some of the

faces from the Fairbridge reunion: it was clear the audience was predominantly from the farm school, and included the president of the Old Fairbridgian Association, Dennis Silver.

The audience was shown *Lost Children of the Empire* and I could see from their expressions that it was a painful experience for many.

Then the screen went blank and the cameras turned to Peter Couchman. He gave a very powerful introduction, summing up the legacy of the child migration schemes.

After asking me several questions, Couchman opened the discussion to the audience. There were some very pertinent comments but then the discussion was set alight by the intervention of Dennis Silver.

'While I admire tremendously the work of the Child Migrants Trust,' he said decisively, holding aloft a sheet of paper, 'I found my own family. I have interrogated and found them.'

When Peter Couchman turned to me for comment, I simply told him that the Child Migrants Trust did not 'interrogate' people. 'Families and parents in the UK are very caring people, who have had very traumatic experiences in losing their children.'

Dr Ron Sinclair, a former child migrant, said, 'The search for identity is very important. If you look at the sort of techniques used in concentration camps, they were designed to take away people's identity. It is the ultimate indignity. So when a person has no identity, this search needs skilled intervention.'

David Hill, the head of the Australian Broadcasting Corporation, and himself a former Fairbridge migrant, was sitting in the front row.

'Fairbridge never thought this far ahead,' he said. 'The schemes were horribly misguided and we will have to pick up the pieces and do the best we can.

'This awareness is thirty years too late. We are being called the lost children of the Empire, but, in fact, we are the forgotten children.'

Mr Hill then posed the question, Why had it taken a British woman to bring the child migration schemes into the open?

The following night, *Lost Children of the Empire* was screened across Australia.

We were ready. Telephone help-lines were open from the moment the show finished.

We took hundreds of calls that night. The phones rang until 4.00 a.m. and would have kept ringing but the decision had to be made to turn them off.

There was obviously a huge need for on-going support lines, which the ABC couldn't provide. Thankfully, ever since my first visit to Sydney, I'd had good relations with Barnardo's, Australia, and it helped find us accommodation and telephones.

John and two other counsellors answered calls from eight the next morning, and they were still there at midnight.

Calls were coming in from all over Australia, hundreds from former child migrants who had been told they were orphans. Extremely distressed and very angry, they wanted immediate answers about whether their parents were alive or not.

A man rang from an oil rig in Bass Strait. He said, 'Tell me it isn't true. I don't bloody believe it. If somebody tells me I've got parents after all these years, I'll bloody shoot myself.'

Others spoke about horrendous acts of physical brutality at Bindoon and other orphanages. There were also calls from men and women who were not migrants but who had also suffered sexual abuse in institutions in Australia.

Ordinary Australians were outraged by the documentary. They couldn't believe that their country could have imported children in such a way. They were ashamed. Others were incensed and distressed that religious orders were implicated.

Over the following days, as I gave interviews to the media, journalists told me that 'this country is in a state of shock'.

Although the main aim of the phone lines was to get a name and address from each caller so we could get back to them, we had to counsel some for long periods. And the stories they told were often so graphic that the counsellors found it hard to cope.

By the end of the week everyone was exhausted. I didn't know how I was going to get home. I still had to travel to Adelaide and then back to Sydney. Life got very difficult. If I went to a restaurant, people would come up to me and say, 'You're that woman who was on the telly last night. We watched you tell Pam about her mother.'

I had to send Penny out when I needed to buy some new clothes because I was being stopped in the street. I didn't appreciate the notoriety, but at the same time, getting the story into the open and seeing the truth becoming more widely acknowledged, was long overdue.

In what was described as a positive response to the documentary, Catholic diocesan welfare agencies throughout Australia offered their services to anyone involved in the child migration schemes who had lived under the 'auspices of the Catholic Church'.

A statement released by the Australian National Catholic Association of Family Agencies said it had been approached by the Catholic Welfare Council in Britain to be the first point of contact for those people who wanted to trace their natural families.

The association's chairman, David Cappo of Adelaide, said the documentary offered a sobering reminder of the 'values which prevailed in the area of child care as recently as twenty years ago.'

'Many of the children who were abandoned to British orphanages were admitted in haste and secrecy, without any professional assistance or advice,' he said. 'The British government which was recovering from World War Two, did not recognize the need for quality counselling or other forms of assistance in the decisions to separate children from their origins.'

He said the involvement of Australian government officials and charities like the Catholic Church had been at the request of the then British government. It was the British government's solution to overcrowded orphanages.

I had one last, and very important, interview to undertake before I went home.

A surveyor from Adelaide had read a copy of the book of *Lost Children of the Empire* and suffered a nervous breakdown.

In hospital he pleaded with doctors, 'Get hold of this woman Margaret Humphreys. I want to talk to her.'

When I got to Adelaide I went to the hospital and found Walter sitting on the veranda, looking out on the gardens. He told me a story that had been bottled up inside him for the best part of thirty years.

At the age of three he was told his parents were dead, and he was taken from a children's home in Scotland and put on a ship to Australia. He grew up in an orphanage along with other child migrants.

Walter developed a wonderful voice and when he was seven, a dentist and his wife asked the orphanage if Walter could sing for them on Christmas Eve. They would keep him over Christmas and buy him presents. Much to his delight, Walter was collected by car and taken to this home to join the festivities.

In front of the family and all their friends, Walter sang *Ave Maria* at midnight. Afterwards, three men took him to the bathroom and sexually abused him in turns. He cried and screamed so much that they decided not to keep him over Christmas as promised and instead took him back to the orphanage. They left him on the doorstep. Walter was still crying the next day – not so much because of what had happened, but because he hadn't received the Christmas presents they had promised him.

21

My own Christmas was easier that year. I could watch the coloured lights go on at dusk in the cosy sitting-rooms along my street and not feel anger or helplessness for the child migrants. When I sat down to dinner with Mervyn, Rachel and Ben, I felt the desperation of the previous year had gone. Life was more settled and normal.

I had even managed to buy a few Australian treats for the children and had successfully hidden them from Ben, who usually rifles my bags the moment I get in through the door. I brought back some Australian Christmas tree decorations – dried berries and pine cones – and the tree looked splendid. All over the house there were hundreds of Christmas cards from around the world; cards with kangaroos in red hats or pulling a sleigh – and not a snowflake in sight. The messages were full of hope tinged with despair.

Christmas is a very difficult time for people without families. The child migrants had experienced many sad and lonely Christmases in the past. One woman had spoken to me of spending Christmas on a bus, crying as she rode around looking in windows at people having fun.

The telephone began ringing at 5 a.m. on Christmas morning.

'G'day from Australia!'

It went on until lunch-time and began again in the evening. For many it was the first time they'd rung the UK, and someone explained, 'Margaret, I've never had anyone to ring before.'

The calls continued through to the New Year but I didn't mind. I walked around with a huge smile on my face, and in my heart, there was a determination that many would hopefully be ringing their own families in the UK next year.

The broadcast of *Lost Children of the Empire* had been a turning point for me. Suddenly I wasn't alone any more; I wasn't imagining what had happened to the child migrants. It was no longer just my responsibility because I had helped bring it into the open. By sharing the problem, I helped share the burden.

The response was incredible. The Trust had letters from as far away as Canada and Kenya, from grandmothers, academics, students and former welfare officers. Some sent small donations, or offered to help. Others asked if we could possibly find a brother or sister who they feared had been sent abroad.

And for the first time, I began to find out about the child migrants that had been sent to New Zealand.

After we had received more than a dozen letters from New Zealand, Merv did some more research and discovered that the New Zealand schemes involved an arrangement between the British and New Zealand governments. The Royal Overseas League, a British pro-Empire charity, organized the parties of up to twenty children who travelled six weeks by sea to new homes.

Records also show that between 1948 and 1954 about 300 British children, aged from three to seventeen, were sent to New Zealand, and all were placed in foster families. They were overseen by the Child Welfare Division of the Education Department.

The schemes were abandoned in 1954 because the 'right type of children' were unavailable. These were children under ten years of age, girls aged fifteen to seventeen, or boys old enough and strong enough for farm work.

Initially, I was relieved when I learned that the children were sent to foster homes, but this changed when I discovered evidence that more than a third of the children involved had to be transferred from their first foster parents and many were transferred several times.

An official report blamed the problem on unsuitable foster parents, interference from birth parents, children with illnesses or behaviour problems not reported to the foster parents in advance, and unrealistic expectations as to the abilities and qualities of the children.

In one 1953 newspaper article, a sixteen-year-old boy alleged he was treated like a child slave by his foster parents on a North Island farm. The boy said he had worked eighteen hours a day and been beaten often. Another child, debilitated by a hernia operation and with an arm and leg wasted by polio, found himself unable to do the farm work expected of him.

There were also complaints by foster parents of 'chronic bed-wetting'.

I didn't have the time or the resources to begin investigating what had happened in New Zealand, but resolved that one day I would go there and interview former child migrants. It was a difficult decision, but I had no choice but to wait.

The charities and child care agencies weathered the storm surrounding *Lost Children of the Empire* remarkably well. In truth, they had escaped lightly. I was astonished that nobody questioned them further. There wasn't one independent journalist who had the courage or the nous to go to the agencies and say, 'Look, this is a bloody outrage. How can you plead ignorance? How can you say you didn't know? Tell me, why didn't you know? And what have you done since 1987 when you were told?'

Anthony Meredith, the director of the Catholic Children's Society, formerly the Crusade of Rescue, told reporters, 'We are talking about forty years ago. One has to look at all the child care legislation in those days. We did not have the expertise we do now. It's easy in hindsight to say that a mess was made of it . . .

'We get about 1000 enquiries a year from former clients about their origins. It is upsetting that we cannot give them more information, but we cannot be held responsible for things that were done forty years ago . . . children's homes were bursting at the seams. It was a way of making vacancies.'

This became the standard response.

Caroline MacGregor of the Fairbridge Society agreed.

'Earlier in the century attitudes to children were very different, so to a large extent we are talking about children who would have been institutionalized for most of their young lives anyway . . .

'In general it was pre-1950 and before the welfare state, when the country did not take responsibility for each individual child as it does now. Now sending children into care and thus abroad has been replaced by fostering or trying to deal with the family situation.'

The Christian Brothers had to be more aggressive than simply firing off letters to the newspapers or issuing press releases. The allegations of child abuse were far too serious to be ignored, particularly after what had happened in Canada only a few years earlier. Similar claims had cost the Order more than eighteen million dollars in compensation payments to victims, and led to a Royal Commission of Inquiry.

Amid the growing calls for a full and independent investigation, the Christian Brothers launched an internal one, appointing one of their own, a historian called Dr Barry Coldrey, from Victoria, to investigate the allegations of sex abuse and brutality.

Coldrey, a Christian Brother, referred to himself publicly as a troubleshooter and a fair-minded academic who would put a stop to the peddling of rumours and hearsay. He would also compile a history of the Order in Australia and its role in child care. In the meantime, the Order's stance remained one of outright denials and claims that stories of brutality and neglect were grossly exaggerated.

Amid this virtual silence, I was caught in a dilemma. Part of me wanted to confront the Government and the charities head-on, but what practical use was a row over morals and ethics? What more could be done to convince them?

Maybe the child migrants would be better served if I put my head down and worked solidly on their individual cases. Others could judge while I made sure that child migrants got home to their families while there was still time. People like Harold Haig.

22

Finding a link to his childhood had made matters more complicated for Harold. By finding his ex-neighbour I had found someone who could remember his family, but in the same breath she'd described a loving, caring mother who would have fought for her children and would never have let them be taken away. Harold suddenly wanted to find 'the bastards' who had forced his mother to give him up. He wanted to find them almost as much as he wanted to find his mother.

With new clues, I began searching again.

So far, I hadn't found any record of his mother's birth or death, but the woman from Acton had told me she was probably from the North of England and his father from Scotland. I also knew for certain that they hadn't married in England, Ireland or Scotland under those names, so I made an assumption that they weren't married.

Why would a couple who lived together and had two children, particularly in those years, not be married? What would stop them? Perhaps, I wondered, one of them was already married to somebody else – or maybe they both were.

I went to St Catherine's House again, spending weeks before abandoning this trail. There was no record of either ever having married.

Similarly, I trawled the Scottish registers and found only four Harold Haigs – none of whom was Harold's father. It was bizarre. I could find no record of him being born, marrying or dying. It was as if he hadn't existed at all.

Perhaps I had the wrong spelling of the name, I thought, and began again.

Twice a week Harold and I caught the train to London and walked through the doors of St Catherine's. Harold would stand there, looking along row upon row of bound volumes, and knowing that within one of them was the answer. In desperation and pain, I would hear him say, 'Where are you? You're in these books. For God's sake tell us where you are?'

By that time, he was spending hundreds of pounds a month on marriage and birth certificates. I was working with him thera-peutically and all the time thinking that if we didn't find something soon, he was going to hurt himself. We were clutching at straws all over again and I said, 'Right! Bugger this, I want every marriage certificate of anybody whose maiden name was . . .' And we'd investigate every one of them. Different spellings, different com-binations, different ages. We tried absolutely everything. Elizabeth Ellen Johnson became Ellen Elizabeth, became Betty Ellen, became Betsy Helen, and so on. Instead of being a mother at eighteen, we tried her in every year until she would have been forty-five.

Twice we found families that could possibly have been right. I wrote letters and they rang back but each time it was obvious that they were the wrong families.

Finally we had to give up and admit that St Catherine's House held no joy for Harold and Marie. Their mother was as lost as she'd ever been.

The breakthrough that helped me find Elizabeth Ellen Johnson came from a totally different direction. David Spicer suggested that we should look more closely at Marie's adoption. If we could convince a judge to release her adoption papers, these might have important background information.

For years Marie had continually written to the Salvation Army asking if her mother had agreed to her adoption, but the replies were always the same: 'By law we cannot reveal any details of your adoption.'

Marie had been adopted in 1947, when ten years old, by a couple in their fifties who had changed her name from Elizabeth. David weaved his legal magic at the court that had approved the adoption and unravelled the red tape that bound up Marie's file. The Clerk of the Court eventually agreed to let me look at the records.

This was to be the day of days. I could see from Harold's and Marie's eyes that they imagined all would be revealed, although I refused to let my hopes be raised too high. We knew there should be records on Marie's adoption and that the Salvation Army, which arranged her adoption, would have to have supplied the court with details of Marie's mother and father.

At the very least the Salvation Army would have had to submit a report to the court to give the circumstances and reasons for the adoption. My biggest worry was that these records would no longer exist. It was outside the time period for them to be kept.

The day I made the trip to the court, Harold was desperate to come with me but I told him no, I needed to go on my own. As it turned out he went to St Catherine's House that day and I asked Yvonne to keep an eye on him. By chance we met on the same train from London back to Nottingham.

I had already said to him that morning, 'Now look, Harold, if you happen to be on the same train, I don't want you asking any questions, because I'm not saying anything without Marie being there. This relates to both of you.'

Harold's whole body just about exploded out of frustration. He sat opposite me, muttering dark thoughts and contemplating darker deeds, with his head pressed against the train window.

I got home at about seven, had a bath, changed, and arranged to meet them. It was important to remember every detail, because I knew they would want to know everything. I described how I met the Clerk of the Court in her office. She was extremely helpful. She arranged for me to sit in a small room and then brought in the file which contained only a few sheets of paper. I had a notebook in which I had written down every word. I had clung to the book all the way home, terrified that I might lose it. Information, however little, takes on this priceless significance when dealing with child migrants.

I went through all the information slowly, leaving time for Marie and Harold to ask questions.

The file contained quite a lot more about Harold's and Marie's mother, but it didn't tell us where she was now, or why Harold went into care.

Elizabeth Ellen Johnson had been living in a place called Ventnor Villas in Hove, East Sussex when Harold was three years old and Marie four.

There were very few details that could help us now, but at least with a new address, I could begin searching the electoral rolls, looking for people who had lived in Ventnor Villas in the early 1940s. Over the next three months, I actually found every person who had lived there, including the owner's daughter who now lives in Northern Ireland.

I flew to Belfast with Marie to meet her. She couldn't help us very much, but she did remember a couple living on the ground floor who had two children including a little girl who went away with the Salvation Army.

It had been four years since we began the search for Harold's and Marie's mother. Four of the most complicated and painful years of Harold's life. During this time he'd become a virtual founder member of the Trust, spending long periods in England, watching our workload increase and many other migrant children successfully reunited with their families.

Each time another migrant heard the good or bad news, Harold became more disconsolate. He wondered if it would ever happen to him.

I sat down with him, trying hard to sound confident, and we talked about the early days and what we'd been through together. He said to me, 'You taught me how to live. You showed me how to relate to people. Before I met you, I just lived in despair. There was no time sequence to my life. Nothing concrete. There's not even a piece of paper to say I arrived in Australia – I'm not even on the shipping list of the boat that took me.'

Since the break-up of his marriage, Harold had drifted away from his three children. They didn't know he was a child migrant. His daughters, both in their twenties, saw him on a television chat show with me and one of them rang me up and said, 'That was my dad. My dad was on telly with you.' She was shocked.

I had to spend a lot of time helping Harold understand that he was important to his children. Even though he realized he'd abandoned them, he had to face up to his own hurt before he could begin to understand how they felt.

After so many blind alleys and wasted months, St Catherine, the patron saint of all child migrants, finally yielded a first marriage for Harold's mother.

We waited three days for the certificate, although I don't know how Harold contained himself.

There were two daughters from that marriage, both born in Oldham, near Manchester. Neither of them was Marie.

Harold and Marie had two half-sisters, and I hoped that if we could find them, they'd know the answers to our questions.

Elizabeth's husband had died, but I found an address for the house they had shared in Oldham. That weekend, Harold and I decided to drive to Manchester to have a look. Bricks and mortar are a poor substitute to finding a mother, but at least they provide something tangible.

When we got into Oldham, Harold had the map across his knees, directing me. I remember driving up to an intersection and saying, 'This is the road, Harold! This is the road!'

And he said to me, 'Don't get excited.'

'Why?'

'You see where the road goes straight over, don't you?'

'Yes.'

'Well, that's where my mother's house used to be.'

I don't know how Harold held himself together. This was the umpteenth time we'd set out full of hope and found only dis-appointment. Harold had a look of total desolation as he stared at the four lanes of Tarmac and concrete. I wanted to scream at the unfairness of it all. I parked the car at the side of the road.

'Right! You sit here,' I told Harold. 'I don't know how long I'll be gone, but just sit here.'

And I began knocking on every door in the road while Harold sat in the car or paced up and down the gutter. Northerners are very welcoming and over the next four hours many people said, 'Oh yes, come in, come on in, dear. How can we help?'

Eventually I found an elderly lady who vaguely remembered

the family. She was sure that one of the two girls was called Barbara and still lived somewhere in the area but couldn't say where. I didn't find her that day but each time I returned, Harold would wait in the car, while I went from door to door. It probably seemed insane but I was prepared to check every house in Oldham.

Finally, in January 1990, I found Barbara living in a bungalow not far from where she'd grown up. After writing her a letter, she agreed to meet with me and listened, wide-eyed as I told her she had a half-brother and half-sister.

Sadly she knew as little about her mother as Harold and Marie. Barbara had been brought up by her father and had been absolutely devoted to him, so much so that she had never once considered searching for her missing mother. She didn't even have a photograph of her.

Harold's other half-sister – his mother's first child – had emigrated to South Africa. I started searching for her, hoping she might know where her mother had gone. I was prepared to fly to Johannesburg, if necessary, when I discovered that she'd died two years earlier.

Again, after so much hard work and heartache, Harold and Marie were no closer to finding their mother.

It was time to make some new assumptions. I suddenly wondered if Elizabeth Ellen Johnson had married again. Maybe that was why I couldn't find any trace of her.

I guessed correctly, although immediately wished I hadn't. She did marry again – much later. She wed a curate's son, Lionel Maulever Worsop Smith, on 21 June 1948, in Brighton. Geographically, at least, I was back where I started, only five minutes from where Harold had been taken into care as a small boy.

Elizabeth had married a 'Smith' – the worst surname of all from my point of view. She had suddenly disappeared within the biggest genealogical family in Britain.

The marriage certificate had an address, a block of flats in Worthing, so I began checking the electoral rolls all over again, trying to find somebody who might remember her. The owner of the flats was in London and suggested I contact a woman who had lived in the block for about thirty years.

At first she couldn't remember a thing about Lionel Smith or his new wife, but when pressed further she said, 'I wonder if it's the man that died? There was a man who died on his own.'

I began searching for the death certificate and discovered that the dead man was indeed a curate's son.

Someone must have been responsible for sorting out his estate and the local council would have a record. Perhaps his personal effects had been kept in storage? Again, it was a blind alley.

Then came the saddest cut – and one that I had feared from the very beginning. While trying to find members of Lionel's family who might have known Harold's mother, I stumbled across a death certificate for Elizabeth Ellen Smith. She died in Worthing in 1973.

There would be no tearful reunion on a doorstep, or hugs at an airport, or long walks of discovery. Harold's and Marie's mother was dead. This is what I fear for all child migrants when I begin a search, and it's their fear as well. It was still, however, essential to find out what had happened to her.

I rang every funeral director in Worthing and Brighton, trying to discover who might have buried her. Eventually I found the right one and asked, 'Who arranged the funeral? Was it a relative? Was it a lawyer?'

After a string of questions that they couldn't answer, I said, 'Surely you must know who paid the bill?'

'I can't tell you that,' I was told.

'Who's in charge?' I asked.

'The boss is on holiday.'

'Where is he on holiday? Please, can you get your boss on the phone? I need to talk to him. We either do this on the phone or I'll be down tomorrow morning.'

Fifteen minutes later, I was put through to the funeral director at his home. He told me the burial was paid for by two spinsters who lived in a large house in Worthing. He gave me their names but there was no listing in the phone book and, the next day, the electoral roll showed they no longer lived at that address.

They were both elderly and I feared they may have died in the interim. If they were still alive, I had to find them quickly.

I found the name of the new owners of the house they'd owned in Worthing but not their telephone number.

'Ex-directory!' said the operator. I should have guessed it. Taking a deep breath, I wrote a letter asking the occupant to please, please ring me, hoping he could sense the urgency and would not dismiss me as a crank. Two nights later, the telephone rang at home.

'You sent me a letter – what can I do for you?' he asked.

'Did you buy the house from Miss Marjorie and Miss Grace Stephens?'

'Yes.'

'And do you know where they are now?'

'Marjorie died and I bought it off her sister.'

'Oh, and where's her sister?'

'In a home for the elderly. She's quite sick. I don't know where it is precisely.'

I was being incredibly polite, but inside I was screaming questions. Where is this home? Give me all the names, for God's sake!

This man, a wonderful person, thought I was absolutely mad, but still agreed to help. He told me to hold fire while he went round the neighbours asking for more information. He rang back and gave me the name of the nursing home.

'Is she still alive?' I asked.

'I don't know. But promise me one thing: one day will you tell me what this is all about?'

'I'll try,' I said, hanging up.

I called the home and spoke to the matron.

'Do you have a Miss Grace Stephens staying there?'

'Yes. Are you a relative?'

'No! I'm a social worker. Can I come and see her?'

'Well, I'm afraid she is on medication right now and she doesn't take visitors.'

'I'll be there on Monday,' I told her. 'I'll explain to you when I get there.'

It meant catching another early-morning train from Nottingham. I changed trains in London and arrived at the nursing home shortly before midday.

Grace sat opposite me, pleased to have a visitor but looking slightly bemused.

I said, 'Did you know Elizabeth Smith?'

'Yes, dear. She was a lovely lady. I knew her for a long while.'

'Did you pay the bill for her funeral?'
'Yes.'
'Please tell me how you knew her?'
'She married my nephew who was a real no-gooder. A terrible, terrible man. We managed, my sister and I, to get Betty away from him and helped her live independently in a flat. We felt sorry for her.'
'What was she like?' I asked.
'She was a quiet lady, who kept to herself. I think there was something in her past that made her very, very sad.'
'Did she have any children?'
'I remember she talked about having a little boy.'
'And what happened to her boy?'
'She said he died when he was ten.'
'Did you ever see the boy?'
'No. We didn't know her then. That's all she said about him. He was a little boy who died when he was ten.'

By now, Harold was back in Australia. I'd always told him that whenever I found his mother, whether she was alive or dead, I would never write or telephone. I would come to see him.

On my next planned visit to Australia I arranged to meet him in the Southern Cross Hotel in Melbourne. Because of what I had to say, I chose a room with a nice view and filled it with flowers; white carnations and pink roses. I knew Harold would remember every detail of that day as if he were painting it on one of his canvases.

I'd always prepared Harold for the possibility of such a sad outcome. But I also knew that he lived in hope. I guess he realized what I was going to say. He admired the view of the city but he was preoccupied.

It was not just about revealing that his mother had died; it was telling him that there was no hope. The search that had dominated his life for forty years was over and there was nothing more he, or I, or anybody could do.

I could see tears welling up in his eyes, each of them brushed aside by his shirt sleeve. He didn't know what to do with himself.

I wanted to tell the story from the beginning; I wanted to

tell Harold about Elizabeth Ellen Johnson, who died a lonely, heartbroken lady, without her children. But I knew he wouldn't last. I said to him, 'Harold this is the day that we all dreaded, I'm afraid.'

He looked up at me through the tears. 'Have you found my mother?'

'Yes,' I whispered.

'She's dead, isn't she?' he muttered.

'Yes, she is.'

I could say no more. In a breath all hope had gone. There was no more searching; no more clutching at straws; no more turning it over and over again in my mind, trying to find the answers.

Harold had always said that there are two levels at which people search. On the one hand he talked of searching all his life for his mother, but on the other he also knew the 'practicalities' that prevent people looking when they live 12,000 miles away.

There are so many imponderables left by such a search. They are the legacy of the child migration schemes and the policy which sent children to the other side of the world, away from their families. Years of heartbreak and years of yearning for mothers, fathers and children. And to what end?

Harold asked me whether I'd been to see his mother's grave. 'That's a journey you have to make,' I told him.

He flew to England and I drove him to the train station.

'I felt bloody sad,' he said later. 'I had desperately wanted her to be alive, after all those years of wishing for her and being told that I was an orphan. The longer I sat by her grave, the more confused and angry I became. I was illegally sent from my country and, like thousands of others, was the victim of a cruel conspiracy of silence and deceit, but I did feel some peace – the peace of mind that at fifty-two years of age, I finally knew where my mother was.'

He didn't have a photograph. He'd give anything for that. But the urgency was over.

When the Trust opened its office in Nottingham, we had had a giant cake decorated with all the flags of the countries where child migrants had been sent. It was quite symbolic and I had cut it in pieces and sent a slice to Harold.

He kept his piece and when he came to England to visit his mother's grave, he brought it with him and buried it in a box beside her.

23

Nearly four years after the Trust had started we had several thousand clients and a workload massively beyond all our expectations. We had reunited over a hundred families.

Yet it was only with the help of my anonymous benefactor that we were able to move out of my home in West Bridgford to suitable offices near by – somewhere that child migrants would feel belonged to them.

My attempts to get official funding had also started to show results, but it was never sufficient to carry out the work quickly enough. Those who held the purse strings didn't seem to understand that we were racing against time to reunite families before elderly mothers and fathers died.

In April 1990, after several meetings and countless letters to the Department of Health, the Child Migrants Trust was awarded a one-year, £20,000 grant. We had applied for funding over three years, needing £111,000 in the first year and £92,000 in each subsequent year.

The news from Australia had been more positive. Early in the New Year, I was surprised to receive a telephone call from the Federal Government's Department of Immigration and Ethnic Affairs, in Canberra. A senior civil servant in Minister Robert Ray's office introduced himself and said simply, 'What can we do to help?'

This was the first time that anyone had approached me from any government. I didn't need to be asked twice. 'We need an office and a qualified social worker.'

Without hesitating, he said, 'I'll see what we can do.'

Within days he rang again and told me to submit an application for a grant; approval would be a formality. The Trust was given just enough to cover the salary of a social worker for three years with a small percentage for accommodation. It meant that I could start an office in Australia and appoint someone.

While I'd been in Australia before Christmas, the trustees and Yvonne had been busy looking for an office in Nottingham. Philip Bean had resigned as a trustee due to his work commitments, and a local businessman, Manfred Dessau, graciously took up the position. He had first approached me after *Lost Children of the Empire* was screened and asked what he could do to help.

Eventually, we found rooms in a large Victorian house that had been converted into offices in Musters Road, near the cricket ground at Trent Bridge.

We begged, borrowed and called in favours to get office furniture, and then loaded up my battered Renault with boxes of files and dozens of notebooks, transferring them from the house to the new office.

The premises were neither large nor lavish, but they were warm, welcoming and homely. There were two rooms set aside for meetings and interviews, neither had any office equipment, just soft furnishings, attractive lamps and many photographs and paintings. The black-and-white photographs on the walls showed scenes of children leaving Britain on different child migrant schemes.

The office was practical and conventional but I also hoped it would become a kind of spiritual home for the child migrants.

Similar accommodation had to be found in Australia so I flew out with Manfred Dessau to formalize the arrangements with the Immigration Department and to look for an office.

I decided to base the Trust's first Australian office in Melbourne which could service the eastern states, while I would continue to focus on Perth.

It took two trips before the right location could be found, a two-storey terrace house in Canning Street, North Carlton, an old suburb with well-established gardens. Inside, it looked almost English with its comfy sofas and the landscape paintings on the walls.

I didn't want a formal-looking office. This had to be somewhere that child migrants could feel welcome and at ease; where there was tea in the pot and biscuits in the tin.

The second priority was to recruit a qualified social worker – someone with the experience and personal qualities to withstand the inevitable emotional onslaught of dealing with so many painful stories. I knew that many of the child migrants wanted a British worker as a tangible link with the land of their birth, and eventually appointed David, who was well qualified and experienced.

David had been to Australia before and was very relaxed and easy going. He would have no support staff and could rely on my being there only three times a year. The rest of the time, aside from the telephone, he would be alone.

Although Canning Street wouldn't be opened officially until January 1991, David went to Australia earlier to make the final plans. I flew out in the New Year and we met in Perth so he could watch me working with former child migrants. We'd talked a lot about the problems, and he seemed confident, but I don't think anything could have prepared him fully for the emotional impact of what he had to face within a few weeks of his arrival.

The Child Migrants Trust was finally on a firm footing – at least while the funds lasted. As it turned out, this was not to be for long. In March 1991 I received a letter from the Department of Health in London. Our application for a further grant had been refused.

This was a major blow. I had already appointed Joan Kerry, a qualified social worker, to counsel and prepare mothers and families of former child migrants. She had travelled thousands of miles in England, Scotland and Ireland, helping mothers deal with their sense of confusion and betrayal when they learned that their children had not been adopted in Britain but had been shipped to children's homes in Australia. This work was vital but I had no idea where I would find the money to keep it going.

*　　*　　*

In the meantime, another unforeseen development had arisen: I received a call from an Australian television producer called Penny Chapman. The name meant little to me, but Penny explained that she was coming to England to try to arrange a co-production deal for a drama that she was very excited about.

'It's about the child migrants. We're going to dramatize their story, the voyage, the abuse, the anger. Can I come and see you?'

Penny had already sold the idea to the Australian Broadcasting Corporation and was hoping to talk with the BBC about a joint production deal.

The writers, Sue Smith and John Alsop, wanted to consult with me for the programme but my commitments were already daunting. I was dealing with reality. The people who could tell them what really happened were the child migrants themselves.

I had other, more urgent, matters to worry about. Thankfully, my frosty relationship with the charities and agencies was beginning to thaw. After being initially very antagonistic and uncooperative, there was a definite move to mend bridges.

Over time it became easier to ask them for information about individual child migrants. There was a recognition on their part that it was a situation that would not go away. Those agencies that employed professional social workers began to change their policy. Gradually they grew to recognize the needs of the child migrants, and to appreciate the work of the Trust.

Unfortunately mistakes were still made and some charities found it difficult to change their attitudes and develop more flexible policies.

Joan Corby is a child migrant who first wrote to me in July 1988. Born in 1936, she was eleven years old when she left a children's home in Birmingham and was sent, on board the *SS Ormonde*, to the Fairbridge Farm School at Molong, NSW.

Joan was told her mother had died in a bombing raid during the war and that she had no brothers and sisters.

She wrote:

> My chief grievance is that I was sent from my native land after the war, when there was no longer any danger of England being occupied by the Germans. Therefore, unless there was another reason for migration, I needn't have been sent away. I still

passionately love my native land and I feel as if I have been exiled unnecessarily and through no fault of my own, and I wish to return to the land of my birth.

Another grievance is the fact that we were torn from our relatives and never had the chance to maintain family ties. Consequently I have walked through life as an orphan under great hardship, mainly spiritual hardship. I am grieved also that it is forty years now since I was exiled and till now nothing has been done to right what I see as a wrong. And, in fact, the wrong until now has not even been acknowledged.

I cannot make head or tail of the reasons why I should have been sent away in the first place and ask you if you know of any reason for this, legally or socially, bearing in mind that England's doors have been open to refugees from all parts of the world and yet we child migrants have never been invited back officially. This seems unjust to me.

If you can help me, please do so as I don't know where to turn. This exile lies very heavy on my heart.

I wrote back to Joan, assuring her that I would do what I could to find her family, but that it could be a long search and I needed her help. She had to give me as many details as possible about her childhood in England – names, dates, addresses, etc.

Unbeknown to me, Joan had already approached the Fairbridge Society and asked for her personal file. When I heard from her again, the inconceivable had happened. Fairbridge, despite my warnings, had simply sent Joan her file through the post. Their only effort at minimizing the impact was a crude and cruel blacking out of important information.

Joan was faced with a censored file, attached to which was a letter from the Fairbridge Society which stated: 'I hope you find this interesting rather than upsetting.'

Joan quoted from the censored letters. One line read: '. . . as you say —— point in disclosing all the facts —— would not help Joan to know that —— had six illegitimate children by —— others.'

It made no sense, but the implications were obvious. The Fairbridge file gave the unmistakable impression that Joan's mother had six illegitimate children by different men.

Joan also learned that the maiden name she had kept until her marriage was different from that on her birth certificate. Instead of being Joan Haymes, she was Joan Haynes.

Her devastation was not surprising. She wrote to me: 'I fear there is insufficient time to right the wrong done to my mother – I can only pray that she or some of her other children are still alive . . .'

In the subsequent months, the Child Migrants Trust could find no evidence of Joan having any brothers or sisters. Although the search continues, I seriously doubt that her mother had six illegitimate children. I think Joan is probably an only child.

Perhaps there was a mistake due to poor record-keeping, or a clerical mix-up. Similarly, her details may have been deliberately falsified, years earlier, to prevent Joan ever finding her mother. Whatever the reason, it was cruel blow to a very vulnerable human being.

24

On Australia Day, 26 January 1991, I flew to Perth, arriving in the early hours of the morning. The receptionist gave me a smile and a stack of telephone messages from former child migrants who were eager to see me. Some simply said, 'Welcome to Perth, call me when you can.'

I couldn't sleep. Perhaps my body was telling me that it was the early evening in Nottingham. I decided to order a pot of tea from room service and unpack some of my clothes until the tea arrived. I would need a jacket, blouse and skirt in a few hours' time and I could see that they would need pressing. I always feel awkward calling housekeeping at three in the morning for an iron and ironing-board. By the time the tea arrived, I had fallen asleep on the bed.

Australia Day was to be one of the hottest on record in Perth and when I woke, I could already sense the furnace being stoked by the early-morning sun. There was one particular child migrant whom I had to see that day, Michael, who first wrote to me in November 1989.

Dear Margaret,
I realize the difficulty you must face in putting the jigsaw

together for those who seek your help. I would like to add my case to your already overloaded list. Thus, I seek your help.

I was brought out to Australia at the age of nine years, arriving in Australia during 1947 on the ship *Asturias* and went to a Christian Brothers' institution, where I remained until 1955.

I am writing to you seeking your assistance and that of the Child Migrants Trust in the hope that I may know who I am, to whom I belong and who might belong to me.

I am encouraged in this by the programme *Lost Children of the Empire*. The work and research you are engaged in gives me the first hope I have ever had in my quest to the answers I seek about myself. I have for the first time in my life been able to talk about my past. Prior to the screening of the programme I was embarrassed to do so. Now I am not.

To assist you I enclose a copy of my birth certificate.

I recall, whilst in a children's home in Lancashire, England, in the 1940s, a lady (my mother?) visited me. I enclose a small note the nuns gave me when I returned to the children's home in 1972 in the hope of finding my mother.

After more than forty-two years, it would be nice to know that I belong to someone, someone belongs to me and that I can share myself with those who are mine, thus giving me a peace of mind and a joy that I have never known and, up to now, I never thought could be mine.

A letter such as this has not been easy to write and is difficult to conclude. I close by saying what you are doing is appreciated. I hope to hear from you soon.

Yours sincerely,
Michael

It was a rather formal sounding letter, but I sensed an unwritten urgency between the lines. Yvonne and I began the search for Michael's mother in St Catherine's House. We began with a long list of birth registrations over a twenty-five year period of women with the same name as his mother. Nothing looked immediately hopeful. There was a registration for a woman with three Christian names, but Michael's mother only had two; Michael was born in Highgate, London, this lady was born in the North of England.

The problems were compounded by the fact that Michael's documentation contained conflicting information. His surname was spelt differently on important documents and his date of birth was also incorrect on papers he received from the agency who had arranged his migration. To make matters worse, the records contained no reference to Michael's mother or father.

Michael recognized me when we met in the hotel lobby. He complained about the hot weather, which he still found oppressive, and I noticed he bore little trace of an Australian accent.

'The heat hasn't been a problem to me so far,' I explained. 'I usually only travel from the airport to my hotel.'

Michael was surprised that I hadn't seen anything of Perth on my previous visits. In my room on the eighth floor, he stood at the window enjoying the view over the river and pointed out to me various places of interest. He told me how the city had changed since the America's Cup yacht races were held off Fremantle several years earlier. It was more vibrant now, he said, there were more tourists and taller buildings.

Settling into a chair, he asked if he could smoke.

I handed him an ashtray and smiled, saying, 'Most smokers need a few cigarettes when they come in here.'

Despite the relaxed introductions, I didn't find it easy to get Michael to talk about his early childhood and the search for his mother. It touched a raw nerve and eventually he explained that he had decided many years ago to suppress his feelings of hurt in order to survive. This was his way of coping. However, I knew he wouldn't be ready to undertake the painful journey to find his mother until we developed a trusting relationship.

Over tea, he told me of his interest in politics, current affairs and history – especially British history. He held firm views about his British origins.

'Do you consider yourself British or Australian?' I asked.

He firmly put me in my place. 'British, of course!' he insisted, as if there was only one possible answer. 'I'm only domiciled here. It's not my home, I am trapped here, my home is in England. They took our childhoods, our identity, our families. But they can't take my nationality from me.'

His anger and sense of injustice were suddenly exposed and it gave me the opening I needed to gently explore his childhood.

He told of arriving in Australia at the age of nine and being subjected to the humiliation of being fingerprinted.

'I felt like a criminal,' he sighed, looking at me for some reaction.

'It's not the first time I've heard about it,' I said. 'I'm not surprised you remember it so clearly.'

Michael was anxious to know if I had any news of his mother. I handed him a copy of her birth certificate. 'That's the first hurdle,' I smiled.

Michael was thrilled. It was the first tangible piece of evidence he'd ever seen that proved she was a real person and not just a figment of his imagination. He felt optimistic and confident that she would be found.

'This is still only the very beginning,' I warned him. 'We could find no trace of a marriage for her or any subsequent children. We are now searching for other family members who may be able to help.

'And you have to remember, your mother is now over seventy years old. There are no guarantees that she's still with us.'

Michael nodded in agreement. When he left the hotel he looked reassured and relieved. The search was going forward and every day brought us closer to the truth.

In March, when I returned to the office in Nottingham, I was immediately given two new pieces of information uncovered while I was in Australia. They concerned the woman with three Christian names whom we were seeking as possibly being Michael's mother.

'Would you like the good news or the bad news first?' Yvonne asked.

I hesitated. In our work 'bad news' is often a kind way of saying that someone has died.

I replied, 'It's not Michael's mother, is it?'

'I'm afraid so.'

These were the very words I was dreading. A death certificate had been found which was almost conclusive; only a few minor details had to be confirmed. The 'good news' was that a distant relative had been located. But this relative by marriage had never met Michael's mother and had no information to give us about her.

Michael had told me of his plans to visit the UK at the end of April. It meant that I had less than a month to establish without any doubt that his mother had indeed died. In view of the need for more personal enquiries, I decided to take over the research myself.

After meeting Michael, I knew that he would find it exceptionally difficult to come to terms with the fact that his mother had died. In fact, she'd been dead for over thirty years.

A friend, rather than a relative, had registered her death, so it was quite possible that Michael would not even meet someone who had known her. I needed to try to find someone who could at least tell him a little about the mother he never knew; somebody who could describe her as a real person, a living, breathing human being.

I telephoned three cemeteries before I managed to establish where Michael's mother had been buried. I also made several enquiries to firms of undertakers. Eventually, I was given some details of those who had attended the funeral. I travelled by car to Leeds to find the street where Michael's mother had been living some thirty years ago. I found the street quite quickly but to my utter dismay a small block of offices occupied the space where the house should have been. Only four houses had been demolished along this narrow winding road; Michael's mother had lived in one of them.

I called at the main library and consulted the electoral rolls to discover which adults had been living in the house at about the same time. There were four listed. I also checked neighbouring houses to see if there was anyone still living on the street whose names appeared in the earlier records. No such luck.

It was almost dark when I left the library in Leeds. Light rain began falling and I hurried to my car. Twenty minutes later I was standing outside the main entrance to the cemetery, knowing that I would venture no further. For me, this marked the boundary of what was private to Michael and his mother.

I telephoned him in Australia and wrote to him. I didn't mention his mother and nor did he. He knew that I wouldn't tell him anything over the phone.

Michael confirmed his travel plans and I agreed to meet him at Heathrow Airport.

A few weeks later, I made the journey south and found Michael standing by his luggage trolley. We shook hands and he seemed pleased when I welcomed him 'home'.

We had a cup of coffee, then took the underground to St Pancras Station to travel north to Leeds. Michael became relaxed and lively as the journey progressed, and enjoyed the changing view from the window seat. We discussed a variety of topics but Michael never mentioned his mother.

She was, of course, the main reason for his visit home; yet I knew that Michael wasn't ready to face all the implications of our research, especially the possibility that she was no longer alive. When he was ready, I would break the news to him.

For the next two weeks, Michael visited friends and was introduced to a distant relative we had found for him. He would telephone me every couple of days and I told him that I was prepared to see him whenever he was ready.

Finally we met five days before he was due to return to Australia.

Michael came to the Trust office and when I asked him where he wanted to talk, he chose to sit in the room with the family dining table and its four matching oak chairs. He put the table between us. It was just as I expected. He needed to stay in control of his feelings and emotions and the distance helped him do that.

We faced each other and as soon as Michael had finished his cup of tea, he said, in a direct, firm voice, 'I think you've been trying to prepare me for something. Come on then, tell me, I'm ready now. I can be stoic when I have to be.'

I knew that Michael's mother had been dead for more than thirty years, but for him she would die that day. The moment the death certificate passed from my hands to his, all Michael's hopes would be lost for ever.

'I have a certificate,' I said, 'sadly, a death certificate, which may well be your mother's – but I would like you to look at it and give me your opinion.'

Michael studied the document for some considerable time before he looked up and said quietly, 'Yes, it's her.'

He had several questions about how and where his mother had died and where the funeral had taken place. Fortunately, I was able to answer most of them, because I had contacted the coroner's office to obtain all the available details.

Sadly, I had also discovered that Michael's mother had returned to the children's home looking for him. She went to collect him only to be told that he had been sent to Australia.

Michael was devastated. He imagined that his mother had led a lonely life as she had not married. He felt that he should have been with her. He wondered whether his mother had spent her days looking at other boys and wondering what had happened to her own son. He tried to make sense of it – why had he been sent to Australia and his mother left behind without her only child?

He seemed to hold himself together well during this discussion which lasted nearly three hours. He had booked into a comfortable local hotel, where I arranged to meet him during the evening for supper.

'Will you come with me to visit my mother's grave?' Michael asked.

'Wouldn't you prefer to go with a friend or relative?' I said.

He shook his head. It was clear that he'd given it a lot of thought, so I agreed to go with him.

We met at the railway station the following morning. Michael seemed shocked, but in control of himself. From Leeds station, we took a taxi to the cemetery. As the driver pulled up at the large ornamental gates, Michael leaned forward and said, 'We won't be long.'

There were a few dark clouds scurrying across the sky in the wind and occasionally there were splashes of sunshine.

The cemetery administrator had told me where the grave was situated and it didn't take Michael long to pinpoint it.

'I've found it, it's here,' he called over to me.

Not wishing to intrude on his grief, I kept well back as he stood next to the grave. After more than forty years of pain and separation, the search for his mother had ended at last.

He knelt down and I saw his shoulders shaking. I wondered over and over what could possibly have justified so much human suffering. The desolation of a nine-year-old boy, the grief of a fifty-year-old man and the lifelong pain of an estranged mother.

Just as Michael was arranging a small bunch of flowers beside the headstone, a huge clap of thunder bellowed out above our heads. It seemed to come from nowhere, catching me completely by surprise.

Michael turned round to me and shouted, 'It's Shakespeare! It's my mother saying, "Avenge my death!" '

25

From the very beginning, when Madeleine first wrote to me and described herself as an orphan, I wondered how she could have believed such a story. Yet she insisted that on the voyage to Australia, a woman had told her that her mother was dead.

Many of the former child migrants told similar stories, including Joan Corby and Harold Haig. As I gathered more and more newspaper reports, newsreel footage and political speeches, the children were invariably described as 'war orphans' arriving from Britain.

Unfortunately, time and again, I had discovered that the child migrants were not orphans. Similarly, I learned that more often than not they had been sent abroad without their parents' knowledge or consent.

When a child migrant learns for the first time that he or she has been so outrageously deceived, he usually reacts with confusion and distress. Knowledge that one's mother is still alive comes as a shock and a relief. The anger frequently follows, with a stream of questions: Who sent me here? Who signed for me to leave Britain? Were my parents told?

I would sit with them, trying to explain that a nun or priest or bureaucrat or welfare worker had signed for them.

Inevitably, their next question was: 'Is that allowed? Can somebody just send me away from my country?'

For four years I listened to these questions, not just from child migrants, unable to answer.

The stories of their parents are just as tragic. The mothers of Madeleine and Pamela were both led to believe their daughters were in England, adopted by loving families. The truth was very different, yet there were even more appalling lies. Some mothers who returned to children's homes to collect their sons or daughters were told that their child had died of a disease or in an accident. They grieved forty years ago for a child they thought was dead. Now they had to face the truth when they were elderly and vulnerable.

This silent group of people who lost their children to a scheme and a political cause would ask me: 'Who gave them the authority? Who sent my child away?'

I couldn't answer their questions. I simply didn't know.

At the same time, David Spicer was receiving letters from child migrants asking if there was any legal action they could take over what had happened to them.

David could only advise them to seek independent legal advice. I wasn't satisfied with this. I wanted to be in a position to answer such questions. I was tired of floundering when journalists persistently asked about the legality of the child migration schemes and possible compensation.

David contacted some of his barrister colleagues and asked if they would help us find some answers. It was an area of the law in which very few people have experience but there were a surprising number ready to give it some serious thought.

Eventually we gathered one Saturday morning at the Doughty Street chambers in London – a group of eminent barristers and solicitors, along with David and myself.

We sat around a brilliantly polished conference table, dotted with jugs of water and legal pads. Around the walls stood glass cabinets stacked with legal texts.

The lawyers and QCs who came that day shared an interest in human rights issues and wanted to explore the legal dimension of the child migration schemes. All had read and viewed *Lost Children of the Empire* and a pile of press cuttings. They had all done their own homework.

I sat opposite them taking notes and clarifying dates. I kept wondering what it would normally have cost to gather so many brilliant legal minds in one room for an entire Saturday.

During the course of the day, the lawyers discussed slavery law, shipping law, the Children's Act and the statute of limitations. Every so often, somebody would get excited and follow a strand of argument while the others raised objections or singled out possible flaws.

That statute of limitations was a stumbling block – dictating that legal action had to be taken within a set number of years of an alleged offence having taken place. Depending on the jurisdiction, it was normally within three or sometimes six years.

It seemed ludicrous that such restrictions could apply to child migrants. Many had only recently become aware that they were orphans. Until I found their families, they hadn't fully realized what they'd lost or been denied.

When the day finished, I still didn't have the answers. Some lawyers were very confident that the child migrants had a case while others wanted to do further research. From my point of view, I was simply delighted that for the first time a group of people with some expertise had sat down and thought about the child migrants. It was an historic event.

Some months later, I heard that a London firm of solicitors, Leigh, Day & Co, had been instructed by a former child migrant to act on his behalf. The news caught me by surprise but the possible ramifications were obvious.

None of this was my concern. I had to deal with the search to find families while there was still time and I couldn't afford to be diverted into other areas.

But I wasn't surprised that child migrants were considering legal action. When somebody discovers that they have been denied their family for decades, their anger and sense of injustice is understandable, and it is not surprising that they should wish to seek legal redress.

Although no precise date can be put on it, there was an important sea change beginning to happen around the world, involving the clergy and allegations of abuse and betrayal. It was to have a profound effect on the child migrants who experienced the horrors of Bindoon, Clontarf, Castledare and Tardun, in Western Australia.

Clergy at the very top of their respective churches could no longer ignore the growing number of complaints about physical and sexual abuse against their priests and ministers. Lawsuits had been lodged in America, particularly in New York and Chicago, and the Catholic Church was under attack for having allegedly covered up allegations and hampered police investigations.

Bishop Peter Connors of Melbourne was appointed by the Australian Catholic Church to manage the paedophile issue. This included taking out an insurance policy against being sued for 'any actual or attempted sexual activity with a child' and the drawing up of a draft protocol for dealing with such incidents. These details were not made public.

Several other churches were looking at similar schemes. There were no such overtures from the Christian Brothers, however, who seemed to ignore any calls for public inquiries, apologies or possible compensation. Their one concession had been the appointment of Dr Barry Coldrey to research the allegations of child abuse and prepare a history of child migration to Australia.

I expected our paths to cross. Surely, I thought, Dr Coldrey would want to talk to the Child Migrants Trust. But for some reason Dr Coldrey proved to be rather reticent about meeting me.

I learned that he was in Nottingham, not five minutes from the offices of the Trust, researching the child migration schemes and he failed to visit us.

In fact, I only learned of his trip to Nottingham when he rang me from London four days later.

'I've been to Malta researching the migration schemes for the Christian Brothers,' he said. 'I was in Nottingham last week. It was suggested that I give you a call, although I can't see why I need meet you. No idea, really. Can you think of any reason why we should meet?'

I was so astonished that I simply said, 'Whatever you think is best.'

I thought it strange that a man would come 12,000 miles to investigate child migration and fail to visit the one agency in the world that deals specifically with the subject. I could only shake my head in disbelief and speculate on what sort of 'history' this man intended to write.

26

Desmond McDaid was two years old when his mother left him with the nuns at Nazareth House, in Termanbacca, Ireland. 'The penguins' – as he calls the sisters – and the teenage girls would come in and care for the toddlers.

'I remember one day this girl had a few of us lined up and she began picking us up and throwing us into the air and letting us fall to the floor. I remember the floor was waxed and I sat there, waiting to be picked up and dropped again. I was resigned to it.'

Desmond retained many such memories from his childhood – disjointed images and sensations that flashed back to him as he talked.

Between the ages of four and eight, Desmond lived in another institution, sleeping in dormitories run by older boys and nuns.

'There were twenty-five to thirty beds with one bucket at the end of the dormitory for a night toilet. And when we had a bath, the nuns made us wear a slip covering our genitals, for modesty's sake.'

From Monday until Friday Desmond walked the mile and back to Bishop Street School. The first lesson was Catechism, where the nuns told him that he was a 'soldier of Christ, fighting the good battle'. He had food in his stomach, clean clothes on his back; what else did a soldier need?

'Some nights I remember leaning out of bed, almost falling out, hoping that one of the nuns would see me and put me back in – just to have someone hold me – to touch me,' Desmond said.

No institution can replace a family. It can provide clothes, food, knowledge and good manners, but it can never give a child love. Desmond eventually got attention, but not the sort he craved.

'I never saw their faces. Hands would come into the bed, playing with me at night. I was too frightened to open my eyes. They would roll me over on my face, pulling my trousers down and playing with the cheeks of my backside.'

When Desmond was eight, a priest came to his school and gave the boys a talk about Australia. That night he dreamed about a white sandy beach and a group of aborigines carrying a coffin into the waves.

'I'd never seen an aborigine before. No-one had told me about indigenous people, so I don't know how I could possibly have conjured up this dream.'

The following day, Desmond was measured for a new set of clothes – the first he'd ever owned.

'No-one told me I was going to Australia. No-one asked me. We were made to line up and taken to the railway station. I was crying my eyes out. We crossed the Irish Sea by ferry, sleeping on bare wooden bunks with one blanket between two of us. Then we boarded another train for a long journey, through lots of tunnels. I guess we must have gone to London.'

Another train took Desmond to Southampton where thirty-two children, half from Ireland and the rest from England, were marched up a gangplank. They were allowed to stay on deck as the ship pulled away, waving from the railings at imaginary friends and family. In truth, there was no-one to see them off.

'The boat trip was nice,' recalled Desmond. 'I remember people having birthday parties, with special treats to eat. There was a social worker, Theresa, looking after us and she used to give me a hug before I went to bed. I had a big crush on her.

'You know, I remember the name of every kid on that voyage. I remember telling them, "I'm never going to forget you." And I didn't. Every name. There was this one kid I remember best. On the day we arrived in Fremantle, they put him on the back of a truck and he disappeared. His name was Jimmy Quigley and I never saw him again. I always remember thinking, Whatever happened to Jimmy Quigley? He was just thrown on this truck and taken away.'

Desmond talked of how the children were split up and put on buses when the boat docked. Some went to Clontarf, others to Tardun and the older boys to Bindoon. Desmond was taken to Clontarf.

'I remember going down the plank, then getting on a bus. I put my face against the window waving to Theresa to say goodbye. I didn't get any sort of immediate impression of Australia – I was too busy crying, crying from deep inside. It took days before the contrast sunk in. Ireland was green, cold and wet, Australia was brown, hot and dry.

'Smell is very powerful for me, and Australia smelt different. I remember smells from Ireland, they're very strong in my mind now.

'We got to Clontarf and I was crying so loudly that I didn't hear the others crying. I drowned out the sound. We were taken to the refectory and given a plate of thick cold stew. The flies were horrendous and you couldn't help eating them every time you took a mouthful of food.

'But we quickly learned never to push our plates away. We had a joke about the porridge served on Fridays. We weren't supposed to eat meat because we were Catholics, but there were so many weevils in the porridge, it was impossible. It's a Boys' Town joke.'

Desmond was nearly nine years old when he started his new life. He remembers the heat and alien landscape; waking up to the sound of magpies and sometimes a kookaburra.

'The day after we arrived, they took us to the zoo and we had a ride on an elephant. It made good pictures for the newspapers. And the following Saturday I was set to work, barefoot, in the baking heat, cleaning up an army rubbish tip.

'Within a week my back was like one big blister, a water blister, burned by the sun. We slept on a veranda and rain would slant in when the wind blew, making the beds sodden.

'I can't remember any brother telling us why we were there, or what the rules were, or welcoming us. I was lost in every sense.

'There was no-one we could go to when we were hurt, scared or sad; no adult we could turn to for comfort, consolation or information. We just had to rely on each other. The only stabilizing factor in our lives was that we were all together.

'A part of me died at Clontarf in those first few weeks. I was nothing. I was sitting on a small wall at the front of the main building, beneath one of the arches and I suddenly realized that I was no longer a human being. I became a nonentity. Life was never going to be what I wanted. I was going to be nothing.

'From the age of eight to thirteen the brutality compounded that hopelessness. The core of me had died and I had this shell; the shell of God's brave little soldier. A mechanical toy.'

There were no women at Clontarf, except for a group of Hungarian nuns who spoke little English. They worked in the laundry.

Desmond's teacher was a lay person and former Boys' Town boy. He didn't belt the children, which made him popular.

'We had our own way of judging people,' said Desmond. 'The difference between a good person and a bad person was that a good person didn't belt you. That was how we measured good and bad.

'The brothers never gave opinions on people unless it was with the strap. Troublemakers were punished, the rest were ignored. I kept my mouth shut. We were taught to keep our mouths shut.

'In that first year, when I was nine, I was accused of doing naughty things with another boy. I didn't understand what I was supposed to have done, but it was something to do with having played with his penis. This brother accused me and I couldn't answer. I didn't understand what he was asking.

'When you were hit at Clontarf it was called a dong. Six dongs meant you were hit six times. This particular brother used a bamboo cane that he would buy long and get cut to length. He kept hitting me until I confessed. I got belted into submission because I knew he wouldn't stop unless I admitted it.

'Another time I was hit until I cried. But I couldn't. I had to make myself cry; to squeeze out the tears so that he'd stop beating me. I forced this noise out – a noise that sounded like submission.

'The reason no-one fought back or complained is that nobody would listen. You couldn't stand up to the brothers.'

Desmond found a routine in his life by going to school and

Both born in 1944, but our lives turned out so differently. Desmond McDaid and me as children.

ABOVE: Sir Joseph Cook, High Commissioner of Australia, addressing Barnardo boys leaving for Australia in 1925. *(Hulton Deutsch)*

BELOW: A party of boys preparing to leave their children's home in Liverpool for Canada in 1929. *(Hulton Deutsch)*

Florence Aulph, who was sent to Canada as a child.

JOURNAL; ... RNING, AUGUST 2 1947

migrating To Australia

These boys, ages ranging from five to twelve years, will shortly leave St. Joseph's Home at Termonba... Australia, under an emigration scheme which has the approval of the Catholic Hierarchy. In the adoption most of the boys will be placed under the ... of the Irish Christian Brothers, and the yo... continue under the ca... ...zareth Sisters.

ABOVE: Irish boys aged between five and twelve leaving for Australia on a scheme organized by the Catholic Church. (Derry Journal)

RIGHT: Leaving Nazareth House, Hammersmith, London, after the Second World War, for Australia.

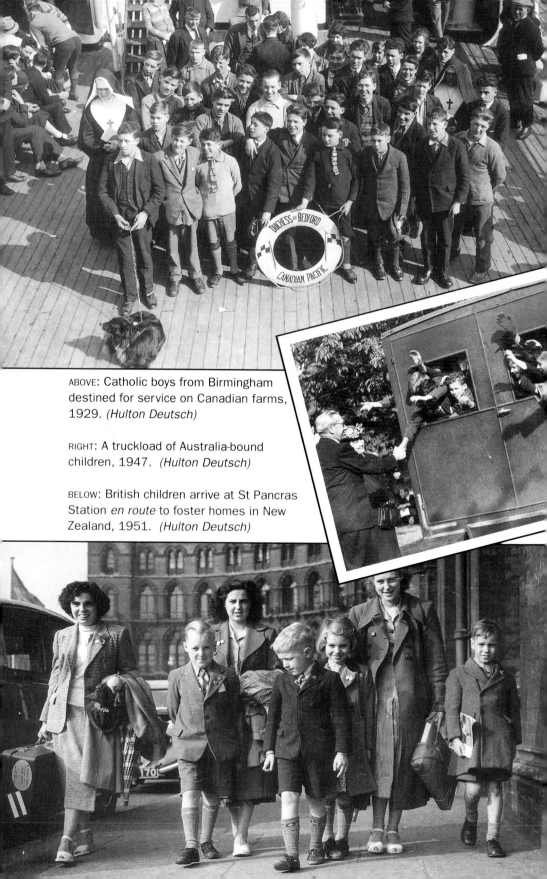

ABOVE: Catholic boys from Birmingham
destined for service on Canadian farms,
1929. *(Hulton Deutsch)*

RIGHT: A truckload of Australia-bound
children, 1947. *(Hulton Deutsch)*

BELOW: British children arrive at St Pancras
Station *en route* to foster homes in New
Zealand, 1951. *(Hulton Deutsch)*

C1253

ABOVE: Arriving at Fremantle aboard the *Asturias*. *(Courtesy Battye Library)*

LEFT: 'Children under the Church of England Scheme (deprived of normal home life) who are going to Homes in various parts of Australia.' 1955. *(Hulton Deutsch)*

BELOW: First look at Melbourne for British child migrants. *(The Age)*

ABOVE and BELOW: British child migrants as young as eight, labouring on the construction of Bindoon Boys' Town. *(News Ltd and courtesy Battye Library)*

RIGHT: Brother Paul Francis Keaney. *(Courtesy Battye Library)*

ABOVE: Boys working in the Bindoon woodwork shop, early 1950s. *(West Australian Newspapers)*

LEFT: Statue of Brother Keaney – 'The Orphans' Friend' – erected shortly after his death. Many child migrants find it offensive and want it removed. *(Select/Tony Ashby)*

BELOW: Barefoot boys at Bindoon shortly after its completion in 1953. *(West Australian Newspapers)*

GLOBE HOTEL,
Albury
Portals of Hospitality
PHONE 67-68
LICENSEE: K. D. BRODIE

CITY AND DISTRICT FORECAST : Fine and Cool.

Border Morning Mail

Registered at G.P.O. Sydney, N.S.W.
for transmission by post as a newspaper

Subscriber to Aust. Assoc. Press which
provides Overseas News in this issue.

Audited Daily Circulation :11,543

'Phone 51   ALBURY WEDNESDAY, MARCH 15, 1950

VOL. XLVII
13,912

2d.

Orphans Arrive Here To Start Their Life Afresh

Representing the youth of England, Ireland, Scotland, and Wales, 22 war orphans, aged from five to 15 years, arrived at St. John's Convent Orphanage, Thurgoona, yesterday, to be schooled and trained as young Australians.

The children left London by the liner Asturias on February 8, and upon arrival at Sydney were welcomed by Father Crennan, priest in charge of Catholic immigration, and Sisters Mary Rita and Bernadette, of St. John's, Albury.

Two Sisters of Nazareth, Sisters Terese Benedict and Ethelreda, travelled from England with the children, but upon arrival at Sydney left for Brisbane, where they will follow their calling.

The children are all girls, and are war orphans of World War II.

With a charming personality, they have already won the friendship of those who have met them, for with the hint of a brogue—and the smile of the highlands—they shyly endear all.

Mother Gertrude, Mother Superior of St. John's Convent Orphanage, said yesterday that she was very pleased to have the children.

The children are well spoken, and have little accent in their speech to identify them with their native land, but a hint of the broad Scots or the lilting Irish brogue will be noticed now and again.

SCOTS LASSIES

Five-year-old Patricia McNaught, of Aberdeen, and 13-year-old Josephine Carvill, of Glasgow, are among the Scottish lassies.

Patricia said that the Bay of Biscay was very rough, and Josephine agreed that the Great Australian Bight could be the same, but, "It wasn't as bad as the Bay of Biscay," neither would say, however, that they had been seasick during the trip aboard ship.

Margaret Coyne (9) of Birmingham, and Elizabeth Finan (7), of Isleworth, said they enjoyed the trip, especially the tour of Sydney beaches.

Geraldine Fitzgerald (10), of Cardiff, Wales, was particularly anxious to know if there were any children's swings in Australia, and was happy when informed that there were plenty.

Three sisters, Stella (6), Constance (7), and Maureen (8) McGreevy, of London, pleased with St. John's, said it was a very beautiful school.

Charming little Pamela Hall (5), has a delightful personality. She said the trip to Australia was wonderful. Pamela's mother was killed during the last war.

Ten-year-old Eileen

Children and Nuns

Sisters Mary Rita (back left), and Mary Bernadette, with their new charges after their arrival at the Albury railway station yesterday morning.

of Birmingham, asked Sister Bernadette if there were any little girls at St. John's. Eileen adores the younger children.

Mary Molohan is from Ireland, and although aged 10, has the trace of a delightful Irish brogue, and her accent adds further to her charm.

"MADE THEMSELVES AT HOME"

At St. John's yesterday they all made themselves at home, and were shown around the convent buildings by other girls.

Convent will prepare them for their future life in Australia by teaching them music, dressmaking, nursing, and sport.

Sports will include basketball, softball, tennis and vigoro.

Education, however, will be the main concern, and the children will be fully qualified for their new Australian life after they have left St. John's.

Huge Subs; P[...] Fast As So[...] To Attack [...]

Submarines as big as aircraft carriers ... Arctic ice, to attack Russia if war broke o[...] Australian explorer (Sir Hubert Wilkins[...]

And, according to newspaper columnist Dr[...] is designing a supersonic B36 bomber to fly [...] the speed of the sound.

Sir Hubert Wilkins said the submarines would carry guided missiles and planes.

Soviet industrial centres, he added, now were situated east of the Ural Mountains.

Her Arctic coast was protected by radar air stations, and U.S. bomber attacks would be difficult and risky.

Warships would be opposed by Russian submarines,

(the huge submarines he[...] mind could lie secretl[...] the Arctic Ocean ice.

The crews could c[...] with electrically hea[...] to get air and dischar[...] or planes.

Sir Hubert, who is [...] to the U.S. Army [...] were no waves un[...] so that the sub[...] but be as large as [...] if desired.

He said Amer[...] hoped to send [...] the centre of th[...] "We are no[...] gress," he added[...]
Drew Pears[...]

Albury Woman and Husband at Law

Property Disposal
... urities,

SYDNEY, Tuesday.
... which a 77-year-old re[...]
... fe for the re[...]

playing sport. He was obviously a bright kid, but the motivation wasn't there, and slowly his grades deteriorated.

'I often thought about Ireland and my mother. Who was she? Why had she left me? But mostly I wondered what I'd done wrong. I reckoned I must have done something wrong to be sent away.'

A week before Christmas in 1955, when Desmond was eleven, the boys piled onto a bus for a journey to a place where Catholic families were waiting to billet them over Christmas. Brother Doyle was driving and as the bus crossed a narrow bridge it collided with a truck.

'I remember this smashing of glass and it was cascading over me in tiny pieces. I woke up with something on top of me. There was a big hole in the bus. I was lucky. Where I was sitting all the seats were pushed up into the back and I was buried under them. I was one of the last people off the bus.

'I remember looking across and seeing poor Davey lying there, bleeding, and I felt sorry for him. Brother Doyle pulled some seats off me and carried me to the shade of a tree. A group of boys were there, saying the rosary.

'Cars were pulling off the road. Two of us were put in the back seat of this green car, Lawrie Tormey was next to the driver in the front. Dessie McMullen was sitting next to me and his leg was hanging on by nothing more than a piece of skin. I kept wondering if I should pull his leg off rather than leave it dangling there. His face was bloody and he couldn't open his eyes because they were covered with dried blood.

'I remember the driver was upset that we were putting blood all over his car.

'He took us to the Princess Margaret Hospital. They thought Dessie was going to die so they put him in a special glass room which must have been intensive care. Tony Bugeja and I were in Ward One. Dessie lost one leg, but Tony lost both of his.

'I was lucky. I had these flaps of flesh hanging off my knee. They thought I would lose the leg but instead they put in ninety stitches. You can still see the scars, and afterwards, I couldn't even kneel down in church.

'I remember lying in casualty for ten hours, because there were so many people injured who needed treatment more than I did. A nurse called Jackie came down and sat with me. I'm still good friends with her. They had to cut my clothes off and I was frightened because I had no underwear.

'I spent five weeks in hospital and it was a good time. There was no fear. We had nice meals and goodnight kisses from the nurses. I don't remember the brothers visiting us, not until days later. A Maltese priest arrived one day.

'The bus crash was a big story in Western Australia. One kid died and four boys lost limbs. We used to laugh when Tony would say, "Scratch my feet, go on scratch them," but, of course, he had no feet. I would pretend and he'd sigh and say, "A bit harder, scratch a bit harder." '

I asked Desmond if anybody had told the boys' parents about the accident. Were they notified that their sons had died or been injured?

He looked at me. 'We were orphans, Margaret! As far as we knew, we didn't have families.

'The crash was an accident – I don't blame the brothers. But afterwards there was no acknowledgement of trauma or grief, even towards the boys who lost limbs. They could have shown us some compassion and caring.'

Desmond reminded me of a story that I'd heard about Douglas Bader, the British war hero, visiting Clontarf about ten months after the bus crash. He came especially to see the boys who, like him, had lost limbs and were learning to cope.

One child migrant, Charlie Gatt, who lost a leg in the accident, had told journalists how he was given new clothes before meeting the Battle of Britain pilot. Bader gave each boy a signed copy of his autobiography, *Reach for the Sky*, but Charlie said the books were taken from them afterwards and he had not seen his copy since then.

For Desmond, the bus accident became symptomatic of his loveless childhood.

'Not long after the crash, I remember being asked in confession, "Do you love God?" I couldn't answer. I didn't know what love meant. How could I know what love means?'

When Desmond was fifteen, a local factory owner, an Aquinas old boy, came to the school, looking for an apprentice to learn how to sharpen tools. It wasn't an official scheme but Desmond could see his grades weren't getting any better.

He took the job and unsuccessfully tried night school. Work took over, although he found time to join the local surf club and become president of the Young Christian Workers' Club. He stopped going to church.

Desmond found a girlfriend, and moved into her parents' house. She soon found another boyfriend but Desmond stayed on as a lodger. Slowly, over time, he became part of their family.

'This family treated me like a son. Here was comfort and protection. Someone concerned if I didn't eat enough. Someone who asked me if I wanted an extra sausage. At Clontarf we got cold stews and the uneaten food was served up again the next day. It came back to the table like a pot of marmalade or a salt shaker.'

Months and then years passed – twenty-two years – as Desmond worked hard and lived with the McAllister family, growing ever closer and feeling a part of their lives.

'The mother asked me to call her "Mum" but I couldn't. Somewhere I hoped that I had my own mother. If so, I still wanted to find her – just to say I was OK. But I didn't think about her as much; not every day.

'It was a long time between leaving Clontarf and beginning the search for my mother. I just put my head down and made some money – I worked up to eighteen hours a day, seven days a week. Life was about paying your way and that's all that mattered. I wanted to make a million quid – not for flash cars, or holidays, or houses. I wanted to make sure that nobody was going to control my life again.

'I never married. It doesn't bother me because I'm quite satisfied being single.

'You see, a part of me died in Clontarf, but I can live with that now. I am what I am. I've managed to make myself into a person out of the left-over bits and pieces.'

Desmond did make his million dollars. He achieved what he set out to do and retired at forty-five after selling his tool-sharpening works. For years he would tell other migrants to forget about their past – 'You're grown up, get on with your life' – yet all the while, he wanted to find his own family.

He would recall how in 1974 he went to Ireland, looking for his mother. He hired a car in Belfast and drove to Londonderry to visit the nuns at Nazareth House where he'd once lived as a child.

'I wanted them to say, "Desmond, we know the problem, we know who you are; here's how you got here," ' Desmond said.

'They're supposed to be an open house with open hearts. That's what they taught me. I was God's little soldier, all grown up – the man they said I should be.

'I sat down and had a cup of tea and the Mother Superior brought out two photographs, one of me at school and the other a going-away picture.

' "Do you know where my mother is? Can you help me find her?" I asked. "We don't know," was the response. And that was it. There were no records or visitors books or school reports. I pleaded with them to look again.'

The next day Desmond went back and the Mother Superior handed him a letter his mother had written:

> Dear Sisters,
> Thank you for looking after me several months ago. I would very much like you to take care of my little boy for two months while I get back on my feet. I'll be back to collect him.

The following day Desmond drove to County Donegal and the area where he was born.

He had no address, or point of reference. He simply drove through the streets, all day and into the night, totally lost in every sense. He was looking blindly for his mother and didn't even know where to begin.

'Finally the police pulled me up and asked what I was doing. "I'm looking for my mother," I said. "Where does she live?" they asked.

'I didn't know what to say. It was seven-thirty in the morning and I realized it was hopeless. It was as if this policeman had held a mirror up to me and I had to push it away.'

Eventually Desmond flew back to Australia feeling dejected and disappointed. In Perth, he tried to conceal his pain by telling his friends that he had had a great time.

I first met Desmond in the Parmelia Hilton in Perth in October 1991. He didn't have an appointment. I was due to see another child migrant named Don at 2.30 p.m., but the receptionist rang to say that two men were waiting for me in the hotel bar.

This was unusual. It was the first time anybody had waited in the bar at lunch-time and I wasn't eager to walk in looking for them as I didn't know what either man looked like.

The receptionist eventually pointed out the two men and I introduced myself to Don who was quite nervous. Desmond said, 'I'm coming with him.'

'Well, I normally see people on their own,' I replied. 'You'll be all right on your own, Don. But if you want your friend to come that's OK.'

'I'm Desmond McDaid,' Desmond said in a matter-of-fact way, as if I was supposed to know him. 'I'm coming with him for moral support – aren't I, Don?'

I wasn't happy about this. Desmond struck me as pushy. As we waited for the lift, I turned to Don and shook his hand and said, 'I'm very pleased to meet you.' When I extended my hand to Desmond he simply ignored it.

When I tried again, Desmond said, 'I don't shake Sheilas' hands.'

I wasn't sure what 'Sheila' meant at that point but I soon realized.

In my room, I felt Don would need a sensitive approach. He was obviously nervous and quite shy. When I sat down I asked him again if he wanted Desmond to stay.

'Any beer in the fridge?' asked Desmond.

'I don't normally offer alcohol during interviews,' I replied.

He went on, 'I've brought Don along. I've picked him up in my car. I don't know if you realize this but I've been trying to make an appointment to see you.'

I politely suggested he make an appointment on his own and I would see him then, but he stayed put.

At that point, Don looked very uncomfortable and embarrassed. I resumed my conversation with him, hoping Desmond would sit still and offer quiet moral support, but every time I asked a question, Desmond interjected. All my non-verbal signals, giving a clear message to Desmond to shut-up, were ignored. I asked him several times if he would be quiet.

Halfway through each question, Desmond would interrupt, talking about his own situation. 'I've been looking for my mother for years. I've spent thousands of dollars and found nothing.'

'We're not talking about you at the moment. I want to talk with Don.'

In the middle of all this, Desmond turned to me and said, 'Have you ever been skydiving?'

Don looked agitated. I put my notebook and pen down, turned to face Desmond and said, 'No, actually, I haven't, have you?'

'No, but I'd love to try. I used to have a girlfriend who was a stripper, and we used to talk about jumping naked to see what we could get up to on the way down.'

Who on earth is this man? I thought. Which planet does he come from? I had never met anyone so blatantly rude, crude and obnoxious. It took everything I had to turn away from him, bite my bottom lip and not react.

Desmond continued to hijack the interview until I told him that if he didn't keep quiet he would have to leave.

I tried talking to Don again. I knew he was desperate to find his mother, and it was entirely possible that she was still alive. I had to listen to his every word and it was very difficult with Desmond present. Every few minutes, Desmond would drop in a reference to how much money he had or how he'd retired in his mid-forties.

He was acting like a child seeking attention. His every action was a plea: Me. Me. Me.

Yet despite the interruptions, I knew that I couldn't simply throw him out. Desmond also needed help in his own right.

When he called me 'Sheila' again, I stopped him and told him my name was Margaret. From then on he referred to me as Mrs Humphreys.

He quietened down a little and I continued to speak with Don. I explained to him exactly how I planned to proceed with his case and that I was hopeful we would find his mother. He was very relieved and seemed unburdened. Unfortunately, I still had this very demanding 'three-year-old' wanting more and more attention.

'Finding mothers is impossible,' declared Desmond. 'I had the best in the business looking for my mother. It can't be done. Nobody could do it better. I've even had private detectives looking and nothing.'

I ignored this statement, but Desmond was undeterred. 'When am I going to see you?' he demanded.

'Well if the experts can't find your mother, what can I do, a mere Sheila?'

Desmond mumbled and stuttered. 'I want an appointment. I need one.'

'I'm sorry, I can't see you this time. But if you would like to send me the papers collected by your experts I'll study them carefully.'

Desmond wasn't satisfied. 'I've had the Catholic Welfare mob working on this, they've had it for two years. I ring them up every two months and there's just nothing, nothing.'

The organization he referred to was, I believed, the Catholic Migrant Centre.

As they left, I shook Don's hand once more. When I turned to Desmond he again refused my outstretched hand.

Going back to my room I shook my head in disbelief at the gall of this appalling man. What lay behind the smokescreen of boasting and bravado?

The following day Desmond's papers were hand-delivered to the hotel. Twenty-four hours later, I opened the door to an obscenely large basket of red roses. I didn't really have to open the card, McDaid's name lit up in neon lights in my head. I sent the roses to a local hospital where they would be more appreciated.

Over the next four months I managed to begin research on Desmond's family background. I wrote a letter to him explaining that there were two possible marriages for his mother. The letter contained a request for twenty dollars to pay for both certificates because I particularly wanted this so-called, self-confessed, 'did-I-ever-tell-you-I-was-a-millionaire' to pay for them. After all, Desmond had made it patently clear that there was nothing he couldn't buy or afford.

On my next visit to Western Australia, early in 1992, I had many child migrants to see, but Desmond wasn't one of them. I did have news for Don – his mother was alive.

I was musing about the twenty dollars, which Desmond still hadn't paid, when another child migrant, Alan Osbourne, invited me to dinner at his home. Alan and his wife Carol had asked me many times before and I'd refused so often that it was becoming embarrassing. In the end I agreed and he arranged to pick me up at 6.00 p.m. from the hotel.

Alan rang me that morning. 'A slight change – we're going out.'

I complained that I didn't want to eat out.

'No, no, you'll enjoy it. I'll collect you. By the way, there's a surprise for you.'

I kept arguing with him, suddenly full of trepidation. I don't appreciate surprises, particularly in Perth where I've never felt comfortable.

Alan picked me up from the hotel and we drove to his house first. While he changed, I wandered through the garden with Carol. By then I'd convinced myself that the surprise was possibly the place he'd chosen for supper. When I heard the crunching noise of tyres on the gravel drive, I knew that it was a large, heavy car. I didn't even look around. I didn't have to think twice.

McDaid! I thought. The evening suddenly had all the ingredients of a major disaster. Dealing with Desmond needed a structured, formal setting, not an evening at a restaurant.

'Mrs Humphreys, Mrs Humphreys,' Desmond said enthusiastically, waving an envelope. 'I've brought you twenty dollars. Here's the money.'

I struggled to smile.

'I've booked us into a lovely restaurant. It's the best in Perth. By the river, of course. Good table and the best seafood in town.'

'I don't eat seafood,' I said. 'Ever.'

'Oh! Well, we'll have to change our plans.'

Desmond disappeared inside and made arrangements to go to an Italian restaurant.

I had to brace myself for what I predicted was going to be one of the worst nights of my life. The women sat in the back of the car – a quaint Australian tradition – and off we went with mixed expectations.

I looked out of the window at the river, totally speechless, listening to Desmond and Alan talking. Carol sensed my disquiet.

As I anticipated, the restaurant was very impressive and Desmond was indeed a 'regular'. This was his territory and he took charge, asking for his favourite table.

I sat next to Alan. Desmond was directly opposite me making

an elaborate performance of selecting and tasting the wine before we ordered our meals.

As the conversation developed, it was punctuated by Desmond ordering new bottles every twenty minutes. His glass was no sooner filled than emptied.

The evening was worse than I had expected. So much so that halfway through Alan asked if I wanted to leave. 'Why bother?' I said. 'Desmond'll be on the floor any minute.'

Surprisingly, Desmond bore no trace of a hangover when I saw him the following day. This was to be our first formal interview.

Desmond sat down in the hotel room, unbuttoning his suit jacket. 'I don't think you like me very much, Mrs Humphreys,' he said.

I was slightly taken aback by this direct approach.

'I don't know about the man,' I said, 'but I think there's a hurt little boy in there somewhere that I'm sure I would like. I guess we'll have to spend some time finding him.'

We talked for nearly two hours, the first of many such meetings. I wanted to discover the other side of Desmond's personality, the side hidden by that brash exterior. I wanted to help him see that there were no hidden agendas, there was no need to try to impress me.

I hoped that he could recognize the child within himself and slowly remove the mask which he presented to the outside world.

In the end, it was his sense of humour which enabled us to work together. He looked at the world in a very dry, ironic way.

By the end of the meeting, Desmond's entire demeanour was transformed. He spoke with a new softness and a gentleness when he described his loneliness. He'd never married – never felt the need – but he had never lost the feeling of inner isolation, despite his many friendships and his social *bonhomie*.

'I feel content. It's like at night, I can get to my toilet without the lights on. I can find my way around in the dark, but I'm aware of my loneliness in those moments.'

Over the next three months I saw a fundamental change in Desmond. We had developed a relationship built on trust and respect. Given his experiences, he didn't trust easily, which was understandable.

I steeled myself for the long haul, for although we found his mother within several months, my work with Desmond would continue for a long time to come.

To use Desmond's own words, 'Margaret, within five minutes you saw through the bullshit. You saw the real person.'

Perhaps he also meant that I recognized his pain.

Desmond and I were both born in the same year – 1944. I found this coincidence enormously significant. It brought our two lives into stark contrast. I grew up in a loving family surrounded by warmth and attention, while he was the son of a struggling single mother in Ireland who asked for help. Desmond was raised in institutions that rarely showed him love, warmth or humanity.

We came into the world in the same year, we listened to the same songs, enjoyed the same dances, watched the same films, yet our lives could not have been more different. This made me realize that it could so easily have been me on that boat to Australia, or any of my school friends. A slight change in our circumstances and it could have been any one of us.

Child migrants were not necessarily poor, deprived, working-class kids. They came from all sections of society and from many different walks of life. It's wrong to think of them all as impoverished and abandoned by their families. This myth must be exposed, just as labels like 'orphans' cannot be accepted at face value.

I telephoned Desmond several times from England, giving him progress reports, and each time he expected to hear his mother on the line. I knew, however, that the approach to her was all important.

I asked Desmond to write a letter to help me describe him to his mother. When I read it, I was amazed. This is a nice bloke, I thought. When am I going to meet him?

The end of the search is enormously difficult for a child migrant. Their fear of rejection is profound, and Desmond was no exception. 'What if she says no? What if she doesn't want to see me?' he asked.

He no longer had to live with the fear that his mother had died, he knew she was alive; but after forty years, he couldn't bear to think that she could reject him.

Desmond flew to England, arriving on a Thursday morning and taking a train straight to Nottingham. I arranged for him to spend two nights in a hotel because I wanted to be sure he was prepared for the reunion. On the first evening I gave him a photograph of his mother. He stared at it for a long while – noting all the similarities.

It took a lot of discipline and self-control for Desmond to wait those two days but he said to me, 'I've lived with this hope for so long; I can wait a little longer.'

On the day we left to meet his mother, I arranged to meet Desmond at his hotel. As I crossed the lobby, he rose from a chair and smiled. He lifted his hand and clasped mine. It was the first time he had shaken my hand.

27

Each time I flew into Australia, and for weeks before I left home, I would begin to prepare myself for what lay ahead. There were child migrants to see for the first time as well as those I already knew who desperately waited for news of their families.

My bags were full of photographs, greeting cards and letters. Sometimes these were written by mothers or fathers, brothers or sisters. At other times I carried a small heirloom like a ring, a watch or a necklace. Often families wanted their newly discovered relative in Australia to have some small object as both a memento and a sign of acceptance.

I never let the bags out of my sight. They were always under my feet or in my arms.

When the plane circled Perth, I would look down and see the lights and imagine everybody asleep. I would think of all the people whose lives would change over the next few days.

When I arrived in March 1992 I had news for two brothers who had been to Bindoon. I would have to tell them their mother had died but that they had two sisters in England. I had with me photographs of their mother, whom the brothers had never seen, and also their father.

For a former Tardun boy, I had similar news. His mother had

died, but he had a brother in England, who had sent photographs, a long letter and his mother's favourite brooch.

For a Geraldton woman, I was able to say that her mother was very much alive in the North of England. In my bag I had photographs of how she looked both years ago and also more recently. There was a very long, loving and accepting letter from her mother.

There was more, but never enough. Still there were too many people waiting for news. And whatever the outcome, there would be joy and pain, regret and despair.

When I arrived at the Parmelia Hilton, I immediately unpacked. As always, I tried to make my room more welcoming by putting up photographs and rearranging the furniture.

On my first Sunday there was a picnic at Pinjarra, outside of Perth, where the Fairbridge Society once had a farm school. The Old Fairbridgians had invited me to a barbecue and I was looking forward to meeting up with them as a group.

There were probably thirty families at the barbecue and their many children danced and played on the grass. The farm school had become a series of holiday cottages rented out to the general public and each building bore an English name.

By late afternoon I began feeling light-headed and weak. I thought it was the effects of too much sun. I'd been working from seven in the morning till eleven every night since I arrived on the previous Thursday.

When I got back to the hotel, I still felt weak and tired and I cancelled two of my evening appointments. I'd never done that before.

My face was absolutely white and all I could do was lie on the bed, feeling terrible.

Eventually I fell asleep and woke at about one in the morning. The bed and my bedclothes were soaked with blood. Disorientated by exhaustion and loss of blood, I had no idea what to do. I could hardly walk to the bathroom.

I thought I was dying: I'm going to die in Perth.

I didn't know any doctors. I didn't know the nearest hospital. I was alone and vulnerable in a city where I'd never felt safe.

I rang my close friend, Susan, who lived in Melbourne and whom I'd known ever since I first went to Victoria. It was three in the morning.

'It's Margaret. I'm in Perth.'

She sensed my anguish. 'What's wrong?'

'I'm sick. I don't know what's wrong. I'm haemorrhaging.'

The fear in my voice was impossible to hide. Susan knew it was serious. To her I had always been this incredibly controlled, capable woman, who is never flustered and always in command of the situation. Now I didn't know what to do. I couldn't even organize a doctor.

'Have you rung for help?'

'No. I don't know who to call. I don't want anybody to know I'm ill.'

'Right,' said Susan, whose husband is a dentist, 'I'm going to ring my own doctor and see if he knows somebody in Perth. The best. Stay calm. You'll be fine. Don't move off the bed.'

'I can't move.'

Susan rang me back within ten minutes. 'There's a specialist who's on his way back to Perth from a conference in Melbourne. He'll be home by now. Call him.'

She gave me his home and hospital numbers. I eventually spoke to his wife.

When the doctor arrived, he gave me a wonderful smile but took one look at me and said, 'Margaret, you have two choices. Either I take you to hospital or you go by ambulance. Can you get to my car?'

Within an hour I was at the women's hospital and he was quietly reassuring me that everything would be fine.

'I've got appointments,' I told him anxiously. 'There are people coming to see me. They've waited a lifetime. I can't stay here, I've got work to do.'

'OK, OK,' he replied, humouring me.

I was frightened that he would tell me that I had to go home to England.

'Margaret, you're not well enough to go home.'

The specialist stopped the bleeding but he warned me that this was only temporary. He still had to discover what had caused the haemorrhage.

'You can't stay at a hotel. Have you any friends here?'

'I've got hundreds of friends, but I'd like to go to the house in Melbourne.'

'All right, I'll make sure you're fit to fly.'

A few hours later I telephoned Merv. I didn't want him to worry, but he dragged the information out of me.

'You're coming home, Margaret. No buts, no questions.'

'I can't.'

'Don't tell me you can't. Come home, get well again and then go back. Don't worry about the cost of another air fare. It's not important.'

'No, really, I can't come home. I'm not well enough to fly all that way.'

When I arrived in Melbourne, Harold picked me up from the airport. 'You look bloody terrible,' he said. 'Are they someone else's clothes or do you like the baggy look?'

I smiled weakly.

'Take me to the house. I'm not my best.'

I wouldn't tell him what had happened. I didn't want any of the child migrants to know that I was sick. I knew they'd make a big fuss and feel responsible. I wanted to carry on as normal.

When we arrived at the house in Canning Street, the child migrants in Melbourne had put fresh flowers in the vases and filled the fridge with food as they always did. There were welcome cards everywhere. The bed was made up for me.

Harold was putting the kettle on when Susan arrived.

'You look terrible,' she said, putting her arm around me.

'Yes, people keep telling me that,' I joked.

'Oh, you poor thing. Are you any better?'

I shook my head.

We began arguing over where I was going to stay. Susan wanted me to go with her. But the child migrants had gone to so much effort getting the house ready, I told her I was staying there.

'All right. First thing in the morning, I'm picking you up. We're going straight to the hospital.'

'Look, Susan, I have to be at work on Saturday. I can't cancel the—' I stopped. There was no point in arguing, Susan was adamant.

*   *   *

The consultant sensed immediately that I was a long way from my home and my family. He tried to be reassuring as he gave me a thorough medical.

'How long are you going to be in Melbourne?'

'Nine days.'

'Well, I want you in hospital.'

'I can't. I've got work to do. People to see.'

I was determined, but the doctor wasn't about to be overruled.

'You've lost a lot of blood. I need to know what's going on inside you. You have to be admitted.'

I tried to protest.

'Listen, Margaret, you're bleeding to death. Do you understand me? You have no choice. I'll arrange your admission.'

The next morning I was admitted for tests and allowed to go home that evening with Susan. Again and again I stressed to her that I didn't want any of the migrants to know. They had their own problems. This was mine.

For the next nine days, at meetings in Melbourne and back in Perth, I was constantly asked what was wrong. I told people that I was tired and nothing more. But they knew it was more serious. For the first time I realized that I was very important to them and that they cared deeply about me.

When I arrived back in England at least the bleeding had stopped but my problem was one of sheer exhaustion. I was half a stone lighter and my hair was falling out in large clumps. After five years of working long hours, my body was trying to tell me something.

My family and colleagues were obviously concerned, and for the first time I began to feel despondent. I had failed to convince the British government of its responsibility toward the child migrants. The trustees convinced me that it was through no fault of mine, but I kept asking myself how much longer the Trust could struggle to survive financially.

I was at home only a few weeks, and still catching up on my sleep, when Penny Chapman, the TV producer, telephoned. Her drama, *The Leaving of Liverpool*, was to be broadcast nationally by the Australian Broadcasting Corporation (ABC) on 8 and 9 July.

'No!' I cried. 'You can't mean it. I've only just left Australia. What about my family? The office?'

I knew it was pointless complaining. Penny had no idea what I'd just been through. I simply would have to drop everything and go back. Merv smiled weakly. This would be my fourth trip to Australia in twelve months. If this went on, I'd come home one day and he'd ask, 'Have you had a nice year, dear?'

Shortly afterwards, the head of drama for the ABC called and said there was going to be a major launch for the TV drama in Sydney and they'd like me as a guest. I told her, 'Hang on, I deliberately kept right out of this. I don't know anything about the drama.'

She said, 'The tapes are on their way. You can look at them before you arrive.'

Sure enough a courier delivered the video cassettes to my home. I didn't want to look at them, especially when the kids were around, so I had to find a time when they were out of the way. Finally, two days before my departure, I got up at five o'clock on a dark, cold morning and turned on the television.

I knew I couldn't sit through five hours, I had no time, but I thought I'd watch enough to get a feel for the drama. Unfortunately, ten minutes was all I lasted. I couldn't bear it – the music, the laughing kids skipping through the streets of Liverpool carrying a Union Jack, the playground scene where they were beaten with canes.

I knew all those children – I knew them now as adults. But here, vividly portrayed, I saw their childhoods. They were singing familiar songs in the streets, and skipping just as I had done as a child. It was no different. The same as all of my generation.

I ran upstairs, trying to get as far away as possible.

'I can't go! I can't!' I said.

Merv grabbed me by the shoulders, looked at me and said, 'Don't snivel! Don't you dare snivel. You're going on that plane. You're going.'

And he was right. I shouldn't snivel. How dare I get upset when I think of what the former child migrants have been through.

'OK!' I said. 'I can't watch the rest of it, but I will go.'

Merv smiled. 'Good. But not on your own – not this time.'

* * *

223

Until then, I hadn't even considered how I was going to get to Australia. This was an unexpected trip and the Trust simply didn't have the money to pay for the air fare.

Nottinghamshire County Council had generously renewed my secondment for another two years but the Child Migrants Trust had received no funding from the Department of Health, or any other department, since the £20,000 they had provided in 1990. Every application since then had been refused.

I argued that for the first time in over 100 years the child migrants and their relatives now had an agency specifically designed to meet their needs, but the Trust had only managed to provide 'a basic level of service to a particularly disadvantaged group of clients'.

When all else failed, I asked the British government to match the commitment of the Australian government which had provided us with £23,000 a year since 1989. We were only asking to employ one social worker for a year.

Again we were refused.

I wrote to the Department of Health in April 1992:

> Time is running out for many thousands of former child migrants if they are to be enabled to meet their relatives before their parents die . . .
>
> The history of child migration is not one which casts either governments or voluntary agencies in a positive light. It is a history which few wish to repeat and its many flaws and occasionally tragic consequences are often explained away as the result of a mixture of good intentions and ignorance.
>
> This sad chapter in our history of child care policy can either be extended or reversed. It is clear that the Australian government has made a positive commitment to confront the results of a policy which failed to protect the interests of this vulnerable and disadvantaged group of children. The opportunity for the British government to make a similar commitment is in your hands.

On 13 May, the application was refused.

*　　*　　*

Eventually, I approached my local bank manager, explained the situation to him, and he allowed me to take out an overdraft to pay for the flight to Australia.

The trustees were worried about my workload and were relieved when John Myles, the Trust's most experienced researcher, volunteered to accompany me and managed to find the money to buy himself a ticket. Everyone at the Trust had been working horrendous hours and few had taken any leave for over two years. We all knew that *The Leaving of Liverpool* would trigger another barrage of enquiries from former child migrants and increase the workload.

From my point of view, I was more worried about the pain and anguish it would cause when the migrants saw the horror of their childhood dramatized before them. They would grieve for the child within each of them.

Before I left, I had a call from Frances Swaine, a lawyer working for Leigh, Day & Co, in London. This was the firm that had been preparing a case on behalf of a child migrant and had since had many requests for legal advice.

Frances intended to go to Australia to interview migrants, and wanted her trip to coincide with the screening of *The Leaving of Liverpool*. The publicity for the drama would help raise public awareness that a legal campaign was underway.

As always, I left for the airport when the children were at school. I never want them to see me leave. I say goodbye in the morning and by the time they get home from school, I'm gone and Merv takes them out for dinner as a special treat.

John and I caught the three o'clock train from Nottingham to St Pancras and then the underground to Heathrow.

We flew direct to Melbourne and stayed that first night at the house in Canning Street. There was no social worker there because David had finished his contract and I was still looking for a replacement.

That night, I managed to watch a little bit more of *The Leaving of Liverpool*.

The story is told through the eyes of two children, Bert and Lily – played by Kevin Jones and Christine Tremarco – who meet in the Star of Sea Orphanage in Liverpool in the early 1950s. Bert believes he's an orphan but Lily has been placed there by her mother, who promises to come back within six months once she is on her feet financially. Before she can return, Lily and Bert are packed off to Australia.

The first half of the drama follows Bert as he arrives, tired, hungry and frightened, at a rural quarry where he's set to work cutting and carrying stone that is destined for a new church. Brother O'Neill, the man in charge, is a bully who breeds bullies.

Although the ABC stressed that the drama was set in New South Wales, the media pointed out the similarities between Brother O'Neill and Brother Keaney of Bindoon, and also the depiction of children hauling stones and making bricks as they had done at Bindoon.

Meanwhile, Lily is sent into domestic service in the outback, where she is exploited by her employers.

Sustained by their friendship, both eventually rebel against the brutality and find each other, but their escape is tinged with sadness. Although Lily does eventually find her mother, there's no salvation for Bert. Embittered and angry, he lashes out and ends up in prison.

John watched the programme with me and was incredibly moved. Often he shook his head in disbelief. 'What is this going to do to them?' he asked.

I shared his reservations, but told him, 'We mustn't look at it like that. It's not what it will do to them but what it can do for them.'

Before we left England, John had insisted that during our trip we were going to eat three proper meals a day, sleep regularly and not work too hard. He wasn't going to let me fall ill again. On the first morning in Melbourne, he went out to buy utensils for the kitchen and stock up the cupboards. I came downstairs and walked into the kitchen to find the table beautifully set with fruit juice in glasses, and bacon and eggs frying on the stove. I couldn't help laughing.

It was the last proper meal we had in the next fortnight.

On Friday, John and I flew to Sydney, ready for the launch. I had no idea what was planned. I thought there'd be a few people, the obligatory case of warm white wine and some sandwiches from the ABC canteen. Then I'd stand up and say, 'Yes it really happened, it's all true,' and sit down to watch a preview of the show.

Not quite!

The Intercontinental Hotel in Sydney has one of the finest locations in the world. Perched on one corner of Circular Quay, it stands guard over the ferries that fan out across Sydney Harbour. The hotel offers views in all directions; over the Opera House, the Bridge, the harbour sweeping up past Fort Dennison towards Watson's Bay and Sydney Heads. This is where the ABC chose to launch *The Leaving of Liverpool.* That evening, a specially invited audience arrived, many of the men in dinner jackets and the women in their outfits from David Jones or the boutiques of Double Bay. There were celebrities, drama critics, ABC executives, journalists, old Fairbridgians and Catholic clergy. John Hennessey was there, a child migrant and former mayor of Campbelltown, he had written to me years earlier. So was Harold Haig, looking decidedly uncomfortable in such a large crowd.

Stunned by the scale of it all, I was handed a glass of champagne and ushered between fully laden tables. A teenager came up to me with a Liverpudlian accent. It was Kevin Jones, who plays Bert in *The Leaving of Liverpool.* Many of the cast had been flown over for the launch, and Kevin was very excited.

'Everybody talked about you. I couldn't wait to meet you.'

Eventually, I found my place card at a table. I remember sitting down and then glancing at the cards around me. Somebody with a very warped sense of humour or a grasp of the absurd in the ABC's promotions department had decided, not only to invite a prominent churchman to the launch, but to sit him next to me.

I thought of Merv, back in Nottingham. 'Just you wait!' I muttered. 'You talked me into this.'

When Penny introduced me to the minister, she said, 'This is Margaret Humphreys, the director of the Child Migrants Trust . . .' but before she could finish he said, 'I know who she is.' He didn't even raise his eyes to meet mine. That was it. We didn't exchange another word through a four-course meal and coffees. It felt a little like the Last Supper on our table.

The ABC were paying and it must have cost them thousands. I

just kept thinking about the money being spent and the Trust's pitiful finances.

I sat there through this astonishing evening, with people telling me about this wonderful drama that would win all the awards, and all the while I was thinking about what a painful impact it would have on the child migrants. But the show was artistically brilliant, and it was courageous of the ABC to confront the shameful issue head-on.

Penny Chapman gave a speech about how difficult the programme had been to make and then she said, 'May I introduce Margaret Humphreys, who's going to tell you all about it.'

I could see John looking at me and thinking, Wrong!

He could see I was angry. I stood there watching all these people drinking champagne, eating their free meals and talking, laughing and joking. Among them, was Harold. Our eyes met and I thought, This is appalling! This isn't right! This room should be full of politicians not celebrities. We should be in Parliament House in Canberra or the Houses of Parliament in London. Those are the people who should have been watching this drama.

I cleared my throat and said I thought the ABC had shown enormous courage in making the programme. Immediately, I sensed that the audience understood my disquiet.

I told them, 'This would be enjoyable if it were only a drama, but unfortunately it depicts the lives of thousands upon thousands of British children. And although it shows young Lily finally meeting her mother, there are still thousands of people who are yet to meet their families, who are yet to go home, who have yet to get so much as a birth certificate to confirm who they really are. This isn't a period drama, it's real. These people are still suffering today.' I wanted to say, 'Now get on with your duck and lamb,' because that's how I felt.

As I sat down, the applause carried on and I had to go back up again. I wanted to say, 'How dare you clap that?' I wanted to shout: 'Put your champagne glasses down, get off your backsides and do something!'

Instead, I strode forward, waited for silence and said, 'Now, what are we going to do about it?'

When I got back to the table, I downed a glass of wine to steady my nerves and then noticed that the prominent churchman was finally looking straight at me.

'It was your country that sent them over here,' he said. 'What kind of country sends their children over here?'

I frowned slightly and, as evenly as possible, replied, 'Well, I suppose it's the same sort of country that sexually molests them when they get here.'

We didn't exchange another word.

28

The man's voice on the telephone was calm, detached and determined. He spoke without a trace of urgency or emotion as he explained how he was going to kill me.

'Leave Perth immediately,' he said, 'or you'll be leaving in your coffin. You have been warned before but you didn't listen. This time we know where your children are. You'd better find them quickly.'

The line went dead.

I had been unable to respond. I felt almost paralysed.

I'd been in Perth for three days, having spent a week in Melbourne after the launch party for *The Leaving of Liverpool.*

I'd left John in Melbourne handling the media. He released the press statements, arranged the interviews and gave nobody direct access to me. I don't think he went to bed for the first three days but he did the job brilliantly, sometimes literally banging on the bedroom door at five o'clock in the morning saying, 'Thirty minutes to the first meeting. Get moving, Margaret.'

In the midst of all this I told him, 'I must go to Perth. I have to tell some clients that I've found their families. If I go now, I can be back before *The Leaving of Liverpool* is screened.'

I went on my own, booking into the Parmelia Hilton. The staff, by now, knew me and made me feel welcome.

From the moment I got to my room the telephone started ringing. In all the years I had been coming to Perth, rushing in and out, I had never developed any attachment to the city. It wasn't that I didn't feel safe or thought it was particularly dangerous – I just hated the place. There were too many ghosts and too much pain.

Suddenly, in the space of a single phone call, it all changed.

Somebody had threatened not only me but my children. I went cold, immediately wondering where they were. Was Merv with them? Were they safe?

Not for the first time, I realized that I was fast becoming a severe nuisance to a lot of people. But this time I was more than uneasy.

In a hotel room, thousands of miles away from my family, I was vulnerable and angry, but I couldn't panic; I had no intention of giving in to this faceless, anonymous threat. I had come so far, and still had too much to do.

At any moment a taxi was due to arrive to take me to the studios of ABC radio for an interview with Verity James. I knew her by reputation to be astute and probing. I needed to set my own agenda but I couldn't concentrate.

Instead, I sat on the end of my bed and stared out of the window, gazing over the palm trees towards the sunlight on the Swan River. How did it happen, I thought, this beautiful place, with its awful history?

Questions flooded through my mind. What should I do? What could I do?

The phone rang again. The taxi was waiting to take me to the studio.

I was fifteen minutes late getting to the ABC – the first time I'd ever been late for an interview. I told nobody about the phone call, but as I answered Verity's questions I wondered if my caller was out there, listening to me.

When I left the studio, I launched straight into my appointments and it was only late in the afternoon, that it suddenly dawned on me that I wasn't in Australia on my own. Why hadn't I let John know about the threat? He was at Canning Street. Alone. Perhaps he too was in danger.

'Either you get on the first plane to Melbourne,' he said, 'or I'm coming over to Perth.'

I tried to explain that I couldn't run away; I had to carry on as if everything was the same. Somebody wanted to frighten me.

Without my knowledge, Verity James had also interviewed Brother Gerald Faulkner of the Christian Brothers and she played his interview after mine. I was surprised to hear him talking publicly but, over the next few days, I sensed that the Christian Brothers had embarked upon a quiet offensive to limit the impact of *The Leaving of Liverpool*.

Dr Barry Coldrey had almost finished his investigations. The Catholic Church had flown him to Europe so that he could produce this report. This was not immediately made public.

At the same time, there had been growing calls from the media and many child migrants for a criminal investigation into the sexual abuse allegations, with mention made of possible compensation.

Dr Barry Coldrey told journalists that the Church condemned any examples of ill treatment of children, but stressed that the British and Australian governments were to blame for what was a 'social experiment gone wrong'.

'It is high time the churches stopped taking all the can and the stick for this. The fact is, we are dealing with government policy that our churches co-operated with . . . government inspections, government supervisions and government subsidies.'

Brother Gerald Faulkner continued the counter-attack: 'We are being, I think, unfairly criticized because we tried to do what was thought best at the time, under government supervision . . .

'We were acting, in a sense, as agents of the Government.'

The Christian Brothers were obviously trying to deflect the spotlight and the blame away from themselves. Yet their comments did not ring true.

Over the previous two years, I had been given an enormous amount of historical material which had been collected and collated by child migrants. This consisted of old newspaper cuttings, brochures, books and official histories of the Christian Brothers' orphanages, published to commemorate anniversaries.

I now knew far more about the child migration schemes to Western Australia, and I also felt that Brother Faulkner's and Dr

Coldrey's press statements bore little relation to fact or to their own order's literature.

Governments may indeed have been behind the schemes, but the Christian Brothers were eager participants.

The first account of children being brought to Western Australia by the Christian Brothers was in an article published in the Catholic newspaper, *The Record*, on 11 August 1938. It announced the arrival in Fremantle of the ship *Strathaird*, which had left Southampton on 8 July 1938, carrying a party of thirty-seven boys, the eldest twelve and youngest only eight.

'37 Catholic Boy Migrants Welcomed', declared the headline and I could picture the bewildered children being shepherded down the gangway, clutching tight to their battered suitcases and to each other. A brass band playing, drowning their sobs, I suspect.

The boys were accorded a civic reception in the Fremantle Town Hall, and were later received at Clontarf Orphanage by an official party, including the Archbishop, a Minister representing the Federal Government, another Minister representing the State Government, and the Leader of the Opposition.

His Grace the Archbishop of Perth gave an address and thanked 'the Imperial Government, the Federal and State Governments, which had made possible that immigration scheme.'

He described it as an historic event in the history of Australian development and one that must exercise a far-reaching influence on the progress of the Commonwealth.

'At a time when empty cradles were contributing woefully to empty spaces, it was necessary to look for external sources of supply. And if we did not supply from our own stock we were leaving ourselves all the more exposed to the menace of the teeming millions of our neighbouring Asiatic races.'

My blood ran cold. Empty cradles! How empty were the cradles these children had left in England? I wondered. How empty were the hearts of their mothers and fathers?

The Archbishop continued: 'In no part of Australia was settlement more vital than for Western Australia, which, while it contributed only one-twelfth of the total population, occupied one third of the whole Commonwealth . . .

'The policy at present adopted of bringing out young boys and girls and training them from the beginning in agricultural and domestic methods, was a far more common-sense procedure. It had the additional advantage of acclimatizing them from the outset to Australian conditions and imbuing them with Australian sentiments and Australian ideals – the essential marks of true citizenship . . .

'. . . those boys who had landed that day, and others who would follow in time to come, would be Empire builders in the truest sense of the word; they would be a credit to the land of their birth and a credit to the land of their adoption.'

Where was the mention of deprived children, or waiting foster parents? This wasn't about giving kids a new start in life. It was a blatant piece of pragmatic social and religious engineering to fill rural Australia with bright, white British stock.

When I first read this story I felt I was suffocating. I gazed out of my hotel room window at the Swan River sparkling in the sunshine and dotted with yachts and catamarans. I wanted to shift the glass and feel the same breeze on my cheeks that filled their sails. It is called the Fremantle Doctor and arrives at about four o'clock every afternoon, gusting in from the sea and cooling things down. Yet, as I turned away, I knew that if I had been able to open the window that day, I would have drawn no comfort from the breeze.

But there was more – much more. As I read further, it became clear that the Catholic Church actively went looking for child migrants. Its claim that boys and girls were foisted upon them by governments just wasn't true.

In 1933, Archbishop Clune of Perth wrote to Cardinal Bourne of Westminster and suggested the possibility of Catholic children being sent from England to be trained as farmers. Children, he said, were cheaper to transport and transplant.

The Catholic Emigration Society, based in London, approved of the plan but five years later the proposals were still bogged down in bureaucracy and red tape. Prominent Church leaders in Western Australia then established the Catholic Episcopal Migration and Welfare Association to lobby the British and Australian governments.

Still the plan moved slowly, until February 1938, when Patrick Aloysius Conlan, a sixty-three-year-old Christian Brother from

Perth, was sent to England to cut through the bureaucracy. Conlan had a reputation as an achiever. He got things done, and within weeks of arriving in London he had obtained permission from the British government and arranged passage for more than a hundred boys mainly from the Nazareth Homes.

On that first morning in Fremantle Town Hall, Brother Conlan was called on to speak, and immediately attributed the success of the migration scheme to His Grace the Archbishop and the Bishop of Geraldton.

These men of 'foresight' had seen it was necessary to people Australia with 'the right type'.

He said he could have picked up hundreds of adult migrants but he could not conscientiously encourage them. 'Their ideas were formed and their sentiments attached to home; but he could recommend English parents to send out little boys under twelve. Some of these were orphans, some sent out voluntarily by their parents to settle in this beautiful country.'

Brother Conlan went on to describe what awaited the new arrivals, calling it a 'complete vocational system'.

'The boys were taught religion down to their very souls. Some were selected for suitable trades. Those who had no bent in this direction were sent to Bindoon where the brothers had a property of 17,000 acres. To train boys to take up farming on their own account they must first be educated in history, science and mathematics. It was necessary first to cultivate the mind . . . History would teach them that there were difficulties in other countries that we do not have here and there were many advantages in Australia.'

Of course, the Catholic Church wasn't the only organization to see the benefits of child migration – particularly when the children were 'sponsored' by governments and a subsidy was paid for each of them.

The first government-assisted migration of children to Australia started in 1912, when the Fairbridge Farm School was established at Pinjarra. In 1929, Barnardo's established a farm school near Picton, NSW, and a children's home in Sydney. In the 1930s, the Fairbridge Society opened its farm at Molong and a similar 'school' was founded by the Lady Northcote Emigration Fund at Bacchus Marsh, outside Melbourne.

The list grew longer every year.

The logic behind the schemes was becoming clear. Britain paid money to remove a social welfare problem; Australia increased its population. It fitted perfectly into the rationale of the charities, many of which believed that urbanization and industrialization were the roots of all evil. What better way to reverse this trend than to take children from the slums and turn them into farmers?

A week after the *Strathaird* departed, another thirty-one child migrants left England on the *Otranto*, and, in May 1939, a third group of forty-two boys arrived in Fremantle on the *Strathnaver*. Those who were too young to become apprentice farmers were sent to Castledare, the remainder to Clontarf or Tardun – all Christian Brothers' homes.

More were expected, but the Second World War intervened. Brother Conlan wanted to encourage wartime shipments but couldn't find the necessary transport, or a way past the German U-boats blockading Britain.

However, on 28 November 1945, *The Record* newspaper reported:

> Readers may remember that just before the war, the Christian Brothers in Western Australia had all the machinery working for receiving orphans and other poor boys from England and Ireland, and one considerable batch of boys is all the happier for it today in this State . . .
>
> And now, with the war over, it is the desire of His Grace (the most Rev. Redmond Prendiville, Archbishop of Perth) to renew the stream of new Catholic life to Western Australia, and in consequence consultation has been made with the other bishops of the state and as a result an association of the bishops has been effected . . . the first objective will be to renew agreements with the Commonwealth, State and Imperial governments in respect to the migration of boys, and to establish concurrently the machinery to receive girls too.

A week later, an editorial in the same newspaper made the migration sound like a piece of Orwellian social engineering.

The plan of the Westralian Hierarchy, outlined in our last issue, to bring to the State some 2000 war orphans and poor children of both sexes, represents a commencement in the most pressing of our national problems. Not only have we to replace the tens of thousands of young men who fell in the recent titanic struggle but also the six divisions of potential citizens who have been lost through contraception over the past sixty years . . .

The Church was far ahead of the present-day radicals in the enunciation of social theory, and it is both fitting and pleasing that it is able to give a bold yet prudent and practical lead in this most urgent problem of repopulation. At best the war with Japan is postponed. Asia presses from the north and the most effective rampart we can raise is a human one.

Immediately after the war, Australian political leaders had cried: 'Populate or perish!' as they glanced nervously northwards fearing that the Asian hordes were waiting to sweep down and seize rich, virginal Australia. After all, the Japanese capture of Singapore and bombing of Darwin had reinforced Australian fears that it did not have the resources or population to defend such a large continent.

Immigration was the answer to the problem. On 15 August 1947, the second wave of child immigrants left Britain. A band played jaunty sea shanties and children waved paper Union Jacks from the decks as the *SS Asturias* set sail for Fremantle with 147 boys and girls on board. Six weeks later, when she arrived, a headline in *The Record* announced: 'Church Aids State in Population Problem', and the State Minister for Immigration, Mr Thorn, told the bemused children, 'Your parents worked hard for their country . . . now it's your turn . . . you are the right type of people, and we want as many as we can get.'

It is ironic to think of Australians sleeping safer in their beds at night, knowing the security of their vast land was being bolstered by a bewildered army of children who were 'conscripted' from British institutions.

29

Although Desmond McDaid had been reunited with his mother, my work with him continued. It is the same with many child migrants. The search for family is also a search for their true identity.

Desmond had become an entirely different person to the man I first met. He still struggled to understand the brutality of his childhood, but I had helped him find the small boy locked inside himself.

'Margaret, I want to take you to Bindoon,' he said. He was looking across the expanse of Perth's skyline at the splashes of green parkland. It was Friday afternoon and the commuters were spilling out of the office blocks in Hay Street and filling the pavements.

'You're part of us now,' Desmond said. 'You're the sister we've never had. Until you go there, you've not fully touched our childhood. The old boys would expect you to go there. You have to think carefully about what message it gives them if you've never been to Bindoon.'

'I have been there,' I said defensively, hoping that he understood. In my mind I'd been to Bindoon countless times over the past five years. I had the men's reality to draw upon. Through them, I could picture it already and had never felt the need to go there.

Desmond wasn't satisfied. 'You've not touched the place. You've not felt the place. You've not smelt the place. And you should, you know. It's time, Margaret. Let's go up to Bindoon. I'll pick you up in the car. I can come early Sunday morning, at four o'clock, if you want. It'll be dark when we arrive.'

I gave him no answer.

Desmond called me the following morning and wanted my decision. I told him I was very undecided and had lots of mixed feelings.

He said to me, 'Margaret, I don't like to think of you walking around with demons in your head. They can become monsters.'

'OK, and what sort of monster would this be?' I laughed.

'Bindoon,' he stated boldly. 'While you don't go to Bindoon, you've only met us halfway.'

I was shocked by his reply. 'Do the other migrants think that? Is that what they say?'

Desmond said, 'That's your monster, Margaret.'

I thought, Right, well, you've got quite a few of your own, Desmond.

But I couldn't forget his words; all day they played in my mind – the thought that some child migrants might feel as if I'd not met them all the way.

Desmond knew I was giving it serious thought and rang again that night. 'Look, I'm free to go any time. You pick that phone up and we're off down the road. I tell you what, why don't we go very early in the morning? We could just quietly slip out of Perth into the bush. What's the problem, eh? We take it as it comes.'

As I put the phone down, it rang again.

'What have you forgotten?' I laughed.

A well-spoken, cold, calm voice said, 'You've been warned. Get out of Perth – and stay out. I hope you know where your children are. You should take them to their last confession.'

He hung up.

My first reaction was fear. I knew that at home in England Ben was on a school trip with his class. It was the first time he'd been away from home on his own.

I rang Merv. He listened quietly and was obviously worried.

'What should we do?' I asked. 'Will Ben be OK?'

'I'm sure he'll be fine but let me think about it and I'll decide if I should pick him up and bring him home. You've got enough to worry about.'

After the call, I stood in my room and wondered what was happening. I'm not a threatening figure. I'm very careful about what I say in the media. I choose every word carefully. I don't apportion blame. Why would somebody want to hurt me and my children?

It was dark when Desmond arrived at the hotel. Reception rang me. 'Mr McDaid is in reception. He says to take your time.'

I came down, blinking through red-rimmed eyes. I hadn't slept.

Desmond said, 'I've got the Sunday papers in the car, but I suggest you don't look at them.'

'Why?'

'Don't look at them yet. Just get in the car and we'll get up to Bindoon.'

As we found the highway heading north, I leaned over the seat and grabbed a bundle of papers off the back seat. I quickly turned the pages, scanning the headlines and then stopped suddenly.

Dr Barry Coldrey had been interviewed by the *West Australian* newspaper about the sexual abuse allegations. First he defended Brother Keaney and the Boys' Town and then he suggested that British child migrants were already sexually active when they arrived in Australia. They were products of English child care institutions where, quite frankly, everybody knew that 'boy-on-boy sex' could be a problem.

There was a tendency, he said, for the Irish-Australian staff at Australian institutions to believe that the British children were more prone to boy-on-boy sexuality than the 'decent Australian kids'.

'Our own records presume that the British kids would require closer supervision.'

The facts were being twisted beyond recognition. Dr Coldrey had basically intimated that the innocent young children who had been brought to Australia were sexually perverted when they arrived and brought these terrible practices with them as part of their baggage.

The hurt these comments would cause was enormous. It was so

unnecessary. What else had to happen before everybody stood up and owned this piece of history? Before we accepted it and dealt with it?

Desmond was not shocked. It didn't surprise him at all.

Neither of us said much as we drove towards Bindoon. I think Desmond feared that at any moment I would ask him to turn round and go back. We watched the sky grow light and shadows begin to creep. We passed through Bullsbrook East and followed the Great Northern Highway through the Chittering Valley.

I find some parts of Australia quite pretty, but others are rather burnt and unattractive. There's so much contrast, but on this journey I could take no comfort in the scenery. All I could think about were the small boys who travelled this same road on the back of pick-up trucks or in buses, bound for a new life. How would I have felt, aged six, arriving at Bindoon?

The journey seemed to take all morning, but in reality we covered the fifty-six miles in an hour and a half.

'We're coming up to it shortly,' said Desmond, turning off the road beside huge iron gates on stone pillars. I expected that beyond these gates, the buildings would appear, but instead we drove down a rough dirt road that led to another gate. As we travelled further and further from the main road I grew uneasy. I realized that I hadn't told anybody where I was going. The office might ring the hotel. What would they think when I wasn't there?

My decision to visit Bindoon had been a difficult one. Finally I had decided that it might do some good – not just for the child migrants but also for the Christian Brothers. Perhaps they would see that I wasn't a monster; I wasn't a threat. If I could go to them, perhaps it would lessen the fear and distrust.

I asked Desmond, 'What happens if they won't let us in?'

He laughed. 'If they turn you away, they turn me away. If they turn me away, they turn every old boy away. They've got to let us in. I've been on the Old Boys Reunion Committee. I've helped them all these years. I've paid everything back.'

Paid them back? I thought about this. Desmond used to repair all their farm equipment and sharpen their saws at his factory. He would never ask to be paid. He felt that if he owed them anything at all, he'd repaid it in full.

'Did you notice those electricity pylons about half an hour back?'

he smiled. 'Didn't you see the fire blazing down those hills. That's the message to say Margaret Humphreys is on the way. You're the devil, Margaret, you can do that sort of thing.'

We both laughed.

After opening another stock gate and bouncing down another rough track through farmland, Desmond gazed over the paddocks and said, 'It's all owned by the Brothers. You should take in this atmosphere.'

It was quiet and still so early in the morning. Occasionally, I heard a magpie or caught the sunlight bouncing off the corrugated iron water tank of a distant farm.

Glancing up, I saw a statue on a hill. Jesus, starkly in silhouette, looked down over the valley, watching the mists burn away and the bare ground begin to shimmer. It was a breathtakingly powerful image – the towering symbol of a holy place. Desmond asked if I wanted a closer look but I declined.

'Do you know what all these things are on the right?' he asked. 'All the boys built these.'

I recognized them immediately. They were the Stations of the Cross – stone monuments marking the stages of Jesus' final journey to crucifixion – as large as a man and elaborately constructed. I remembered the migrants telling me how their knees and toes were burnt by the lime as they made the cement; and how their knuckles bled. I could picture the small boys hauling the stones into place. God's little soldiers.

My stomach churned.

'I want to go back, Desmond. Let's stop now.' I could see no point in continuing. But it was out of my hands. Desmond drove on.

When I saw the main administration building, I was astounded by its beauty. It was far bigger than anything I had imagined and dominated the surrounding countryside like a castle.

Before I could say anything, Desmond motioned towards the middle of a courtyard. There stood Brother Paul Keaney, cast in bronze, with his chin thrust forward, surveying his kingdom while one hand rested on the shoulder of a young boy and the other clutched what appeared to be a diploma or building plan.

When Keaney died in 1954, aged sixty-six, the business community in Perth paid for the statue. The obituaries were glowing in their praise for 'the Orphans' Friend', 'Man in a Million' and 'Keaney the Builder'. He was described as 'one of Australia's best-known educationists in child welfare work', and as having given 'a life of devotion to the underprivileged boys . . .'

I looked at the statue and remembered a picture I'd seen of Bindoon's opening day in 1953. More than 5,000 people attended what the newspapers had called 'a red letter day for the Christian Brothers'.

Standing on the steps of the administration building, Brother Keaney, founder and principal, had told the crowd, 'It is an overwhelming day for me. I cannot describe my feelings at seeing such a great concourse of people.'

The State Premier opened the technical school, and the Federal Minister for Territories opened the administrative building. He read a special message from the Immigration Minister, Harold Holt, who was later to become Australia's Prime Minister.

'To the Christian Brothers I express admiration for their devotion to the task of training the young.

'It is splendid testimony that now, only six years from its beginning, Bindoon is able to accommodate 180 boys.'

Desmond parked the car. There was no sign of life. I expected to see children in the grounds and hear choristers singing in the church, but the dormitories, classrooms and pews were silent.

Bindoon was renamed Keaney College, and in the late Sixties became a fee-paying boarding-school for Catholic graziers' sons. On this Sunday the children were on holiday.

As the car doors closed, an elderly brother with sleep-tussled hair appeared on the steps. He recognized Desmond immediately.

'Hello, how are you?' he said, as they shook hands. He didn't look at me.

'Very well, fine, thank you,' said Desmond. 'I've just brought Mrs Humphreys here to see the place. Is it OK to look around?'

I don't know if he recognized me.

The brother said, 'Well, go on in – through that door – and have a cup of tea with the brothers. They're in there having breakfast.'

I didn't say a word.

This wasn't what I expected or wanted. I was hoping to look quietly around the college. I didn't anticipate being invited to have a cup of tea. I didn't want to place people in an uncomfortable position. Now I felt uneasy. I wasn't on my territory and I feared a confrontation, although I knew that I wouldn't be the cause of it.

Desmond took charge. We went through the door and found the brothers sitting down at a long refectory table. They were dressed in their black robes, eating toast and marmalade with mugs of tea.

They looked up as we entered and Desmond said, 'Hello, everyone. I've just brought Mrs Humphreys to have a look around.'

A falling pin would have sounded like clashing cymbals.

For a long while we stood there. A half-dozen brothers, most in their sixties, sat at the table, with several more visible in the kitchen, washing-up.

Finally, a younger brother broke the silence and asked if I'd like a cup of tea.

I didn't want a cup of tea. I didn't want to be there. I simply wanted to walk around and see what I came to see, and leave. I was Desmond's guest, not theirs.

'Come and sit down, Margaret,' said Desmond, leading me towards a bench. I was sure that the brothers knew exactly who I was.

One brother went off to put the kettle on. He was gone a long time and came back with two cups which he put down in front of us. I could see that Desmond had noticed one of the cups was chipped. Desmond is very particular about such things. He would never let somebody have a chipped cup. Without saying a word, he simply picked it up, disappeared into the kitchen, and came back with another.

Desmond poured. He swirled the teapot a little and tipped it up. I watched in amazement as only clear boiled water came out. They'd forgotten to add the tea leaves. Desmond just looked at me and then he said, 'You know, Brother, if you don't mind, I think I'll just go into the kitchen and make a fresh pot of tea.'

There were actually five attempts to make me a cup of tea. The brothers couldn't manage it. They seemed even more nervous around me than I was in their company.

'Would you like breakfast?' I was asked.

'No, thank you,' said Desmond. 'We might take a stroll. What time is mass?'

'We don't have mass on a Sunday. We don't open the church,' said a brother. 'We have it on Saturday evening.'

This surprised me a little. I expected the Christian Brothers to be far more traditional in their worship, or at least to leave the church open on a Sunday.

'Can we look at the workshops?' Desmond asked.

'If you wish,' came the reply.

As we left the dining-room, Desmond shook hands with several of the brothers he knew well and then stayed by my side as we emerged outside. It was barely 8.00 a.m., but the temperature had already begun to climb. We kept to the shade of the administration building and began walking.

I was very quiet. Desmond said I just grew smaller and smaller like Alice in Wonderland. He thought I might disappear. I was tiptoeing, as if in a church, while Desmond pointed out different buildings and told me stories.

As a boy, Desmond had visited Bindoon regularly, normally on weekends because there was work to be done or sporting events being arranged. Later, when he left Clontarf, he would attend the Old Boys' reunions to keep in touch with friends.

As we walked, Desmond would say things to me like, 'Of course, loads of fiddling went on in there.' That's how he described the sexual abuse.

It was hard to believe that over a decade successive boatloads of boys could have built the great central building, plus the church, school, farm buildings and a dam for irrigation. They dynamited rock from the quarry, loaded it on trucks, unloaded it at the building site, chiselled it to size and put it into place under the supervision of two Italian stonemasons.

Because the migrants had told me so much, Desmond assumed that I'd know every brick in every building. He was nearly right. As we walked, all the stories came back to me. The descriptions given by so many men over the years were so accurate, that I felt as if I'd been to Bindoon hundreds of times. I could have found their dormitories and probably identified individuals' beds.

There is a grandeur and serenity about the buildings which is totally at odds with what happened there. On one level it was quite beautiful, but at what cost? Here was this wonderful place surrounded by trees and rolling hills; with handsome buildings and cooling shade. For a moment, its beauty made me forget – but only for a moment. I reflected that flowers can grow everywhere, even in an unloved garden.

Desmond led me to a large classroom with lathes and benches that looked quite old. This was where the boys had learned woodwork. At the front desk, an elderly brother seemed quite shocked to see us. He was shaking, and I thought perhaps he was unwell.

He wouldn't look up as we walked between the benches toward him.

'Hello, Brother, how are you?' said Desmond. 'I'm just showing Mrs Humphreys round the workshops. Do you mind?'

We all shook hands and they began talking, about the weather, the school and farming, until the brother lapsed briefly into silence and raised his sad eyes to Desmond's.

'You're that man with the factory who has done all the repairs for us over the years and never charged us.'

Desmond said, 'That's right. That's me.'

'Have you found your family then?' he whispered.

'I've just come back from England. I went over to meet my mum.'

There was absolute quiet. Even the clock on the wall seemed to slow.

'And this is Mrs Humphreys who found my mother. She's the lady who takes the boys home.'

The brother appeared uneasy and we all stood in silence.

We left soon afterwards. The car sent a cloud of dust drifting on the breeze and carried us away as fast as Desmond dared drive over the ruts and potholes.

On the way back to Perth, Desmond persuaded me to visit Clontarf, the orphanage where he had spent most of his childhood. Initially I refused to go through the same experience again. I was happy to rest and listen to Mozart on the car stereo. At the same time, I was worried about the impact of Barry Coldrey's insensitive remarks in the morning's papers. There would be calls waiting for me at the hotel from outraged child migrants. But Desmond was insistent, and I sensed that he wanted me to see the place where he'd grown up because it would help me understand him and what he had been through.

St Joseph's Clontarf, like Bindoon, is set in beautiful surroundings on the banks of a river and surrounded by well-established trees. Desmond told me that some years earlier it had become an aboriginal college, still run by the Christian Brothers.

The buildings weren't built on such a grand scale as at Bindoon but it still looked idyllic. We drove through the large stone pillars along the straight driveway and parked in front of the main building. The college was almost deserted.

Desmond was full of stories, pointing out familiar places. He told me how he would wake each morning to the sound of birds in the gum-trees.

I asked him, 'Where are the verandas where the rain used to slant in and wet your beds?'

'You're walking on them. You're walking in the puddles.'

As we left, Desmond picked some flowering gumnuts from the trees and gave them to me as a reminder of my visit.

We sat for a long while saying nothing after he parked at the hotel. I leaned against the car door, staring up at a clear sky. I realized that Desmond, too, had been disturbed by the visit. For the first time he'd seen Bindoon through somebody else's eyes. The unquestioning loyalty, his enormous capacity to forgive, his unwillingness to look back in anger, were all brought sharply into focus.

Maybe some good will come of it after all, I thought.

'I put you in a difficult position out there at Bindoon,' he said, obviously upset.

'I was expecting it,' I told him.

But I wondered, with a shudder, whether one of the brothers I had shaken hands with had been involved in the abuse.

I decided I'd rather not know the answer.

30

I arrived back in Melbourne nine days before *The Leaving of Liverpool* was screened. My plane touched down only ten minutes before Yvonne's flight from England.

It was obvious that John and I weren't coping with the demands created by the TV series – the media and political interest were both greater than anyone had imagined. The trustees decided to send Yvonne out to help.

John and Harold met us at the airport, both anxious about the death threats in Perth. Harold explained things to a bemused Yvonne as they drove to Canning Street. It was a terrible beginning to her first trip to Australia.

We were staying at the house – John and I each took the bedrooms and Yvonne had a camp bed downstairs in the office, near the fax machine which beeped and hummed through the night. It didn't matter – none of us caught much sleep in the next fortnight.

Frances Swaine arrived a day later and began interviewing the child migrants. Frances had asked if she could use our offices to ensure that counsellors were near by if a child migrant became distressed.

For legal purposes, it was essential to obtain very detailed histories and discover the precise circumstances under which each child migrant was sent to Australia. Frances believed they deserved to have the circumstances of their emigration and the damage they suffered investigated fully, and the question of compensation explored.

The traffic coming through the house made it difficult to work. I was also worried about the Trust in Nottingham. Our full-time social worker Joan Kerry was virtually holding the fort on her own. What I didn't need was a problem with the ABC.

'Auntie', as the corporation is affectionately known, had not budgeted for a telephone help-line service. I knew *The Leaving of Liverpool* was destined to cause an enormous stir and I wanted trained counsellors to field the calls.

In a series of angry exchanges, I made it clear to the ABC that it was uncaring and potentially dangerous to put such an emotive programme out and not provide facilities to cope with the reaction. Eventually, the funds were found.

We were given eight lines in the corporation's Melbourne studios, and after the first episode, a message was screened stating that counsellors were available on certain numbers.

If anything, the reaction was more powerful than the response to *Lost Children of the Empire* in 1989.

When the drama finished, shortly after 10.00 p.m., the phones began ringing. There were tears and pleas for help; more stories of abuse and desolation. Our lines were so jammed that people began calling the ABC's general switchboard – not just in Melbourne, but in Sydney, Brisbane, Adelaide and Perth.

The flowering gumnuts that Desmond had given me from St Joseph's Clontarf were sitting on the tables as the counsellors began taking the calls. It was bitterly ironic. I listened to old boys talking of their abuse and desolation, and in front of me were these flowers that could easily seduce one into thinking that Clontarf was a lovely place.

'It was like a bloody concentration camp – floggings unlimited,' said one man who had suffered abuse.

A young woman rang: 'I'm ringing on behalf of my mother who was a child migrant. She's dead now but she always wondered why she was sent. Why? Why?'

Another woman wanted to tell us about her old school friend, Margaret, who was from the UK. 'Nuns would strap her all the time, mercilessly. Welts all over her. They wouldn't feed her. We tried to give her food. We used to save our collection money to buy it. Poor Margaret. She'd done nothing wrong. The nuns wanted to break her spirit.'

A wife rang to say her husband still had nightmares about his life as a child migrant. 'Inside he's still just a little boy,' she said.

In the early hours of the morning, I turned the telephones off and went back to Canning Street to sleep. There, the answering machine was full and the telephone rang all night. By morning, child migrants began arriving. Some of them had driven hundreds of miles.

John answered a knock at the door and found an anxious man on the doorstep with tears rolling down his face. Another had driven about 250 miles from Holbrook in NSW; and one arrived on a flight from Brisbane. We invited them inside and gave them cups of tea while they waited.

I will never forget one particular child migrant who arrived that day. I hadn't met him before but he had this terribly haunted look. Immediately I knew that I couldn't ask him to wait, or to come back later.

I showed him into the back sitting-room, the quietest place, and made him a cup of tea. As we sat down, he turned to me and said, 'You know what they did to us, don't you? You know! You know what happened to us. Have you been there? Have you been to that bloody terrible place?'

He was talking about Bindoon.

'I'm in a terrible mess. A terrible mess. I was five years old and a brother put me on the back of his horse and took me out to the country and tied me to a tree and just raped me time after time. Then he left me there – tied to this tree – and just rode off. I was crying and bleeding. When I got free I ran to this convent, to the nuns, to the women. I ran there and they put me to bed.'

I was perfectly still. I didn't blink, or reach out to him, or utter a word. When somebody tells you that he was tied to a tree and raped by somebody he trusted, and then left there, crying, you don't move an eyelash because he's looking to see if you're disgusted. He wants to know if you find it repulsive or degrading. You don't move. You sit still to show him that it doesn't matter; that he's still the same person. You accept him as an individual who needs to share his pain.

No matter how many stories of abuse I hear, I am always shocked. You can't be prepared. I'm not shocked by the knowledge that brothers or priests or others are capable of such brutality. It's the total devastation of the victim that stuns me; the fact that he has held on to his pain for all these years. It humbles me.

When you think of that raped child being eight years old, and then ten and fifteen and then being a young man and going to work for the first time; and finding a girlfriend, becoming a husband and a father – all those phases of life that we go through – and this is his baggage; this is what he takes with him through all those changes. And then suddenly there is a programme on the television and he somehow finds the courage or the anger, or whatever it takes, to come and say, 'I'm giving you this. I've carried it for long enough. I'm giving it to you now.'

It's no good sitting there saying I don't want it. You take their baggage because you know it's too heavy for one person to carry through a lifetime.

31

The headlines said it all.

'Liverpool the Best', 'Gripping Tragedy of Child Migrants', 'Castaways of Empire in an Inspiring Drama'.

Every major newspaper carried the story, publishing interviews, location reports or television previews and reviews.

The Leaving of Liverpool became one of the ABC's best-rating series ever and took top honours at the Australian Writers' Guild Awards, picking up the prize for best original mini-series.

Philip Adams, one of Australia's leading social commentators, wrote in *The Australian*: 'If this isn't a masterpiece, it's the next best thing. *The Leaving of Liverpool* is so compelling, so beautifully crafted, you view it with a mixture of anguish and wonderment, wishing you could disbelieve it, looking for flaws that might allow you to escape its pain and sadness . . . '

Of course, the child care agencies were less enthused. The Catholic Church displayed an uneasy mixture of defence and concern, learning perhaps from past mistakes that outright denials won it few friends. Far better to display a sense of sadness and an eagerness to help.

Dr Barry Coldrey fielded most of the calls from the media, and described the drama as powerful but 'unbalanced'. At the same time, he continued the quiet offensive, directing blame to the British and Australian governments.

The Editor of the *Catholic Record* was more outspoken, telling readers: 'A very small group of complainants are riding on the back of Liverpool and the earlier BBC production *Lost Children of the Empire* to captivate press, radio and television with their selective defamatory reconstruction of documented history . . .

'The smug middle-class Australian critics of today had best go back to what their parents were saying about migration in the 1950s and whether Australia House London is to be indicted for the millions of Britishers who landed with a jolt in Australia's so-called post-war "paradise".

'In what passes as a media debate in the late 1900s the Christian Brothers will have to live with being damned whether they do or don't reply to these cultivated impressions . . .'

By September, Western Australia's State parliament was drawn into the debate. Philip Pendal, a Liberal Party MP and 'product of a Catholic education' told the House he was fed up with 'Kick a Mick Week'.

'Over the last 160 odd years, Western Australian society has bled dry the services of Catholic institutions that were among the few to minister to outcasts in our society.

'Thousands of priests, nuns and brothers have devoted their lives to lepers, drunks, orphans and rejects at a time when those people were abandoned by most sections of society, including successive governments. The efforts of those people are unquestionably being denigrated because of an errant few . . .

'I am sure that some misfits crept into the priesthood and the religious life of the Catholic Church. The bad-apple syndrome is as old as time itself. Those who know their Bible history from a Christian perspective will know that our friend Judas was only the first weak link. To the extent that misfits creep into the system, I do not condone their actions and neither does the Catholic Church.'

The media debate raged on. My main concern was that in the furore surrounding *The Leaving of Liverpool*, everybody was focusing on the involvement of the Christian Brothers and the Catholic Church. The child migration issue was not limited to one country or one agency. Western Australia wasn't the only place where children were sent and suffered hardship, degradation and abuse.

I also stressed to journalists that not all child migrants complained of such harsh treatment. Some felt they were treated with kindness and compassion in the children's homes. They did not witness or suffer abuse or cruelty and had fond memories of their childhoods. This, however, did not stop either their longing to find their families or their anger at having been told they were orphans.

In the first forty-eight hours after *The Leaving of Liverpool*, we received more than 700 calls on the hotlines – increasing the backlog of missing families. When I returned to Perth before flying home, my hotel room floor was littered with new files.

Amid this organized chaos, a large brown envelope was delivered to the hotel. I didn't have time to open it or recognize the handwriting. I simply assumed it contained documents sent to me by a child migrant who wanted to find his or her family.

I slid the envelope into my briefcase, hoping to read its contents during the flight or when I got back to Nottingham.

32

It was wonderful to be home. I wandered through the house, constantly ambushing Mervyn, Ben and Rachel with unexpected hugs. I needed the reassurance and comfort of holding them close.

By now Rachel was old enough to understand. While she wanted us to spend more time together, she appreciated that time was running out for many child migrants and that our family sacrifice was minor compared with their problems.

But not long after I returned, Rachel said something that stopped me in my tracks. She had noticed that my hair was falling out again – it was all over the towels and the bathroom floor. Putting her arms around me, Rachel whispered, 'Oh, Mum, it's time somebody said to them that you belong to us.'

I was deeply upset. It was not the child migrants' fault. The Trust's lack of funds had ensured that we had to work twelve hours a day, most days of the week.

I had missed Rachel's birthday almost every year except one – her eighteenth – in the previous five years. I had missed anniversaries, school concerts, fêtes, football games . . . the list was shamefully long.

And no matter how hard I tried to acknowledge that failure when I returned home, it was never the same. You can't make up for missing a birthday – that special day is gone for ever.

On the other hand, I was working with people who sometimes had never known, with any certainty, on what day they should be celebrating their birthday, or even their correct age. I've often sent people their first birthday card. It is my way of letting them know how important they are to me.

My children have grown up in the real world. Thankfully, they understand the sacrifices our family has made. And they know that I would never let the child migrants down. I couldn't live with myself.

Soon after I returned to the UK, I was surprised to hear that Dr Barry Coldrey had finally revealed limited details of his 'investigation' on behalf of the Christian Brothers. He admitted to the *West Australian* newspaper that he had uncovered evidence that some brothers may have sexually abused children at Bindoon Boys' Town. Whether his wider findings were made public, he said, would depend upon his 'employer'.

'I am prepared to say that the lines of evidence against certain staff members are strong, but I'm not, at the moment, prepared to go further than that.'

He went on to comment on one brother whose name had cropped up often in the Bindoon old boys' stories, saying, 'There are strong allegations against this chap [Brother] Angus but all I would say at this stage is that if he was living, well, he would have a lot to answer for.'

As far as I knew, this was the first time the Christian Brothers had admitted that there might, after all, be some truth in the allegations of sexual abuse. Dr Coldrey went on to name another brother and a priest, Father William Giminez, against whom there had been 'constant but never precise' allegations.

Playing the fair-minded academic, Coldrey conceded some points and appeared both reasonable and balanced. However, having accepted that the allegations might be true, he then attacked other claims made by old boys.

But research can work both ways.

Perth social psychologist, Juanita Miller, was writing a doctoral thesis on the treatment of child migrants in Western Australia. Ms Miller interviewed 180 former child migrants from Bindoon,

Clontarf, Tardun and Castledare and eventually claimed that in a given year at Clontarf Boys' Home, as many as 50 of the 250 boys were being sexually abused. She collected the names of sixteen Christian Brothers alleged to have been involved.

Meanwhile, the Christian Brothers and many other charities maintained that the child migration schemes were inspired, subsidized and monitored by governments. They had merely picked up the pieces.

I knew this wasn't entirely true, but, inevitably, governments must have been involved. You cannot move thousands of children from one side of the world to the other without it being sanctioned by the government of the day.

33

The plain brown envelope that had arrived at my hotel in Perth sat in a pile of mail for almost a week before I had time to open it.

I was in the office, working my way through the backlog when I picked it up and examined it carefully, looking for an address or some indication of the sender. Since the death threats I'd become very cautious of unmarked packages or unfamiliar handwriting.

As I cut through the tightly sealed flap, it was obvious that whoever was responsible didn't want the envelope to open accidentally.

I soon knew why. Dozens of photocopied Australian documents spilled out across my lap. I took one look at the letterheads and realized that I was holding some very unusual material. There were letters, reports and memos dating from the 1940s, and addressed to senior officials from the Department of Immigration, the Attorney General's Office, the Education Department and the Child Welfare Office.

I burrowed through them, looking for some note of explanation. There was nothing. Whoever sent me this information didn't want to be identified.

As I leafed through the pages, pictures of the origins of child migration schemes began to emerge. Sometimes I laughed out loud, or groaned in disbelief.

An early indication that Australia wished to recruit large numbers of children came in 1922 when the Western Australian State Premier suggested that the nation's war dead should be replaced by 6,000 children from Britain, the mother country.

Some 'private organizations' were already operating their own schemes, such as Dr Barnardo's and the Fairbridge Society and these were encouraged to expand their operations.

The Big Brother Movement and Northcote Children's Emigration Fund were specifically established to meet the need, but many organizations simply transferred existing resources to face the new social challenge. These included the Catholic Child Welfare Council, the Church of England, the Church of Scotland, National Children's Homes and the Salvation Army.

Among the documents was a 1938 letter from the Prime Minister's Office in Canberra to Downing Street, London. It accompanied copies of three agreements. The first was to provide for the cost of establishing a farm school at Molong, NSW; the second to provide maintenance for not more than 300 children at the school; and the third to jointly sponsor the 110 boys about to be handed into the welcoming arms of the Christian Brothers in Western Australia.

The child migrants were to be funded not only by the British government but also by the Australian Federal and State Governments. Together they would contribute 7 shillings a week towards maintenance of each child until he or she reached fourteen.

To qualify for the money, the receiving organizations, like the Catholic Emigration Association and the Fairbridge Society, would provide quarterly reports on each child and, when satisfied, the Treasury would transfer the payments into the association's bank account.

There were more letters – each more damning than the next. There was one document that stood out, perhaps because of its jingoistic language. This, I quickly realized, was a key piece of evidence that identified some of the architects of Australia's post-war migration policy.

In January 1945, the Prime Minister called a conference of State Premiers in Canberra to discuss child migration. The briefing paper, no more than six pages, outlined the problem. Australia had seven million people – a population that increased naturally by only 55,000 to 56,000 a year. To achieve a population of ten million within twenty years, it was necessary to bring in up to 70,000 immigrants a year.

The paper revealed, 'There are special and urgent reasons why a major effort should be made immediately in the field of child migration. The peculiar circumstances of the war have created in Europe a greater number of orphans, stray children, "war babies" et cetera, than ever before. This makes the present a time of potentially unparalleled opportunity for Australia to build up her population with child migrants who, on account of their easier assimilation, adaptability, long working-life ahead and easier housing, constitute a particularly attractive category of migrant for the first post-war years . . . The opportunity must be seized immediately and exploited for two or three years ahead, or lost for ever.'

Conference delegates were told that voluntary organizations like the Fairbridge Society and Barnardo's were to be encouraged to continue their work, but their efforts were essentially small scale. From all the schemes combined, Western Australia had received only 1,255 child migrants between 1924 and 1940.

'Children have apparently not always been well selected; they have often been given inadequate opportunities in life (due to an understanding, in part, that earlier Governments wanted them to be trained as agricultural labourers and domestic servants only); and in the cases of some organizations, have been afforded quite inadequate after-care. Part of the deficiencies can be traced to unqualified and/or under-paid staff. A closer supervision by Governments of their standards of performance should ensure that within their numerically limited scope, they should do good work in the post-war years.'

I read this passage aloud and paused. If the existing schemes were considered small scale, what did the Australian government have in mind? It was soon made clear.

'The present proposal, approved in principle by the Commonwealth Government and now put forward to State Governments on whose full co-operation its success depends, is for an official child migration scheme . . .

'It is proposed that the Commonwealth seek out in Britain and Europe, in each of the first three post-war years, at least 17,000 children a year (ie about 50,000 in three years) suitable and available for migration to Australia . . .'

Fifty thousand? Unbelievable! That's a lot of mothers and fathers without their children. Yet the details of this Pied Piper scheme were even more astonishing.

British children from six to fourteen years and 'white alien children' aged from six to twelve, were to be accommodated in converted military bases and airforce camps. After the first stage of 'education, language mastery and assimilation', they would graduate to hostels housing forty or fifty, based in Australian towns with populations of over 2,500 people.

'The immigrant children should enter naturally and fully into the social and community life of the town. Civic pride and responsibility should be invoked; the townspeople and town authorities should be brought to look upon these immigrant children as a special and honourable responsibility of their town . . .'

The estimated cost of this scheme over eight years was 26.3 million pounds, shared between the State and Federal Governments.

In the minutes of the 1945 conference, it emerged that all the States had agreed to co-operate, but some delegates were unhappy with the plan. A Mr Pittard from Victoria said, 'It savoured too much of the institutional type of treatment,' while a Mr Baker of South Australia said, 'It was better to place children in private homes.'

The possibility of adoption was also raised. NSW had a waiting-list of 500 adoptive families, Victoria 400, and South Australia 200. This was quickly dismissed because of the 'substantial legal obstacles' associated with adopting a British child, and the fact that most families wanted to adopt infants under three years of age.

I smiled ironically. Yes, I thought, it would have been extremely difficult to adopt child migrants legally because many of their parents had not, and would not, have given permission for their children to be sent overseas in the first place.

The scheme envisaged by Australia's State Premiers in 1945 was too ambitious. They did find child migrants, but not the 50,000 in three years they wanted. The number was closer to 10,000 over many more years. But to my mind, even one child was one too many.

There could be no excuses – no cover-ups. The importing of children into Australia was a deliberate social policy. The honourable gentlemen who governed the nation gathered together and planned to populate their country, brazenly talking of acquiring children as if they were the spoils of war. Children made the 'best migrants'. Children couldn't complain.

Ever since the plight of Britain's child migrants had first been revealed, the charities and agencies had accused me of not putting child migration into its historical context. They argued that I had never taken into account the deprivation, poverty and hardship that had existed in Britain following the war; that the children that they had sent abroad were given a new start in life with better prospects and opportunities.

Is this the historical context they referred to? Were the needs of children being fully met by pragmatically using them to boost Australia's population?

Over the next few months, more brown envelopes arrived. Whoever was sending me these documents seemed to know my movements. The envelopes would arrive in Nottingham, in Melbourne or in Perth – wherever I was staying.

I had no idea who was sending them to me but I knew that he or she was definitely a friend of the child migrants; someone who wanted the truth to be fully revealed.

I spread the documents over my desk one afternoon trying to put them in chronological order to see what picture emerged. I particularly wanted to find out if there was any evidence that the authorities had had any idea what was happening inside the institutions in Australia.

The Secretary of the Child Welfare Department in Western Australia wrote a memo to his Minister on 3 July 1946.

'I have been very disturbed in mind about some of the boys who have been brought into Western Australia from overseas . . . [in particular] I have been disappointed in the Roman Catholic Scheme . . . the interests of the boys who came to Western Australia in 1938 and 1939 were not safeguarded; instead of them being placed out in employment they have been retained in connection with building operations for which in the main no wages have been paid them, or if placed out they have rarely received a full wage . . .

'Some of the boys concerned have complained most bitterly at the treatment meted out to them. The Department has a record of such cases. The list is not large but I should say that for each who has complained to the Department there must be a number of others who have not so complained. It has been common knowledge that a lot of the buildings erected at Clontarf, Bindoon and Tardun have been erected with the aid of migrant boys, that without the migrant boys the building operations would have been retarded . . .

'I am of the opinion that something should be done to adequately protect the interests of other children coming to Western Australia whether in connection with the Fairbridge scheme, the Roman Catholic scheme or any other scheme which may arise in the future . . .'

There was a similar memo on 11 August 1947, from another public servant.

'The 1938–39 scheme in many ways was disastrous. Children brought out under this scheme became anti-social, anti-Australian and anti-Christ, and some of them unfortunately have returned to the Old Country, not at all satisfied with the treatment received at the hands of the authorities here. This at all costs must be avoided in the future.'

Sadly, I suspect none of these complaints ever reached Britain. Even if they had, it is highly unlikely, in my view, that anybody would have listened or acted decisively.

Four days after this last memo was written, the SS Asturias set sail with 250 boys and girls destined to begin the new wave of child migration. This time it was the Secretary of State for Commonwealth Relations in Britain who signed the agreement, and again the three governments (British, Commonwealth and Western Australian) shared the cost, contributing eleven shillings a week towards the maintenance of each child and a grant of five pounds for a going-away outfit.

According to the documents, unaccompanied children arriving in Australia automatically came under the guardianship of the Federal Minister for Immigration, who delegated this responsibility, normally to the head of the Child Welfare Department in each State. The child migrants were then indentured to a particular child care institution until they were sixteen years old.

In Western Australia, the Under-secretary for Lands and Immigration became the 'guardian' of the children in the late 1940s, and this later passed to the Child Welfare Department.

Institutions such as those run by the Christian Brothers were initially supposed to be inspected every two months, and later quarterly. Unfortunately, these visits became the exception rather than the rule. A letter from the Director of the Child Welfare Department in October 1958 complained that there had been no inspection of Clontarf for more than three years.

A Commonwealth Migration Officer visited Bindoon Boys' Town on 23 July 1948, and was shown around the school by Brother Keaney.

'The most urgent need of this Institution would appear to be the necessity to complete their building programme to allow proper sleeping and ablution facilities for the students (at present a number of boys sleep on the verandas which in wet weather is not altogether desirable).

'All of the buildings and proposed new buildings are to be of stone and brick and at present the only adults employed are an Italian bricklayer and a British carpenter. Trainee boys are employed on making bricks, plastering and cement work and certain forms of carpentering.'

The Christian Brothers divided the children according to age and ability. Infants went to Castledare Junior Orphanage; older boys who showed any academic bent went to Clontarf, 7 miles southeast of Perth, and boys interested in learning a trade were sent to either Bindoon or St Mary's Farm School at Tardun.

A 1951 report by the Education Department gives this breakdown:

CASTLEDARE: Infant boys, migrants and local, are still being taught by Brothers whose training does not equip them for the work.

CLONTARF: The lowest and weakest grades are still taught by an untrained layman, the bandmaster, and the task is far beyond his capabilities.

BINDOON: The staffing has not been of a nature to handle effectively the serious problem of the junior grades.

In much the same tone, a 1954 Child Welfare Department report criticizes Clontarf for the failure to build a cement floor for the bed-wetters dormitory; to keep a punishment book; and to give migrant children enough writing materials and stamps to send more than one letter a month.

But by far the most damning report was reserved for Castledare Junior Orphanage. Boys as young as three, some migrants and others State wards, were denied even the basic decency of being put to sleep at night in a clean bed.

This is what the Child Welfare Department discovered on 5 July 1948: 'Cubicles generally dingy and in no way bright or attractive; floors stained under the beds by liquid, which undoubtedly was urine which had dropped there through continually saturated mattresses. In several instances there was still a quantity of urine on the floor, which had not soaked away and no effort had been made to mop it up. Under one bed there appeared to be one area where the urine had dried out on the boards, leaving a salty crust. Many of the wire mattresses of these beds showed a rusty tarnish on the area of contact with urine. The mattresses were themselves in a deplorable state . . . dirt had become impregnated on the urine-affected area. The mattress covering was grimy and dirty. The mattresses themselves were torn and in the first right-hand cubicle off the courtyard of the first block, the mattress was nearly torn in half, exposing a mass of brown fibre filling. In this case the Manager, Brother McGee admitted that a boy was using this bed . . .

'The blankets inspected were miserably thin, being, I believe, ex Army and American Forces stock; two and three blankets to a bed and totally inadequate both in quantity and quality to provide necessary warmth for children of tender years sleeping on these verandas subject to the chill conditions of winter . . .

'Practically all pyjamas seen under the children's pillows were grubby and dirty, damp with urine . . .

'It must be remembered that this Home was built for an entirely different purpose from that for which it is now being utilized but its general deterioration must be of concern to the Roman Catholic

Authorities. Castledare is catering for children who are still little more than babies, who need love, affection, care and attention which a child of such age would get from a mother . . .

'There appears to be no organized medical parade nor any woman qualified to attend to the welfare of these young children. Epidemics have been experienced before in institutions and, in particular, Castledare some years ago had an outbreak of "Vincent's Angina" [a type of trench mouth] which caused no end of expense to the authorities and suffering to the children, and it is possible that infantile paralysis would sweep through this Home with disastrous effect, and, in view of the present conditions mentioned in this report, would be difficult to control.

'The children appeared to be quite healthy and it is hoped will remain so, but the fresh complexion may be the result of a new climate and fresh air in a new country. Lying in wet beds and dirty clothes will eventually take its toll.'

Is this the historical context that the charities and agencies claim I had ignored?

I have always accepted that, for whatever misguided reasons, governments and agencies did what they thought was right at the time. But what I can't accept, is that they were warned. They knew what was happening to the child migrants – and apparently did nothing.

34

What began as a trickle of requests for help became a flood. By the end of 1992 the Child Migrants Trust had received more than 20,000 enquiries since its inception. We had two full-time family researchers, a social worker in Australia, another in the UK, and Yvonne.

We were working long hours, piecing together the histories of literally thousands of families. Thankfully, we no longer continually had to travel to London and sift through hefty volumes at St Catherine's House. At great expense, the Trust had managed to buy the birth, death and marriage records on 12,000 microfiche. This saved us a tremendous amount of time and energy, and money in the long run.

Still, I was always conscious of the fact that I lived and worked on the opposite side of the world from the very people we were trying to help. My visits to Australia were always hectic affairs with no time to become a part of the migrants' lives or to understand their way of life.

Similarly, there were some child migrants who I felt would never approach me for an interview in a Perth hotel room. These migrants had suffered more than most and despite my attempts to make my hotel room warm and welcoming, it was still daunting for these people to enter a large hotel.

I felt it was necessary to spend a longer period in Perth and establish myself in a house where child migrants would feel comfortable either just dropping in for a coffee or sitting down for a meaningful discussion.

On 4 December 1992, after months of preparation, I flew to Australia. The Trust team had been working until the early hours in the morning preparing me for the journey. Yvonne, in particular, had to ensure everything I would need was packed safely in the black boxes. Meanwhile, Joan Kerry, our social worker, was criss-crossing the UK, preparing families for the eventual reunions with their sons and daughters. These had been made possible by the work of John Myles and our new researcher Beverly Rutter, who had joined the team when John and Penny married and started a family.

I had to present my annual report to Nottinghamshire County Council in the morning; then catch an afternoon train to reach Heathrow by 8.00 p.m. Whatever happened, I couldn't miss the flight.

Before the meeting at County Hall, I arranged a preview of *The Leaving of Liverpool* for the councillors. This took on a special significance because it was now almost five months since the drama had made such an impact in Australia yet it was still not scheduled for showing in Britain. The BBC had jointly financed an award-winning show, which was now sitting in a vault at Television Centre, London. Why?

Several MPs were among those watching the drama when I arrived. Looking around the room full of familiar faces, I saw a councillor with tears rolling down his face. Here and there, tissues were dabbed at moist eyes.

As I stood to speak, a question interrupted me mid-sentence. 'When is the BBC going to transmit *The Leaving of Liverpool*?'

'I don't know.'

'Have they bought it?'

'Yes. It's a co-production.'

'How much have they paid for it?'

'I don't know.'

'I want that found out this afternoon,' a councillor demanded. 'Has the BBC given you an explanation?'

'No.'

'Right. I want questions in the House about this. Which MPs are here? I want questions immediately. It looks as if this programme is being stopped.'

The Hon. Joan Taylor, the Chair of Nottinghamshire Social Services Committee, tried to explain that I had a plane to catch, but the councillors wanted answers and explanations. Eventually I got away, and dashed for the train.

The cross-party support and affection shown to me at County Hall that day gave me the added strength I needed. I felt that they all knew the personal risks involved in my going to Perth; these didn't have to be spelled out or spoken out loud.

Four months was a long time to be away from my family, but at least I knew that Merv and the children were going to join me over Christmas and New Year. It was the children's first visit to Australia and Rachel and Ben were very excited. At last they were going to see the country they had heard so much about from the migrants they had met in Nottingham or who had written them letters.

While I flew to Perth to organize the rent of a house, Merv and Ben flew directly to Melbourne to be joined by Rachel and my brother-in-law, John. I would eventually join them a few days before Christmas, then we would all fly to Perth for a proper Down Under celebration.

Perth has the ambience of a large country town rather than a city. It dozes on hot days and doesn't wake until the air cools in the evening. For a long time I had little fondness for it – the very thought of what had happened there bleached the colours and almost polluted the air.

I rented a house on Dalkeith Road, in Nedlands, not far from the University. It was a single-storey, brick dwelling, referred to by the locals as a 'Nedlands Fortress'. The art deco interior was cool and relaxing, with fringed lampshades and stained-glass windows.

I knew immediately that the kitchen and family room would be the focal point for visitors, so I filled the large Welsh dresser in the kitchen with photographs of child migrants – both as youngsters and adults. The noticeboard in the kitchen started with only a few notes about local services but within days was overloaded with cards, invitations, press cuttings and letters.

I unpacked my suitcases and then began sorting through the boxes and organizing my office in the study. Suddenly I thought, I've been here before. It reminded me of when I first started working in the upstairs bedroom at my home in Nottingham. All I had then was a telephone, a desk and commitment.

I didn't tell many people initially that I planned an extended stay in Perth, not only for security reasons but also because I wanted to pace myself and not be deluged with requests. It was only when I sat beside the telephone that I realized how difficult it was going to be without some basic office equipment.

Surprisingly quickly, the news spread and soon the house in Dalkeith Road was full of flowers and cards. Everybody wanted to help – perhaps seeing it as their chance to be more involved. I explained what I needed and soon the Department of Family Services provided us with a fax machine, while the child migrants found a filing cabinet, photocopier, word processor, desk fan and a pushbike.

Despite this support, it took all my courage for me to stay in Perth. I knew that I couldn't afford to be intimidated by the threats. The only way to feel safe was to confront it – to brazen it out. I wanted to give out the message: 'I'm here! I'm staying! I'm going nowhere!'

When I flew to Melbourne, the family were already settled in Canning Street. A group of child migrants who had met through the Trust were excited that we were spending Christmas in Australia as a family. To welcome us to Melbourne, they invited us to a meal at an Italian restaurant in Lygon Street, not far from Melbourne University.

It was a light-hearted evening and at some stage one of the child migrants mentioned a raffle they were holding to raise some much-needed funds for the Trust in Melbourne. Although every bit of financial support helped, I felt sad to think that migrants had to raffle a bottle of whisky to help somebody find their mother. Governments should have been paying for this, not the child migrants themselves.

During the meal, a friend leaned across the table and jokingly asked Ben, 'What are you going to give this raffle then, young man? What are you going to give?'

Ben looked up at her and without drawing breath, said, 'I gave you my mother.'

He was twelve years old and he managed to stun the table into silence with his razor-sharp reply.

All I could think was, Out of the mouths of babes . . .

The woman put her arms around Ben and said, 'Oh, you did! That's right, you did and we love you for it.'

In the previous seven years, we had not been able to take a family holiday. I had never taken leave. Yet even then, with the whole family in Australia, I managed only a few days off.

We flew to Perth for Christmas. Desmond delivered a tall Christmas tree with lights and decorations; Jackie and Ron gave me house plants, Eileen and Pauline baked cakes and provided extra bedding and blankets for the house. It was, to us, something quite special and unexpected. The child migrants were all pulling together and it created a different kind of family gathering, born out of an unspoken optimism and a shared faith.

On Boxing Day, I took a photograph of Merv and Rachel relaxing on the bedspread as they did the crossword. It was very important to me. After all that had happened, my family was still intact. We were still very close, so together and weathering the storm.

I thank Mervyn for that. He has always been such an enduring source of quiet strength and altruism over the years. His sense of justice was as deeply affronted by his research into child migration, as mine was by meeting those affected by it.

After my second trip to Perth and that terrible Christmas in 1988 I remember asking him one morning, 'Why me? How did I get so involved in all this?'

He was shaving with his back to me, but I saw his smile in the mirror. He said, 'It's that well-known mixture of the right person, in the right place, at the right time, with a smashing family.'

After the New Year, the family slowly returned to England. Rachel and John were the last to leave. I remember walking to the taxi queue at the airport and thinking, The house will seem completely empty. Last week there were five of us, now there's just me.

The taxi-driver said to me, 'You look as if you have the worries of the world on your shoulders.'

If only he knew. I had to go back to this empty house, and I didn't know if I could put the key in the door, let alone walk inside.

Merv had sensed my trepidation when he left, but he also understood that I couldn't run away. I couldn't live my life being scared of a place or a person.

35

I didn't think it possible for me to feel comfortable in Perth. I
always arrived from England in the small hours of the morning
when it was dark, still and hot. All I could ever see as we came in
to land were the street lights and occasional cars; there were few
other signs of life. My mood was always sombre, for I knew I was
bringing so much with me that was going to change so many lives.

This time it was different. I got to know the people. I lived among
them and made Perth my home. I wanted to be able to work more
normal working hours and do ordinary things like cook and shop,
and meet people who weren't child migrants. I wanted to get
physically fit by running every morning.

I should have known that this sounded too good to be true, but
it all seemed possible at the outset. For the first few days I was able
to get up early and run along the beach. Even at six-thirty in the
morning the sand was dotted with people, jogging, fishing or
walking their dogs.

I had brought with me a large selection of tapes of my favourite
music and a trunk full of books. At five in the morning the classical
music began playing. The builders working next door would yell
over the fence, 'What was that you were playing this morning,
Margaret?'

After those first few days, I thought everything would be all right. I could not have been more mistaken.

On the first weekend after Merv and the children had gone, I spent Sunday evening listening to some opera and reading. It was such a luxury.

I went to bed feeling relaxed and ready to sleep. I had chosen a bedroom at the front of the house which had a window overlooking the veranda and the large front garden. The house was set well back from the road so there was no traffic noise, particularly when the curtains were drawn and the windows closed.

When I'm away from home I leave the bedside lamp turned on. I like the soft light because I don't want to wake up suddenly in a strange room in the dark and forget where I am.

I woke from a deep sleep at about one in the morning. There was a loud banging.

Disorientated and anxious, I couldn't tell where the noise was coming from but I knew it was very close. The hammering began again and I looked towards the window. Somebody was outside.

The blows grew louder and the window rattled. Then I heard a man's voice.

'We've found you! We told you we would. We'll find you anywhere. You've been warned. You're dead this time! We'll fucking finish you off for good!'

I didn't think, I just moved.

Jumping out of bed, I ran through the hall into the kitchen and family room. There were french windows which led on to the back garden. These were open but the mesh screen door to keep out insects was closed. Blinded by panic I ran straight into the door and was thrown backwards on to the floor.

Dazed, I crawled to my feet and threw open the screen door. The voice was shouting from the veranda.

The garden was in darkness and I ran blindly through it. At the bottom, near the fence, there was a bench. When I reached it, I somehow felt safe. I sat down and froze, turning to stone.

Somewhere, in the back of my mind, I heard a car start up and drive away, but I didn't move. I couldn't move.

It was daylight when I finally stood up and walked towards the kitchen. I had been sitting on the bench for seven hours. I could hear the sounds of people going to work and children going to school.

I can't totally comprehend what happened to me that night. The shock has never gone away.

The Federal Police were very helpful and supportive, but they could do little to comfort me or to make me feel less vulnerable.

I told very few of the child migrants what had happened and they each found their own way of dealing with it. Every day people rang, often just to check if I was OK. Alan Osbourne would visit around lunchtime, checking the gardens and gates. Desmond, Eileen and Jackie called most days. Harold flew over from Melbourne and spent ten days in a self-contained granny flat in the back garden.

That night changed me; it affected me deeply. Someone had come to my home, to my veranda, to the window beside my bed, and threatened to kill me.

How did they find me? What would have happened if the window was open?

Any thoughts that I had about leading a normal life in Perth totally disappeared. I was never going to be completely free to run in the mornings or leave the windows open to catch the breeze. Whenever I left the house, I couldn't come home without first checking it room by room, the doors and windows, the gate. It was the same before I went to bed. I would leave the lights on and re-check all the locks. I never had a full night's sleep again. And soon the workload became so heavy, that my hours were as long as usual, and as tiring.

The telephone barely stopped ringing; I was nervous about picking it up. I had an answering machine, but I didn't want child migrants to call and hear a disembodied voice on a machine.

In January, the *7.30 Report*, a current affairs show on ABC television, produced a report on the men from Bindoon talking about the abuse they suffered. I left the house during the programme and returned to find a death threat on my answering machine. It wasn't the last. The calls would come at unusual hours late at night and early in the morning.

I was determined to keep the dark side of Perth in perspective. It was something that I had to deal with.

When Frazer Guild of the *Sunday Times* in Perth came to

interview me, he asked, 'Is your life being threatened, Margaret?'

He was sitting on the very veranda where the incident had occurred. 'I'm sorry, but I don't want to answer that,' I replied.

Frazer knew the shorthand answer was yes, but I am indebted to him for respecting my wishes not to give these cowards, whoever they were, any news space. It also allowed me to continue with my work and not alarm the child migrants.

Elsewhere, and similarly out of my control, a storm was brewing over child abuse and the clergy. It was already headline news in America, where the Archdiocese of New York was being sued for telephone number amounts. There were similar allegations in Britain against a handful of clergy.

Victims were accusing Church leaders of shielding offenders from the law. Some suspects were simply moved to another parish. There were allegations of delays, threats and bribes.

At first, reports and documentaries were picked up from America, and then Australian journalists began looking to see if they could find any home-grown examples. It wasn't hard. Support groups like 'Broken Rites' and 'Project Anna', both Melbourne-based, had been formed to provide counselling to victims, and in Perth a lobby group called VOICES (Victims of Institutionalized Cruelty, Exploitation and Supporters) had been established to put pressure on the police and politicians to investigate the abuse allegations.

Two current affairs reports on events at Bindoon thirty years earlier were prepared: the *Sixty Minutes* special, aired one Sunday night, and *Inside Edition* on the following Tuesday. One man described being raped at the age of nine and a half while at the Castledare Boys' Home. He was sodomized twenty times in the following twelve months.

Another, was penetrated eighteen nights in a row and had to plead with the brother to stop because he was falling asleep in school.

'That's him. That's the bastard,' he said, looking at a recent photograph of a former Christian Brother. 'If I saw him now I'd put a bullet in his guts for what he did to me.'

The *Sixty Minutes* documentary revealed that in the 1940s this particular brother was moved from Western Australia to an orphanage in NSW because of complaints made against him by a boy. He was later allowed to return to Perth but in 1956 the Christian Brothers transferred him again, this time to a South Australian orphanage, because of further complaints.

Brother Gerald Faulkner was questioned about the wisdom of such a decision.

'I didn't hide the problem. My Order hid the problem,' he said. 'The way of dealing with allegations then was quite different. People assumed that a new start in life at a new place would bring about a different sort of life.

'It is silly in our circumstances or with our knowledge now, but it was not quite as silly in 1950.'

Brother Faulkner complained that the term paedophile was 'thrown around too loosely'. When asked for his definition of the word, he said, 'A paedophile is a person whose sexual love is expressed in terms of interfering with children.'

When the journalist quarrelled over the use of the word 'love' to describe sex with an eight- or nine-year-old boy, Brother Faulkner eventually conceded that he should have said 'sexual appetite'.

Eventually, however, a semblance of the truth seemed to emerge.

When asked how many Christian Brothers had sexually abused child migrants, Brother Faulkner said, 'It seems to me from our research that it's probably nine or ten but they fall into different categories. Some of those – three or four – are dead.

'I have a great feeling of sorrow for those who have suffered, and for the fact that some of my confreres in the past have betrayed the trust that was placed in them.'

I, too, felt some sympathy for these abusers. I regarded them as victims also. These were young men with no training in child care. How could they possibly be expected to meet the most basic needs of young boys who were already traumatized by the time they arrived in Australia? That does not forgive or excuse the abuse. Nor does it exonerate the decisionmakers – whether in the Church hierarchy or governments – who put them in positions of trust.

Brother Faulkner looked remarkably different from when I first met him in 1989. His belligerence had diluted. Back then he had said that the 'outrageous' claims of sexual abuse were totally untrue and that stories of brutality had been 'grossly exaggerated' and 'blown up out of all proportion'.

It was a different story now and, I felt, a different man. Yet despite his admission there wasn't even the hint of an apology. If Brother Faulkner was ashamed and repentant, it didn't come across. The following week, on the front page of *The Record*, he launched an attack on the media's portrayal of the Christian Brothers.

'They are determined to portray some alleged occurrences as proven evidence of widespread and continual and systematic abuse throughout all of our institutions over their long history.

'There is no excuse for abusing children. There is no condoning of criminal offences.

'Nor, on the other hand, ought we to condone the power of the media to discredit the work and dedication and reputation of a group of men – literally hundreds of brothers who have worked in WA – because of the behaviour of some of their confreres forty or fifty years ago.'

It was a passionate article, but it could not exonerate the Order for having spent years seeking to discredit the victims of abuse rather than acknowledging their suffering. And how did it intend to deal with the issue now?

When the phone rang early on a Saturday morning in February, I half expected another threat. Thankfully it was Merv, which was unusual because he normally called during off-peak hours.

'I've got a letter for you. It's from the Australian High Commission.'

'Oh God! What have I done now?' I replied.

'Do you want me to open it?' he asked. 'I could read it to you.'

'No. No. Give me fifteen minutes. I need a coffee and some music.'

I put on Mozart's *Ave Verum Corpus* and boiled the kettle. The coffee was strong and as I nursed the cup I suddenly wondered what I'd said or done to warrant a letter from the Australian High Commission.

When Merv called again, I told him to open the envelope.

'I already have,' he said. 'I think you'd better sit down. It's a letter from the Deputy High Commissioner.'

Dear Mrs Humphreys,

I have the honour to inform you that your name is being considered by the Australian government for submission to Her Majesty the Queen, Sovereign Head of the Order of Australia, for an award of Honorary Medal in the Order of Australia (OAM). The proposed award is for your service to the community, particularly to child migrants . . .

I am therefore requested to ask whether this proposed honour would be acceptable to you, and if you would indicate your wish by completing the attached confirmation of acceptance.

Please treat this matter as confidential until confirmation of your proposed honour is received from the Queen and formally announced by the Governor-General.

I was speechless.

'Are you still there, Margaret? Hello. Hello. Are you still there?'

'Only just,' I murmured.

Merv couldn't hide his excitement. He was thrilled; but I didn't quite know how to react. I needed time to think.

Of course, I could tell no-one about the proposed Honour until it was announced officially by the Governor-General of Australia, Bill Hayden. For the next few weeks I got on with my work in Dalkeith Road pretending nothing had happened. Yet inside I had this huge secret.

In the meantime, there were more child migrants to see, some of whom I'd never met before. Despite having heard hundreds of stories about their childhoods, I could still be shocked. One man described how he arrived in Australia as a young lad, but had fallen ill on the voyage and was taken by ambulance from the dockside to a hospital in Perth. For the next twelve months he remained there and not once did anybody visit him. He was seven years old.

'They forgot about me, Margaret,' he said, without hiding his anguish. 'Even the nurses didn't know where I was supposed to be, or if I belonged to anyone. Eventually, a truck turned up and I was put on the back tray and taken away by the Christian Brothers.'

Another very sad story emerged through a telephone call I received from Marcelle, a child migrant, who had news about a mutual friend named Tony Jones. Tony had first written to the Child Migrants Trust in 1988. He had left England in 1950 and was nine years old when he arrived at the Fairbridge Farm School at Pinjarra, Western Australia.

His childhood was lonely, but he thought the 'cottage mothers' at the Farm School were caring people who did their best in difficult circumstances. If they beat him, it was normally well deserved.

'I didn't understand why I was here, so I kept running away. I couldn't settle down,' Tony told me. 'I was a loner who never fitted in with the regime.

'As I got older, I wanted to know about my past, but all my efforts failed. Sometimes I'd actually pick up the telephone directory and begin calling all the Joneses to see if I could find a relative. Somewhere I had to be related to somebody.'

This desperation to find his family never left Tony. He could remember little about his time in England and had few details to help with the search. Matters were made more difficult because Jones is such a common surname. The London telephone directory contains four thousand Joneses, and nationwide the figure runs to tens of thousands.

It took almost three years of painstaking work and many false leads. When I visited Perth, I would reassure Tony that we hadn't forgotten him and show him details of the search. Finally, late in 1991, I told Tony that his mother was alive and he also had brothers and sisters in England.

There is no way of describing his joy. It was absolute.

Tony has only one kidney, and survives on a modest invalidity benefit. He didn't have the money for an air fare, so desperately began saving. He was prepared to go without everything to get home to his family but still couldn't raise the money. In the meantime, he and his mother exchanged long letters, filling in the details of their years apart.

In his first letter, Tony wrote:

My Dear Mother,
Please, Mum, read this letter and give me the chance to get to know you again. Mum, I love you and always will. You have been in my heart for forty years. All I remember was a funeral,

then I was taken away. I was told you were dead. I will not forgive them for that.

Please, Mum, write to me. Please give me the chance to prove to you that there is no hurt in me towards you.

I have a lovely wife Sue and she has been trying to find my family for twenty years, but the homes would not tell her anything. It was Sue that found Margaret Humphreys from the Child Migrants Trust. When they told me you were alive and well, I was over the moon. But I was very sad when I was told that you broke down and cried.

Don't worry about all the questions of the past. The only things you have to tell me, the things I have waited forty years to hear, are that you love me and you will write to me. And please let me have a photo of you to put on my bed so I can say to my kids and anyone I see, 'That's my Mum and I'm so very proud of her.'

Mum, I'm going to close for now because I keep getting tears in my eyes. I'm lost and I really do need your love to fill that hole in my heart. Bye, Mum.

Your loving son,
Tony.

The love was reciprocated and they began corresponding with each other as Tony continued to save money.

The phone call I received at Dalkeith Road early in January was to tell me that Tony had just stepped on a plane to England.

I immediately assumed that over Christmas he must have somehow found the money to buy a ticket.

'It's dreadful, Margaret,' Marcelle said. 'Tony had a phone call in the middle of the night. His mother is dead. That's why he's on the plane. His brother sent money from England so he could be at the funeral.'

I was absolutely horrified. My worst fear had been realized. Here was a child migrant who had been deprived of his mother for all these years; then they started to write to each other and the pain of a lifetime began to melt away; but suddenly it was all taken away from him. Forty-three years Tony had waited, but instead of a joyful homecoming, he returned to find his mother in a coffin.

Tony met the rest of his family during his time in England but nothing could lessen his bitterness at having missed out on his greatest wish. Like all child migrants, he had left Britain with no return ticket. It was a one-way journey.

When Tony returned to Perth, he didn't try to hide his sorrow. He told me that his mother had died in an armchair and on the floor beside her was a letter from 'Your loving son, Tony'.

I flew to Sydney on the day the Order of Australia award was to be announced. There was work to do and journalists, who had had several days' notice of the award, were already beginning to call. I didn't tell any child migrants, I wanted them to read it first in the newspapers.

I stayed in Sydney for several days and kept wondering if the news had reached Perth. It had certainly been heard loudly in Nottingham, where the team at the Child Migrants Trust was ecstatic. They told me that at Nottinghamshire County Council, Joan Taylor was called out of an executive meeting to be told of the honour and rushed back inside to share the news.

My hotel room in Sydney overflowed with flowers and cards.

When I got back to Perth, I took a taxi from the airport and arrived in Dalkeith Road shortly before 3.00 p.m. As the driver stopped, I thought I was looking at the wrong house. There were balloons hanging off the trees, the windows and doors. A poster draped across the door said: 'Congratulations', and there were flowers and cards filling the veranda. The answerphone was clogged and fax paper overflowed on to the floor.

The messages were all the same – a remarkable outpouring of goodwill, warmth and enthusiasm.

VOICES wrote an editorial in its newsletter declaring that the OAM 'will be enthusiastically applauded by all those Australians who believe in justice and who admire courage and dedication . . .

'VOICES is proud that our Australian government has recognized an issue which for so long has been shrouded in official deceit and even fraud. The British government, for its part, is refusing to accept its share of responsibility in an infamous scheme which inflicted so much misery and hardship on thousands of innocent children. Congratulations, Margaret – Well done, Australia – Shame on you, Britain.'

Alan Osbourne rang and asked me to dinner. 'Just a quiet meal with my wife and me,' he said and stupidly I believed him. I should have known something was planned when he told me not to dress too informally.

When we arrived at a hotel in Fremantle, I saw Eileen and Jackie in the foyer and still didn't grasp what was happening.

I walked into the main restaurant and there, at a long table, a group of very familiar faces greeted me. The warmth and friendship of the occasion was overwhelming. There was a sense of pride and a feeling that the child migrants were now being given recognition.

Two speeches were made, both brief but not lacking in depth or humour. The sentiments expressed were memorable. Desmond said that I was like a sister to them; the sister they had never had.

Maureen Mac spoke on behalf of the women who spent their childhoods at Nazareth House, Geraldton. 'Margaret, you treat each and every one of us as an individual.'

Words like these are not said easily. We were all working together and we shared respect and trust for each other. I remember looking at the faces around the table and thinking what a remarkable journey we had all taken together.

That night I decided I wanted to arrange a celebration, of sorts, for my friends in Perth. But there were so many and I felt the same about all of them. I knew that the garden at Dalkeith Road couldn't cope with more than sixty people, so I left the invitations to Desmond, Eileen and Alan.

In the six years that I'd been visiting Perth I had never been to a traditional Australian backyard 'barbie', but a fortnight later, on a Saturday evening, a large crowd gathered at Dalkeith Road where the garden had been transformed by fairy lights, balloons, tables, chairs and music. Child migrants had come from everywhere – men and women from all the schemes, many of whom had never been gathered together before.

I had a large cake made – a replica of the one which launched the opening of the Child Migrants Trust office in Nottingham, with the flags of all the countries involved in the child migration schemes.

During the evening, the Geraldton women sat in a row and sang the songs from their time together at Nazareth House. Many were the same songs that the boys used to sing and some grew misty-eyed at the familiar words.

The child migrants shared their different experiences; some talked of having returned home to meet their families, sharing the pain and the happiness. We weren't there to fight governments, or to talk about compensation; there was no bitterness or rancour. Instead, only genuine regard and affection. It was a tribute to how they had survived.

The Order of Australia medal was recognition for them. It was an official acknowledgement that the child migration schemes had taken place. At last, their voices had been heard.

Four months in Perth had extended to almost five months. Everybody had worked together, and my time away from home had been worth while. I managed to interview hundreds of child migrants while the team in Nottingham worked tirelessly to find their families. Telephone calls and faxes were flying backwards and forwards both day and night.

Leaving Perth was never going to be easy. Normally, I prefer leaving Australia without emotional farewells. This time we said our goodbyes at the barbecue, with the singing of 'Now is the Hour For Me to Say Goodbye'. The song had become almost our theme tune.

As my sixteen bags and boxes were stowed on my flight, I was happy to be going home and satisfied that the Child Migrants Trust was no longer a distant office in a distant land. It truly belonged to the people it served.

36

I had missed my family, friends and colleagues dreadfully, and when I got home I wanted Ben to recite every detail of his day at school; to catch up with Rachel's life.

I spent a week immersing myself in family life and becoming part of their daily routine again. The house looked different; not in any specific way, just different – I'd been away a long time.

It wasn't made any easier by the fact that I returned to England a slightly changed person. I have never slept properly since that night in Perth. Sometimes I fall asleep and wake in utter panic with my heart racing. For a split second it's all happening again – the banging on the window, the voice. I think I'm going to die – not at the hands of a murderer, but because my heart will beat too quickly.

During my stay in Perth, the Child Migrants Trust had continued the search for families and arranged reunions with mothers, fathers, brothers and sisters. These were now taking place every month.

No matter what was happening politically and legally concerning child migration, the Trust had never been distracted from its initial goal: to reunite families. This was our purpose and, at the end of the day, the only thing that was truly important.

My trip had also shown me that public awareness of the tragedy of the child migrants was far greater in Australia than in Britain. It had become a national issue and it was rare to find anybody in Australia or New Zealand who hadn't heard about the child migration scandal.

Unfortunately, this was not the case in the UK. After six years of endeavour, I still had not had a single meeting with a British government Minister. Finally, on 18 May 1993, Mr Tim Yeo, the Parliamentary Secretary at the Department of Health, agreed to meet an all-party delegation from Nottinghamshire County Council. I had two goals. The first was to explain the needs of British child migrants; the second, to appeal directly to the Minister for funding to help reunite them with their families.

Mr Yeo described the meeting as 'helpful and informative' and released a statement afterwards saying that he intended opening discussions with the Australian government. He promised nothing more.

If I was to raise public awareness in Britain, it was vital that the BBC screened *The Leaving of Liverpool*. It had been almost a year since the drama was shown in Australia and yet the mini-series wasn't even listed in the Corporation's forthcoming schedules.

Joan Taylor of Nottinghamshire County Council arranged for another debate and the councillors went for everybody. Letters were fired off to John Birt, the director general of the BBC, Marmaduke Hussey, the Chairman, Alan Yentob, the BBC1 programme controller, and each of the BBC directors. Meanwhile, questions were tabled in Parliament asking whether the mini-series had been shelved because of pressure from either the Government or the charities involved.

Not surprisingly, I was soon *persona non grata* with the BBC. When the *Nottingham Evening Post* rang the BBC to ask why the programme hadn't been shown, off the record, a press officer said, 'Don't take any notice of that bloody woman from Nottingham.'

The official BBC explanation was: 'The mini-series missed its slot in 1992 because we were looking to do some further editing on the programme to make it suitable for transmission.'

Further editing? There was an unpleasant ringing in my ears.

Eventually, the BBC announced that it would screen the drama. The mini-series was scheduled at short notice for mid-July – TV's silly season – and there were plans for only limited pre-publicity.

This meant no launch, no TV plugs and no cast interviews. For whatever reason, the BBC had ensured that *The Leaving of Liverpool* would struggle to attract an audience.

Martin Jacobs, an actor who played a leading adult role in the drama, rang me.

'They're not going to do anything to help promote it, Margaret. Nothing at all.'

'I know. I know. It's a crying shame. Is there nothing we can do?'

Martin suddenly announced: 'We'll do it all ourselves. We'll start tonight. You and I will do the publicity.'

This was a completely new challenge. In the next four weeks Martin and I cranked up a promotional campaign at no cost to the BBC. The British public were going to know about this TV programme, even if we had to yell from the rooftops or walk down the high street carrying sandwich boards.

Using our contacts in the press we arranged major articles in every national newspaper. We did press briefings, TV interviews, radio spots and previews. The BBC had produced no detailed press packs so we had Penny Chapman send us the left-overs from the Australian launch.

In the midst of this avalanche of publicity, the BBC must have wondered what the hell was happening.

But there was still another unpleasant surprise waiting. I'd always assumed, come transmission night, that the BBC would provide the Trust with phone lines to take calls from viewers. Having seen the impact of the mini-series in Australia, this was vital. I had never lost sight of the fact that there was a large silent Britain-based group of grieving mothers and fathers, brothers and sisters who had lost part of their families. It would come as a shock to many that the children they had become separated from, for whatever reason, had been sent overseas. Sadly, the BBC didn't understand this.

'We have no budget for that,' was the reply.

Right! I thought. I've had enough of this. I requested a hearing and was told that Alan Yentob, the channel's most senior manager, was dealing with the issue personally. I wrote him a long letter, to which I have never received a reply.

Then I wrote to John Birt. Somebody else replied on his behalf and insisted the decision was final.

Nottinghamshire County Council, which has from the very first day been the Trust's most caring and committed supporter, was also appalled by the BBC's attitude. Right across the political spectrum, the councillors and local MPs shared this view.

Defeat loomed. The Trust had no money for switchboards and telephones. We struggled from day to day on a shoestring budget. Now I was in another corner.

Explaining the situation to Joan Taylor, I vented my frustration and disbelief.

Finally, she said, 'Margaret, stop worrying. We're not going to let this happen. We'll fund the help-lines. We'll put the telephones in, we'll pay the charges. You just make sure the BBC put the numbers on screen.'

I was absolutely elated. Yet again Notts had proved to be the conscience of the world on this issue. But soon my mood changed. I couldn't believe it! The BBC refused to screen the numbers. It was regarded as 'not necessary'.

On 13 July, I appealed directly to MPs in a committee room at the House of Commons. David Hinchliffe, a Labour front-bench spokesman on health, chaired the meeting. After years of hammering on these same doors for moral and financial help, I was determined to get a little understanding from Westminster.

As our cross-party delegation entered St Stephen's entrance of the House of Commons, I was besieged by TV cameras and reporters from Britain, Canada, America, Australia, France and Germany.

It was an historic event. To my knowledge it was the first time MPs had been directly told about the experiences of British child migrants. Until then, I don't think they appreciated the horrors of the schemes and the grave injustice.

The next morning's newspapers said it all.

The *Independent* reported: 'A charity representing thousands of child migrants separated from their families after the Second World War has fiercely criticized the BBC over its refusal to publicize a telephone help-line . . .

'The [Child Migrants] Trust is already suspicious about a year-long delay in showing the programme in Britain.

'A spokesman for BBC1 has dismissed any suggestion of a conspiracy and said the corporation did not publicize help-lines after drama programmes . . .'

That afternoon questions were asked in the House of Commons, with two MPs demanding an inquiry into why the BBC refused to screen the help-line numbers. They accused the BBC of 'outrageous and irresponsible' behaviour.

The following morning, less than forty-eight hours before *The Leaving of Liverpool* was due to be shown, a statement was released by the BBC. A spokesman said, 'We are now offering this help-line number to viewers. It was always considered and no decision had finally been taken. Today it was decided to display the help-line phone number.'

37

In late June, the Christian Brothers had quietly arranged advertising space in WA's major newspapers. A message was prepared by Brother Gerald Faulkner, with the approval of his superiors, and delivered for publication on 7 July. The headline, in white on black, read:

THE CHRISTIAN BROTHERS CHILD CARE INSTITUTIONS
Clontarf (1901–1983); Castledare (1929–1983); Tardun (1928–1965); Bindoon (1936–1967)

In the statement that followed, the Christian Brothers finally apologized for the physical and sexual abuse suffered by former children in its care:

Such abuse violates the child's dignity and sense of self-worth. It causes psychological and social trauma that can lead to lasting wounds of guilt, shame, insecurity and problems in relationships.

We, the Christian Brothers of today, therefore unreservedly apologize to those individuals who were victims of abuse in these institutions. We do not condone in any way the behaviour of individual Brothers who may have perpetrated such abuse.

In apologizing, however, we entreat people not to reflect adversely on the majority of Brothers and their co-workers of the era who went about their work with integrity and deep regard for the children entrusted to their care.

The statement went on to launch a spirited, albeit hollow, defence of the child migration schemes and the role played by the Christian Brothers. This, they insisted, was very minor compared to that of the relative governments.

Between 1901 and 1983 some 4,000 boys, mostly orphans, child migrants and State wards, were cared for in Christian Brother institutions in WA.

Most of the children who came to these institutions were from deprived backgrounds. Many were child migrants from the UK and Ireland, brought to Australia in a scheme initiated by the Commonwealth government and with which several voluntary organizations, including the Australian Catholic Church, actively co-operated . . .

We cannot and do not excuse any abuse that took place in our institutions nor do we wish to minimize in any way the damage caused.

However, for those looking to apportion blame for such incidents, the following must be borne in mind:

The events took place mostly thirty to fifty years ago and many of the people named as accused, victims or witnesses, are dead or unable to be contacted. While the passage of time does not diminish the seriousness of the incidents, it does make it extremely difficult to uncover the full truth; and

Regular inspections were made of these institutions by the Government agencies who had ultimate responsibility for the welfare of the children. There is no indication of generalized abuse in their reports.

Humility at last, I thought. If only it hadn't taken so long. The years of silence had been a form of secondary abuse, causing even more heartache and suffering for the child migrants.

The ramifications of this very public apology echoed around the world, particularly in Britain. I had never lost sight of the fact that these were British children whose fate was decided by the British government. They were sent overseas on schemes that were approved and administered by the British government. Their fares and upkeep were partly subsidized by this same government, whose Home Secretary endorsed the emigration of individual children like Harold Haig.

Surely, then, Britain must bear responsibility for ensuring the welfare and safety of these innocents. And the same is true of the Australian government and the charities and agencies who were supposed to care for the child migrants.

Within hours of the Christian Brothers' statement appearing, there were calls for compensation and criminal prosecutions. Bruce Blyth of VOICES appealed to victims to join a register being prepared to assist police investigations.

Now the big question became whether the Catholic Church would voluntarily pay compensation; and, if not, would the victims sue?

The first answer was a categoric 'No!' Deputy Provincial Tony Shanahan told journalists that it was impossible to put a monetary value on the tragedy and, anyhow, throwing money at victims never helped.

Dr Barry Coldrey called talk of lawsuits 'misguided' and continued to lay the blame anywhere but on the Catholic Church.

He reportedly said, 'If they bring it against the British government they should bring it more against the Australian government because we were pulling harder than they were pushing . . .

'We are dealing in a world of government policy. If there is guilt, the forces guilty are government decisions.'

Dr Coldrey's long-awaited research into the child migration schemes had been made public three weeks earlier. Six reports were released, each ranging in size from 30 to 100 pages, but the child abuse allegations made up only a small part of his report. Dr Coldrey had the audacity to suggest that if the Child Welfare Department had been more vigilant, the children being cared for in the Boys' Towns might not have suffered such abuse.

His views were not shared by many. An editorial in Perth's

Sunday Times on 11 July, summed up the general feeling.

'The Christian Brothers have taken only the first step towards righting the wrongs of the past by apologizing to those who were physically and sexually abused in WA orphanages.

'It was an apology reluctantly dragged from the Brothers while they continued to insist that many of the claims were exaggerated.

'But while the Church has bowed to the overwhelming pressure of evidence that some in the Order had shamefully betrayed positions of sacred trust, the Christian Brothers leadership is now balking at paying compensation.

'Offers of counselling and support services for those still in emotional crisis as a result of cruel treatment is all very well, but those who have had their lives ruined deserve more.'

From my point of view, the issue of compensation was less urgent than the need to reunite families. Now, hopefully, the spotlight would shift away from Perth. There were tens of thousands of other child migrants, elsewhere in Australia, and in Canada, New Zealand and Zimbabwe. They, too, had suffered.

The child migration scandal wasn't confined to Western Australia or to the Catholic Church.

Sandra Bennett, the child migrant I met on my first trip to Australia, made this point passionately in an open letter to the Catholic Church. She signed it 'Ann Pritchard' – the name by which she was known at the children's home in Britain.

> One of the disturbing aspects of this story is to know that ill treatment and physical abuse were not peculiar to the institutions in WA. Indeed, my own experiences, at St Joseph's Orphanage in Rockhampton, run by the Sisters of Mercy in the Fifties, were to be similar.
>
> As the scheme under which we children migrated was nationwide, I can only presume that the same excuses will be offered. I reject outright the pleas . . . that 'resources were scarce, Government assistance was minimal, personnel were untrained in child care and were often overworked and specialist help was almost unknown.'

If by resources you mean money, very few would argue that the Catholic Church would be one of the richest organizations in the world. I was never to see the variety and plenty on your tables equally loaded on ours. In fact, we were so hungry and the quality of food so poor, that soon after arriving we began to steal. We had a workload that we had never had in England and the calories just weren't sufficient. Naturally, all of this sort of behaviour got us into trouble, severe beatings being the result. Even during the war in England I was never to know hunger.

The Catholic Church has a tradition of looking after the unfortunate children of free unions and unsettled families. Could it not have drawn on experience for some guidance? I cannot accept that the collective intellect of all the people who came into contact with us could not come up with a better policy of child care.

Orphans learn not to expect too much in the way of hugs and kisses. Nobody else gets them, why should you? What you hope for is not to be treated cruelly and beaten and made to feel even worse about yourself. Statements like 'no wonder nobody wanted you' frequently accompanying the beatings are enormously damaging to the emotions of a child. Your 'circumstances' are already a deep, dark mystery and there is tremendous guilt that you have done something dreadful to have been rejected by your parents . . .

The needs of the institution were all met as far as I am concerned. But what about my needs? Nobody ever asked me. Even the emigration to Australia was against my will, torn from already fragile roots and transplanted into a semi-arid environment with an even more barren policy of child care could be nothing more than shock. Now, astride two cultures, I have roots in none.

Robbed of a past, I was now robbed of a future. No amount of counselling can restore my feeling of worth. 'Like Niobe, all tears' mourning for her slain children, I was to grieve for my unborn children and the loss of a family of my own. Not for nine days and nine nights, but a whole lifetime. And I still grieve.

You may all know the story now. The Catholic Church was directly responsible, in my mind, and indirectly the State. I am weary of the burden and am no longer prepared to wear the mantle of guilt and shame. I pass it on to you.

ANN PRITCHARD

38

In Nottingham, the County Council had stripped down its nuclear bunker, brought in furniture and installed phone lines, ready for the broadcast of *The Leaving of Liverpool*. A computer system was ready to log every in-coming call.

Joan Taylor rang me: 'Margaret, it's ready, come down and have a look. The phones are in. You've got free-phones. We're not having anybody fail to call because they can't afford to.'

The Christian Brothers' statement could not have been better timed to help generate publicity. It pushed the child migration scandal from the review sections onto the news pages.

The charities and agencies reacted quickly. David Skidmore, of the General Synod of the Church of England, wrote to *The Sunday Times*, arguing, 'At the time, emigration to countries of the former British Empire was seen as the best alternative for children who otherwise faced a bleak future of poverty or institutionalized care.

'With the benefit of hindsight, those who engaged in this response to the children's plight can be seen to have been acting out of the best intentions but misguidedly.'

Michael Jarman, of Barnardo's wrote in a letter to the press: 'At the time, Barnardo's believed that it was providing these young people with an enormous opportunity, as well as expanding its capacity to help more children in Britain. This idea is greatly at odds with our emphasis today on working to keep families together.'

The City of Liverpool Social Services had an entirely more helpful response. I had a letter and a telephone call from Councillor Cathy Hancox who wanted me to confirm that child migrants from Liverpool had been sent to Australia.

'Yes,' I said. 'Quite a number.'

Mrs Hancox, along with an officer from Liverpool's Department of Social Services, came to see me to discuss how they could help, and eventually The City of Liverpool County Council provided the Trust with funds to pay a social worker's salary for eighteen months.

I spent most of those last few days before the broadcast in the bunker, dealing with last-minute telephone interviews. The setting mirrored my mood. What better place to be during a siege than deep underground behind walls of steel-reinforced concrete?

I had heard from Western Australia that police had begun investigating complaints filed by child migrants against the Christian Brothers, and there had been calls in Parliament for a full judicial inquiry. Australian lawyers were preparing to lodge claims by more than 250 men who alleged they were abused in Christian Brothers institutions.

Similarly, I had heard that lawyers in the UK were preparing writs against the British government on behalf of child migrants, along with applications for legal aid.

On the afternoon of Thursday, 15 July, before the first episode of *The Leaving of Liverpool*, we did a final test of the telephones. A switch was pulled and all of them rang simultaneously. Rather than wait for the programme, people were already calling, having read the numbers in newspapers and magazines.

We logged 700 calls that first evening and 10,000 over the next five days.

Counsellors struggled to comfort callers and take down their details. We had tearful mothers wondering if the children they gave for adoption could possibly have gone to Australia; brothers and sisters who remembered seeing siblings taken away; and even calls from abusers ringing up to confess that they had molested children and needed help.

My only disappointment was the discovery of just what the BBC meant by 'further editing'. There is a very moving scene in the first episode that shows a ship arriving in Australia and the children disembarking. They are shepherded into a holding area and made to line up beneath large signs naming the charities who were receiving children off that ship.

This brief incident was taken out by the BBC. There was no reference, by name, to any of the charities or child care agencies who participated in the child migration schemes. This could well have left British viewers with the impression that it was only the Catholic Church which played a major role in child migration.

First the BBC had refused us phone lines; then it refused to screen the help-line numbers and finally it decided to edit the mini-series. I wrote immediately to John Birt, the Director General, requesting an explanation.

His reply, drafted by the 'Appeals Secretary' of the BBC, totally failed to address my concerns of bias against the Catholic Church.

> '. . . following transmission in Australia, the Fairbridge Trust contacted the BBC to emphasize that they were no longer associated with this kind of work. In deference to their concern, this small cut [in the film] was made, and included a similar sign to Barnardo's since they were the only other organization identifiable in the scene.
>
> . . . we certainly do not agree with you that to remove the reference amounted to editing the production with bias.

What bizarre logic! Would the BBC edit *Schindler's List* on the basis that the German army is no longer involved in the persecution of Jews?

The second half of the mini-series, on the following night, was even more demanding. Within the bunker we were fighting to stay awake in the early hours of the morning and answer the continuous stream of calls. Amid the commotion, a journalist from Perth managed to get through.

'I just heard on the national news that the Australian flag is flying over Nottingham,' she said.

'Yes it is,' I told her. 'It's flying alongside the Union Jack as a mark of respect for the child migrants.'

The journalist became very emotional. As her voice faltered, she told me that she had never heard anything like it.

39

The Leaving of Liverpool created an enormous sense of outrage in Britain, as it had done in Australia. It touched the hearts and conscience of the nation. Letters poured in, adding to the thousands I had received since the Trust was founded.

Such letters are often moving, but there is one, in particular, that I will always remember. It was written by a former London policeman who, in the early 1950s, found two boys wandering lost and alone near London Bridge. He wrote:

> It subsequently transpired that the boys had absconded from a children's home in Kent. They were two boys of a family of six, three boys and three girls, whose father was a Flight Sergeant in the Royal Air Force stationed in Berlin. As you will guess the marriage had broken up and the children had been put in the care of the local authority.
>
> The lads had got as far as London Bridge Station and after crossing London Bridge and entering the City, I had found them.
>
> Their purpose in absconding was that they were aware that they were on their way to Australia with a view to eventually being put to a career in farming. They had mutually decided – and I can only guess their ages at about ten and six years – to

run away to find their sisters to say goodbye to them before they went.

I subsequently went on to have a happy and worthwhile career in the police service, reaching relatively high rank and to have five children from an extremely successful marriage, but that little incident still brings a lump to my throat. It still causes me to wonder what happened to those young boys. I can only hope they have done well and that they are still in touch with their brother and sisters.

I retired some years ago and from time to time give a little talk to Rotary Clubs, Women's Institutes and the like. I always refer to the incident of those two lads as being the saddest moment of my police career.

The Leaving of Liverpool also touched the hearts of the decision-makers in Britain.

Shadow Health Secretary David Blunkett openly called for a public inquiry into child migration. Labour's Social Services spokesman David Hinchliffe said the Government had a 'clear obligation' to provide proper funding to the Child Migrants Trust.

The plight of the child migrants was now firmly on the political agenda. In some ways, I blamed myself for the fact that it had taken so long. I had simply failed to get my message across to the politicians in the UK.

Despite the barrage of publicity and questions in Parliament, by August 1993 the British government had still not acknowledged the enormous tragedy that had taken place. I was finding it increasingly difficult to keep silent when the child migrants were being treated with such indifference.

In Australia there was a huge sense of embarrassment for a policy of social engineering that had gone so badly wrong, but the British government appeared ready to ignore any suggestion that it was in any way responsible.

During parliamentary question time on 2 November 1993, David Hinchliffe MP confronted the Prime Minister John Major.

'Is the Prime Minister aware that early next month Mrs Margaret Humphreys will become the first British citizen outside the royal family to be awarded the prestigious Order of Australia medal for her work rehabilitating victims of the British child migrant scheme?

In recognition of that award will the Prime Minister set up an independent public inquiry into the operation of the scheme until 1967 and the resulting appalling treatment of vast numbers of British children? In view of his professed commitment to open government, will the Prime Minister end the disgraceful Government cover-up of the issue once and for all?'

John Major replied, 'I am certainly happy to congratulate Mrs Humphreys on her award. I was not aware that that was the case, but I give her my warmest congratulations. As the honourable gentleman will know – for I am aware that he has taken a great interest in this matter – the migration schemes to Australia and other countries were run at the time by respected national voluntary bodies. The Government's concern now is to ensure that former child migrants who want to make contact with their families are able to do so. Any concern about the treatment of the children in another country is essentially a matter for the authorities of that country.'

Mr Major's 'concern' that child migrants were reunited with their families sounded rather hollow when one considered the fact that the Trust had received only two Department of Health grants in five years.

Similarly, his claim that the suffering of child migrants was not the concern of Britain alarmed me. Surely Mr Major wasn't aware of all the relevant facts. I wanted to remind him that these were British children. I wanted him to look at the government documents and social welfare reports which showed, beyond doubt, that successive British governments played a major role in our children being sent abroad.

Under the Empire Settlement Acts of 1922 and 1937, the Government actively co-operated with private organizations to jointly help people who wanted to settle in 'His Majesty's Overseas Dominions'. Although not specifically designed to include children, this legislation allowed organizations like Barnardo's and the Fairbridge Society to begin shipments of youngsters.

Under the Children's Act 1948, the Government had a duty to properly supervise the charities and organizations who were receiving children in Australia, Canada, New Zealand and Rhodesia. But all evidence pointed to the fact that successive British governments had made little or no effort to inspect or even keep track of the children once they had left British shores.

If the Prime Minister chose to ignore such facts, he wasn't by any means the first. For when Mervyn and I began researching Britain's involvement in child migration, we uncovered a catalogue of denials, ignorance and unheeded warnings.

The Child Migrants Trust gained access to the archives of former welfare organizations in the UK. Immediately, it was clear that two organizations in particular had been worried about child migration – the Association of Psychiatric Social Workers, and the British Federation of Social Workers (BFSW). The latter set up a special sub-committee in February 1945 and convened a conference on child migration for December of that year.

Among the recommendations to emerge was that special emphasis be placed upon 'the importance of giving children links with the country of origin and of giving them contacts with persons outside the institutions or foster homes in the receiving country'.

This warning went unheeded.

And then in 1948, a former principal of the Fairbridge Farm School at Pinjarra in Western Australia, voiced his concerns to the BFSW. Mr Paterson complained that the new committees that were running the farm school still retained some of the old people associated with the 'bad traditions of the past', whose first care was not the welfare of the children and who were identified with the policy of cheap labour . . . '

But still the ships left England carrying more and more children.

On 24 March 1948, a letter was published in *The Times* signed by sixteen of Britain's leading welfare agencies.

Emigration of Children.

Sir,

. . . The undersigned have reason to think that the practices of the various agencies for the migration of children overseas vary and that their methods of selection of children, their welfare, education, training and after care in the receiving countries are not always of a sufficiently high standard. We would urge, therefore, that, in conjunction with the Commonwealth Relations Department, an inter-Governmental commission of inquiry be set up to examine the whole system of care of deprived children of British origin in the Commonwealth . . .

On the far side of the world, *The Age* newspaper in Melbourne picked up the story. 'Welfare Officers Seek Migrant Inquiry,' the headline read.

> Sixteen British welfare associations, pressing the Government to investigate present conditions of 300 child migrants from Britain to the Dominions, say they have received adverse reports on children both from individuals and organizations overseas. Many children from seven to fourteen years – orphaned, abandoned or illegitimate – have been sent overseas by charitable organizations within the last eighteen months.
>
> The Government says it has sponsored only 150 such children. It has a complete check on what has happened to them and cannot speak for the other 300 who have been sent by voluntary organizations.
>
> One welfare officer said some of the children were now in institutions less efficiently run than those in England. 'Our greatest fear is that population needs of the Dominions are being put before the welfare of these children,' he added.
>
> Headed by the British Federation of Social Workers the associations claim that many children are undergoing 'a new life of drudgery, with little thought to education.'
>
> They want a Government commission to investigate along the following lines:
>
> Conditions under which these children are selected;
>
> What has happened to them?
>
> What safeguards are there for their well-being?
>
> How can they be protected from blind-alley jobs?
>
> The demand for an investigation comes only a short time before the new Children's Bill comes into force in July. Under this bill the Home Secretary gets power to control all arrangements for child emigration.

There was no official Government inquiry or investigation.

The 1948 Children's Bill contained two clauses relating to child migration, both of them deeply flawed. The BFSW wanted them altered. In particular it wanted a stipulation that the Home Secretary had to give his consent before any child could be sent overseas by a voluntary agency. This regulation already applied to children in local authority care.

If this wasn't possible, the BFSW wanted an amendment to the Bill that would have forced the voluntary agencies to be registered and under greater control.

When the Children's Bill passed through the House of Lords on 13 April 1948, Lord Llewellyn spoke out: '. . . children should not be emigrated willy nilly without much enquiry as to their physical condition or the kind of conditions to which they were going in the Dominions or perhaps somewhere else . . .'

The Lord Chancellor replied, 'I can give an assurance that the Home Office intended to secure that children shall not be emigrated unless there is absolute satisfaction that proper arrangements have been made for the care and upbringing of each child . . .'

Several weeks later, when MPs in the House of Commons expressed similar concerns, the Home Secretary assured them: '. . . the regulations will certainly require adequate arrangements to be made for ensuring that the child who is being emigrated has the same after care as that which is required for the Local Authority child.'

No regulations were issued, no amendment was made, and the 1948 Children's Act was passed. The second wave of child migration now had the green light and over the next five years more youngsters were sent to Australia than had been transported in the previous quarter of a century.

The supporters of child migration breathed an enormous sigh of relief. They had escaped closer control, although some could see the writing on the wall. A memo written by Mr J. East at the Commonwealth Relations Office on 9 June 1948, revealed: 'We are getting into rather deep water with the Home Office over child migration and there is a school of thought in the country which is almost opposed to child migration on principle.'

There were more warnings – each one of them adding to the embarrassing catalogue of neglect. Yet the voluntary agencies seemed beyond scrutiny – almost untouchable – with royal patronage, and their boards bulging with the great and the good. Even today, few people dare to criticize those charities involved.

In the 1950s, there were many critical reports on child migration. A 1951 study by the National Council of Social Services reported:

'Since the general opinion in this country seems to be against any child being brought up in an institution unless he is unsuitable for adoption or fostering, it seems doubtful whether it is in the best interests of children for them to be sent abroad in order to be brought up in institutions, completely cut off from any home ties they may have, and perhaps in very isolated places.'

Despite such expert advice, the schemes continued.

In 1953, the British government established the Oversea (*sic*) Migration Board specifically to promote child migration. It immediately criticized local authorities for not providing enough children.

The Board's first annual report, in July 1954, applauded the schemes and the voluntary societies involved:

> We are unanimous in the view that the United Kingdom authorities who bear a moral responsibility for these children, should not abandon their interest in this way but should renew the agreements with the voluntary societies . . .
>
> Having built up their organizations on the basis of United Kingdom as well as Australian government assistance, many of the societies would find it extremely difficult to continue on their remaining resources. They might be forced to lower their standards of accommodation and training, and the interests of the children already under their care, who emigrated with the help and the blessing, so to speak, of the United Kingdom government, might conceivably be prejudiced.
>
> Apart from the argument of obligation, there seems no doubt that the cost of child emigrants to the economy of the United Kingdom is less than that of adults who leave in the middle of their working life having already benefited from educational and health facilities in this country. Children, on the other hand, not only have not yet begun to contribute to the economy, but they have not completed their education and, as far as the emigrant children are concerned, frequently come from broken homes and might, if they stayed in the United Kingdom, eventually become or continue to be a charge upon the rates.

I wondered again if this is what people meant when they accused me of not putting child migration into its historic context.

The Oversea Migration Board's 1956 report included details from a 1955 Fact Finding Mission appointed by the Secretary of State for Commonwealth Relations to investigate the Australian institutions.

> We heard often in the course of our discussions the widely held view that many children, whom life had treated badly, would benefit by transfer to a new country where they could be given a fresh start, away from old scenes and unhappy associations. Few with whom we spoke seemed to realize that it was precisely such children, already rejected and insecure, who might often be ill-equipped to cope with the added strain of migration.

This, of course, was not what the Oversea Migration Board (or the government of the day), wanted to hear. Its reaction?

> We are quite out of sympathy with the suggestion that children already in care in this country should be restrained from emigrating to Australia because of the conditions in that country.

The Board did, however, accept some of the recommendations – brothers and sisters should be kept together; voluntary societies in Australia should be supplied with full information about each child (although not particulars of family history); and, wherever possible, child migrants should be placed with foster parents.

In my experience the first of these proposals was adopted but the latter two were ignored.

However, it is the main recommendation that was most telling. It had a familiar ring to it. 'Voluntary societies in Britain should obtain the consent of the Home Secretary before any child migrant is sent overseas.'

The Board disagreed.

> We have already stressed the scarcity in the UK of children who are both suitable and available for migration. We fear that if their recruitment was hampered by the need to submit each individual case to examination by the machinery of a

government department the numbers would become pro-
gressively less . . .

We believe that for political, strategic and economic reasons
it is important that migration from the United Kingdom to the
Commonwealth should be maintained.

The British government did eventually regulate the voluntary
societies. Legislation was passed on 7 January 1982 – fifteen years
after large-scale child migration had ended.

As I studied the documents and correspondence, the steady decline
of child migration was painfully plotted out. It slowed in the
mid-fifties when the Oversea Migration Board, among others,
discovered difficulties in finding children.

'. . . the social and economic pressures in this country which led
to the emigration of unaccompanied children . . . have disappeared,'
the 1956 report stated. And it went on to reveal that 'the demand
for children for adoption [in Great Britain] exceeded the numbers
available' and that the great majority of children in the care of the
authorities 'could be placed in this country in what were regarded
as satisfactory foster homes.'

Why then, I asked myself, did child migration continue?

It was the same story when I looked at Australian records. The
Chief Migration Officer of the Australian High Commission in
London journeyed around Britain during 1955 trying to convince
local authorities to send more of their children to Australia.

In Manchester he reported that '. . . great stress was placed by
Child Welfare Authorities in the UK today on a parent substitute,
and the "cottage mother" system had definitely fallen into dis-
favour in Britain.

'The long-term object was to return, if at all possible, the children
concerned to their mothers and fathers . . .'

It was the same story in Birmingham. 'The Town Clerk stated
that even if the parents were bad parents the Children's Committee
was most averse to sending children 12,000 miles across the other
side of the world to Australia.'

Obviously, the local authorities had woken up to the perils and
inherent cruelty of child migration but, sadly, not so the charities.

In December 1954, the Catholic Church asked the Australian

government to lower the minimum age of child migrants from five to three, because the orphanages had empty beds. Thankfully this request was denied because '. . . the long voyage to Australia involves an element of risk with very young children which is not justifiable. Even in the case of infants travelling with their parents, deaths do occur from time to time from shipboard illnesses, and sickness from the rapid climatic changes is frequent . . .

'Perusal of our records show that there are only two current nominations for children aged three . . . On the other hand twenty-six children aged four, and eight aged three have arrived here under the post-war child schemes.'

Australian welfare officers were also beginning to question the wisdom of the schemes. In August, 1959, the Acting Assistant Director of the Child Welfare Department in WA, wrote a report for the Commonwealth Immigration Advisory Council.

'Whilst the standard of institutions receiving children, so far as material needs is concerned, cannot be questioned, there is a deep emotional factor lacking. Children have displayed considerable disturbance . . .

'After-care service for institutionalized children is very important . . . The contact by nominating bodies is not consistent enough, resulting in the children becoming involved in failure to settle in a satisfying home and suitable job and, in fact, in some instances, becoming "drifters".

'. . . the number involved colliding with society is still too high . . .'

The report goes on to say that the Department favoured the use of foster families instead of institutions but unfortunately, 'institutions nominating children are not anxious to pursue the boarding-out policy, although it is felt that practically all children could be adequately fostered if the institutions were not loath to part with them . . .'

Why would anyone in child care want a child to remain in an institution when there was a possibility of a home life? Surely it could have nothing to do with the Government subsidies that accompanied each child?

The Governments, the charities and the churches involved, can not have failed to hear these warnings.

There was now no possible reason to take innocent, defenceless children from their homeland and transport them to institutions on the far side of the world.

So what was done? They continued to send and receive children – not for eight weeks, or eight months, but for another eight years.

40

There was never any doubt in my mind that the child migration schemes were enormously misconceived and had disastrous consequences.

There was also ample evidence of information such as birthdates, names, dates and addresses being totally at odds with the official documentation. I would have liked to put it down to shoddy record-keeping and poor handwriting, but the sheer volume of mistakes made this seem improbable.

Some children were allocated new names and dates of birth when they arrived in Australia because their records were 'incomplete'. One thirteen-year-old actually had his first name changed because too many other children at the home had the same name.

As I battled to find the families of child migrants I began to consider if some information had been deliberately falsified to cover the tracks of child migrants and make it difficult for parents or relatives to ever find them.

Was this also a reason for telling children that they were orphans?

Countless speeches, papers and history books refer to the child migrants as underprivileged, oppressed and orphans.

'Orphans Arrive Here to Start Their Life Afresh', declared one newspaper headline. 'War Orphans Arrive Today', said another.

There is a 1947 newspaper story asking for families to take a migrant child home for Christmas. Three small boys, each about seven years old, are pictured sitting on a motor cycle and the caption announces:

> Look! We're all ready to come. You see there are nearly forty of us who have never had a home. Our Mummies and Daddies were killed during the war and now we have come out here to Australia. We know you'd love to have one or more of us for Christmas . . .

Similarly, a booklet celebrating the history of Clontarf has a cover photograph showing the entrance to the institution. The caption states:

> The portals through which 2,451 Orphan Youth have passed to become worthy citizens of Our State.

The Catholic Church doesn't use the dictionary definition of the word orphan – they consider it to be a generic term that means whatever they want it to mean.

Of course, calling children 'orphans' made the schemes seem far worthier. Orphans tug harder at the heart strings than other children. They're all alone and need to be 'rescued'.

But is it a cruel and calculated deception? The philanthropists and child 'care' agencies appear to have wanted to sever any links the children might otherwise have had with their families or country. They were so successful that many migrants are still totally convinced their mothers and fathers are dead.

Yet after researching thousands of cases in the past seven years, I can safely say that I have found only one child migrant who could properly have been called an orphan.

Many of the charities have been upset by my use of words like 'deceit' or 'deception', but quite frankly I can't think of what else to call it. If you tell a child that his or her parents are dead, when it wasn't true then and isn't true now, then surely that's deceit.

Likewise, attempts by parents to find their children were met with more lies. Many were told their son or daughter had been adopted; or worse still, had died. Few knew their youngsters had been transported out of Britain.

Is that not deceit and deception?

Another disturbing fact emerged when I discovered that there had been approaches from Australian families willing to adopt young migrants. An Adelaide newspaper reported in January 1949 that:

> Several offers have been made to adopt British war orphans who arrived in the *Ormonde* and are now living at Goodwood Orphanage. But they are not available for adoption.
>
> A spokesman for the Catholic Social Service Bureau said today that whether British children were available for adoption depended on the approved organization responsible for nominating the children. In this instance the Catholic Church had no intention of making them available for adoption. The children would be reared at the institution under the care of the Catholic Church until placed in employment under supervision, he said.

Over the years, many migrants tried to retrace their footsteps, but too often the lies continued. Again they were classed as orphans; or told their mothers had abandoned them at the hospital or were killed in car crashes. Many have the evidence of such lies in writing.

One of them is Albert Stanhope, a former child migrant who came to see me in 1993. Albert is quite wealthy in material terms. He's a middle-aged real estate agent now married with three children.

When I interviewed him I found him to be a very articulate man, although quite withdrawn. He perched uncomfortably on the edge of a chair, glancing nervously at his hands, with his briefcase between his feet.

Within about ten minutes he sat back and quietly said, 'I wonder if I have any family.'

Albert arrived in Australia aged seven. He had an appalling childhood and was full of so much hurt that I realized he was going to need a lot of counselling.

On his next visit Albert brought his birth certificate which he had managed to obtain as an adult. I spent a long while trying to draw him out about his childhood, but Albert wouldn't say much.

He just told me, 'If ever those brothers have a go at you, Margaret. If ever they go public and have a go at you. I'll finish them.'

'Why?' I asked.

'Never mind why, I'll finish them.'

He's said the same thing on more than one occasion. I can only assume something pretty terrible happened to him.

As it turned out, I found Albert's family quite quickly. And the search uncovered a series of documents relating to his emigration. The details speak for themselves.

In August 1946, a young secretary and single mother, Patricia Stanhope, wrote this letter to an orphanage in Liverpool.

Dear Madam,

Can you please tell me if there are any places for my little boy in your care? It has been so hard to find work and now that I have a factory job in Bristol I am unable to keep him with me. He is four years old at the moment and hardly any bother. If you could look after him for a little while, until I get myself set up, then I will collect him. I am quite willing to pay for his keep. I hope you understand, I don't want him adopted. Please just look after him for a short time.

This reply was written on 18 September.

Dear Mrs Stanhope,

Thank you for your letter received on Tuesday last. We may have a vacancy for your little boy and I enclose an application form. We require full details of your background and new employment. A reference from your employer would be of assistance.

If these are satisfactory, I can give you a decision at the beginning of October.

There is a memo, obviously written during a conference, which explains why Patricia Stanhope had to put her baby in care. It reveals that her father died in the first World War and her mother raised three children on her own. Patricia, the eldest, took on the responsibility of looking after her brothers while her mother worked six nights a week as a nurse. As a result, Patricia didn't finish school. She fell pregnant not long after her mother died.

A position was found for baby Albert, and Patricia handed him over. She worked hard at her new job, trying to save enough money to bring him home.

She visited the orphanage every fortnight, but the train fares were expensive and the meetings so emotional that she began to visit less and less as the months passed.

Eventually Patricia fell in love with the factory owner's son, who wanted to marry her. She broke down and told him about Albert, fearing he would disapprove but instead he told her to fetch him back. He was part of their family.

> 19 February, 1950
> Memo: telephone call from a Mr Henry Archer, who claimed to be the new stepfather of Albert Stanhope. Apparently, Miss Patricia Stanhope has now married Mr Archer and wants to pick up Albert immediately. She was told that he was no longer in this country.

Four days later, a letter arrived.

> Dear Sir,
> I don't know where to begin. My distress and shock could not be greater at the news that my wife's child has been emigrated without her written or verbal consent. No adoption papers have been signed by her and, in fact, I have a copy of a letter she sent to you on the 6th of August, 1946 in which she expressly states that her child is not to be adopted.
> On whose authority was he transferred overseas? Why was this done without my wife's permission? These are questions to which I demand a full explanation. I also demand that you inform us of his precise whereabouts and begin immediate steps to have him returned.
> He is my stepson and will be brought up in a loving household.
> Surely you must realize that his mother wants him back. She stated as much when he was placed in your care.

I ask you for an immediate reply and return of the child.
Yours faithfully,
H. Archer.

A mother had lost her child. A dreadful mistake had been made. Yet there was no sign of remorse or an apology from the orphanage. This letter was written by the person in charge.

4 March 1950
Dear Mr Archer,
Thank you for your letter dated 23 February, 1950. You may not be aware of all the relevant facts of the decision to emigrate Albert Stanhope. He was placed in this orphanage on November 9th, 1946. Our visitors' book shows no record of anybody visiting the boy between January 1948 and November of that year. We had no letter from Miss Stanhope in that time explaining her absences, nor was any money forwarded to maintain Albert's upkeep.

This was an act of deliberate desertion and it was evident that someone had to assume parental rights and act on the child's behalf. Rather than be upset, your wife should consider herself fortunate. Albert is alive and well and enjoying a far healthier and brighter future. This is in no way due to your wife. Her actions harmed his welfare and we sought to protect him.

Albert was sent to Australia in 1949 under the child migration scheme. He is now under the jurisdiction of the Australian authorities and no concern of ours.

I would warn you against making any attempt to retrieve him. He has settled into a new life and is very happy. Any attempt to remove him would be detrimental to his well-being.

The last document I uncovered was full of frustration and anger. It asks the same questions that I have asked for seven years. Questions that can never fully be answered because there is no defence for what was done to these children.

12 March, 1950
Re Albert Stanhope
Thank you for your letter. It was a foul and appalling attack

316

on my wife. You simply overlook the fact that a child still belongs with his mother, not you or anyone else, and that he has been taken out of this country illegally.

I was shocked to read such a letter from a member of a religious order that prides itself in caring for others and preaches forgiveness. How dare you accuse my wife of deserting her child. How dare you send him overseas illegally.

This surely is illegal and I am already seeking instruction on such matters.

In the meantime, I advise you and your Church to employ whatever powers you possess and return Albert to this country.

Yours faithfully,

H. Archer.

Albert Stanhope didn't come home – not for another forty-three years. As his mother fought for him, he was seven years old and destined to grow up in the misery of an institution.

At some point his parents gave up, bowing to the pressures imposed on them. Patricia, however, never stopped grieving for her son. She, at least, knew he was alive, others were told their children had died.

Until last year, Albert had never even seen a photograph of himself as a child. He believed he was an orphan. Not only does he have a mother, but he now knows that she never wanted to leave him. He could have grown up in a loving, stable family in London, but instead suffered the degradation of institutionalized care.

If you wonder how it feels, here is the very first letter Albert wrote to his mother.

Dear Mum,

I pray that I find the right words – there is so much I want to say to you. When I arrive in England next week, it will be a moment that I've dreamed about since I was a small boy.

We know so little about each other but in a sense we were never apart. I have a beautiful family in Australia and as I watched them grow up, I wondered about my own family in England.

Having waited so long, I can barely contain myself and

hopefully, with the help of Margaret, I won't be a bundle of nerves when I see you.

Before I go I want to mention something which is very important. They're just a few words, but I want you to remember them, Mum. The words are 'No Regrets'. You must always, but always remember that.

All my love,
Albert

EPILOGUE

13 December 1993

Seven years ago, as I stood on the doorstep of a strange house in a strange town facing an elderly woman I'd never met before, I had no understanding that I was about to lift the lid on one of the most appalling and shameful pieces of recent British and Australian social history.

I was a Nottingham social worker who had done nothing more remarkable, I thought, than help reunite a mother and daughter after a separation of forty-five years and 12,000 miles. Naïvely, I believed this was a one-off occurrence, or perhaps one of a mere handful.

Now, seven years wiser and sadder, I was standing on another doorstep altogether different. Government House in Canberra, the home of the Australian Governor-General Bill Hayden.

Several taxis pulled up behind me. Harold Haig stepped from one of them, his grey beard combed and his hair pulled back into a neat ponytail. Pamela Smedley was there, along with her mother Betty, who had flown from England especially for the investiture. There were other familiar faces, like Desmond McDaid and John Hennessey. There were former child migrants from all the schemes and the States concerned.

If possible I would have invited all 10,000 children who were sent to Australia. I wanted all of them to share in the day. They had arrived in Australia as enforced emigrants and many had worked hard, raised families and paid taxes in a country that had never completely welcomed them. Despite having spent fifty, sixty or even seventy years in Australia, some still do not have citizenship.

They deserved to be honoured guests at Government House in Canberra – still a potent symbol of the ties that bind Australia and Britain. The Governor-General is the Queen's representative in Australia. He opens Parliament on her behalf and confirms legislation that has been passed by the Upper and Lower Houses.

It seemed rather ironic. I had often wondered if the Queen realized that her family had, in the past, lent their patronage to charities which were sending British children abroad.

An attendant ushered us up the marble steps to a large sitting-room flanked by french windows overlooking the rain-soaked gardens. There was a piano in one corner, decorated with photographs of the Queen in silver frames, and a Christmas tree by the windows.

The timetable of events was very formal. At 10.00 a.m., the Governor-General would appear and make the presentation. Half an hour later, he would depart and that would be our signal to leave.

When His Excellency Bill Hayden arrived, I was formally presented to him and then he invested me with the Order of Australia medal for services to the child migrants and the community at large.

The medal is a simple convex golden disc with a texture of beads and radiating lines. It was minted from Australian gold and topped by a crown which signified the position of the Queen as the head of the Order. It is very attractive.

Afterwards, as orange juice and wine were served by waiters carrying silver trays, His Excellency and his wife mingled with the child migrants and friends of the Trust. The Governor-General was genuinely interested in each of their stories and quite obviously had read about the issue.

But as the good-natured conversation flowed, I found myself preoccupied with the ironies of the scene.

I had accepted one of the highest honours that the Australian government can bestow on a non-Australian, but my own Government in Britain still refused to acknowledge that it bore any responsibility for sending its children around the world and condemning many to lives of servitude, brutality and loneliness.

The Australian government had been more generous in providing financial support to the Trust, but it, too, had failed to admit publicly responsibility for the role it played in the schemes.

I didn't set out to uncover any shameful secrets. My naïvety was such that it didn't even enter my thoughts when I began looking for Madeleine's mother. And since then I've tried to remain balanced and not apportion blame or publicly condemn any of the architects of child migration.

In a sense child migration has never been a secret. Information has always existed in obscure history books and government archives, or untouched in the records of charities and religious orders.

I simply brushed away the top layer of dust that has covered it since 1967 when the last handful of the child migrants left Britain.

As the power and influence of the Commonwealth waned, the children sent from Britain's shores were forgotten; they faded from the country's consciousness.

I have had MPs say to me, 'Did this really happen? How could this be? Surely we would have heard about it.'

Perhaps that was the idea. Britain sought to rid itself of its so-called deprived children. It didn't expect to hear from them again. Out of sight meant out of mind.

Even now I still ask myself, Why? After years of hearing the stories of child migrants, of having them sob on my shoulder, yell in anger and shake with frustration, I am no closer to understanding the logic of child migration. I know the official line and know the historical context – they chill me to the bone. Paternalism, racism, religious fanaticism and bureaucracy all formed an unholy alliance and this was the result.

Now adults, lost to their families and disbarred from their identities, many of the child migrants will never recover. It has led to enormous emotional problems. Being a child migrant was punishment enough, but some were to face even greater degradation. Some people have argued that allegations of physical and sexual abuse should be separated from the debate over child migration because not all of the children were affected.

I don't agree.

To take children from their families and their countries was an abuse; to strip them of their identity was an abuse; to forget them and then deny their loss was an abuse. Within this context and within our culture, few tragedies can compare.

After the investiture, our party adjourned to the Statesman Hotel in Canberra for a celebratory lunch. There were many familiar faces around the table and I was struck by how they had come together as a family as if they had known each other all their lives. It was entirely different from when I first met them. There was enormous self-pride and self-respect.

Although speeches embarrass me, I was moved by their words.

Desmond made the toast: 'Margaret, there is a timely significance that your investiture should occur on the eve of the International Year of the Family. Perhaps our collective experience, our struggles for survival and emotional growth will, in a very powerful way, remind the wider community to rediscover and revalue their families.'

An emotional John Hennessy summed up his feelings. 'I was always told that I was born in Belfast in 1940 and my first name was John. I had never seen my birth certificate so I went through life believing these things. That was until Margaret sent me a registered letter and inside was my certificate.

'I found out that I wasn't born in Belfast, but in Cheltenham. My first name isn't John, but Michael. And – I will never forgive Margaret for this – I was actually three years older than I thought.'

Pamela Smedley turning to Betty, said, 'I have a beautiful mother, who they told me didn't exist. And what we have to remember is that not only have we suffered, not only were we lied to, but our mothers and fathers were also deceived. They were told lies and we were told lies.

'If it wasn't for Margaret Humphreys my mother would not be sitting beside me today. I'm a different person now. I am whole.'

Geoffrey Gray, from Western Australia, had also been struck by the irony of the morning's events. 'Countless times people have asked, "Why didn't you speak out before?" I'll tell you why. We had nobody to turn to. Nobody wanted us. The only person we could turn to was Margaret Humphreys.

'The Australian government has recognized that these dreadful schemes did take place. But there are still many who think this could not have happened; who think that we could not have done this to children.

'Sadly, it did happen. Her Majesty's Government still does not respect or accept the wrongs that were inflicted on us and our families.'

Margaret Martin, who arrived in Australia aged eleven, described the beautiful feeling of knowing that she was someone. 'Up until the age of fifty I didn't feel this. I wanted to know my roots but I didn't have the courage and I didn't have the support.

'When I was little and very miserable, I used to imagine that my mother was the Queen and wore a tiara on her head. I had nothing else to cling on to except this dream.

'Finally, when I met my Mum for the first time, she was four foot ten inches tall. She was still a queen to me.

It is wrong that child migrants should feel indebted for what are basic human rights. They deserve so much more.

I have done what I can, with the help of many courageous and committed colleagues, friends and supporters.

Where there was only pain, now there is hope and optimism. But sadly, this is not the last chapter. I wish it were. Time is running out for the former child migrants to be reunited with their families and the task is made more difficult because of the constant struggle for funds.

It is time for those who put so much effort into sending innocent children abroad to sit down and put the same effort into repairing the damage they have done.

And it is time for the child migrants to be told that the countries which accepted them are sorry and that the country which abandoned them is ready to welcome them home.

If you wish to contact the Trust, or send a donation, please write to one of the following addresses:

Child Migrants Trust
8 Kingston Road
West Bridgford
Nottingham
NG2 7AQ
United Kingdom

Child Migrants Trust
228 Canning Street
North Carlton
Melbourne
Victoria, 3054
Australia

INDEX

Entry is made under forenames in this index, where the surname has not been given.

ABC (Australian Broadcasting
    Corporation), 165–6, 231
  and *The Leaving of Liverpool*,
    187, 222, 227–8, 249
Adams, Philip, 252
Adelaide, 93–100, 140–2, 313
adoption, rejected for migrants,
    261, 313
The Age, Melbourne, on migrants
    1948, 304
Alsop, John, 187
Angus, Brother, 256
Ann Theresa (migrant), 77–80
Archer, Henry and Patricia,
    315–17
Armstrong, Sir Robert, 13
Association of Psychiatric Social
    Workers, 303
Asturias, SS, 37, 191, 237, 263
Aulph, Florence (migrant), 125–6
Australia, 56, 236–7, 258–62
  MH in, 40, 138–46, 161–8,

    181–2, 186–93, 210–13,
    218–22, 225–54, 268–84,
    319–21
Australia, SS, 89
Australian High Commission,
    London, 21–2, 308
Australian National Catholic
    Association of Family Agencies,
    167

Bacchus Marsh Farm School, 235
Bader, Douglas, 208
Baker, Mr, 261
Baldwin, Eric (migrant), 101
Barlow, Yvonne, 64–5, 66, 112,
    113, 123, 135, 138, 158, 191,
    193, 267, 268
  in Australia, 248
Barnardo's, Dr, 38, 56, 59, 60,
    124, 125, 153–4, 155–8, 259,
    260, 296–7, 302
  farm school, Picton, 235

Barnardo's, Australia, 44, 166
Bayns, John, 126
BBC (British Broadcasting
    Corporation), 153–4, 187,
    268–9, 286–9, 298
    see also The Leaving of Liverpool
Bean, Philip, 58, 75, 111, 185
Bennett, Sandra (Ann Pritchard,
    migrant), 41–2, 293
    open letter, 293–5
Big Brother Movement, 259
Bill (migrant), 75, 76
Bindoon Boys' Town (later Keaney
    College), 80–1, 82–3, 86–7, 88,
    143–4, 238–47, 250, 256, 263,
    264, 265
Birt, John, 286, 287, 298
Blunkett, David, MP, 301
Blyth, Bruce, 292
Boys' Town see Bindoon
Briggs, Maureen (migrant), 89–90
British Association of Social
    Workers (BASW), 36, 43
British Federation of Social Workers
    (BFSW), 303, 304–5
British government, and child
    migrants, 302–3, 304, 306–8
Broken Rites group, 276
Bugeja, Tony (migrant), 207

Caernarvon Castle, SS, 120
Calgary (Canada), 128–9
Canada,
    child migration, 56, 124, 125–33
    MH in, 124–34
Canberra, 52–3
Canterbury (Melbourne), St John's
    Boys' Home, 50–2
Cappo, David, 167
Carden, Stephen, 60–1, 102
Castledare Orphanage, 87, 264–6,
    276
Catholic Child Welfare Council,
    259
Catholic Children's Society, 171
Catholic Church, 38, 56, 87, 151,

155, 167, 201, 233–5, 252–3,
    276, 292, 308–9
Catholic Emigration Society, 234,
    259
Catholic Episcopal Migration and
    Welfare Association, 234
Catholic Migrant Centre, 88
Catholic Record see Record
Catholic Social Service Bureau, 313
Catholic Welfare Council, 167
Channel Nine, Australia, 94
Chapman, Penny, 187, 222–3, 227,
    228, 287
    see also The Leaving of Liverpool
charities, 60–1, 62–3, 69, 151,
    155-8, 171, 187
Child Migrants Trust (CMT), 58,
    60, 61, 62, 64, 69, 74, 94,
    150–2, 154, 155, 170, 184,
    185, 249, 267, 325
    funding, 158–9, 160, 184, 222,
    224
    addresses, 325
child migration schemes, 38, 43–4,
    56, 235, 259–64, 303–10,
    321–2
Child Welfare Departments,
    Australia, 264, 265, 292, 309
Child Welfare Society, 130
Children's Act 1948, 302, 304–5
Children's Society, 56, 155–7
Christian Brothers, 80, 82–3,
    172, 201, 233–5, 236, 256–7,
    259, 264, 276–8, 282–3,
    290–3, 297
Christine (migrant), 105, 109,
    113–14, 150–1
Church of England, 56, 155, 259
Church of Scotland, 56, 259
Clarke, Kenneth, MP, 70
Clontarf, St Joseph's Orphanage,
    87, 205–9, 233, 249, 257,
    263, 264–5, 312
    MH's visit, 246
Coldrey, Dr Barry, 172, 201–2,
    232, 240–1, 252–3, 256, 292

Coleshill, Nazareth Children's
  Home, 41
Commonwealth Institute, meeting of
  charities and Child Migrants
  Trust, 155–8
Commonwealth Relations Office,
  303, 305, 307
Community Services Department,
  Adelaide, 93
Community Services Department,
  Perth, 88
Community Services Department,
  Sydney, 101
Conlan, Brother Patrick Aloysius,
  234–5, 236
Connors, Peter, Bishop of
  Melbourne, 201
Corby, Joan (migrant), 187–8,
  198
Couchman, Peter, 164–5
Crennan, Mgr George, 43–4, 64
Crusade of Rescue Agency, 44

David, social worker, 186, 225
Department of Family Services,
  Perth, 270
Department of Health (and Social
  Security), 36, 68, 69–70, 151,
  159, 184, 186, 224, 302
Department of Immigration and
  Ethnic Affairs, Australia, 184–5
Dessau, Manfred, 185
Devonport, Charles (migrant),
  129–31
Devonport, Nellie, 131
Dodds-Parker, Lady, 156
Domino Films, 64, 74, 138, 140–2
  see also Lost Children of the
  Empire; Mack, Joanna
Don (migrant), 211–13
Doyle, Brother, 207
Duchess of Atholl, SS, 128
Duncan (Canada), Fairbridge Farm
  School, 128–9, 133–4

East, J., 305

East Sussex County Council, 68
Edward (VIII), as Prince of Wales,
  128, 134
Empire Settlement Acts 1922/1937,
  302
Esperance Bay, SS, 59
Evening Telegraph, St John's
  Newfoundland, 126

Fairbridge, Kingsley, 102, 105,
  115–16
Fairbridge Foundation, Australia,
  104
Fairbridge Memorial College,
  Bulawayo, 116
Fairbridge Society, 38, 56, 60–1,
  88, 102–3, 105–6, 107–8, 123,
  128, 150–1, 155–6, 164–5,
  172, 188, 259, 260, 302
  see also Duncan; Molong; Pinjarra
farm schools see Duncan; Molong;
  Picton; Pinjarra; Tardun
Faulkner, Brother Gerald, 161–4,
  232, 277–8, 290
Federal Catholic Immigration
  Committee, 43
Ferriman, Annabel (Observer), 37,
  38, 55, 57, 59, 60
  in Australia, 41, 43–4, 45, 50
Ford, George, 126

Gatt, Charlie (migrant), 208
General Register Office see St
  Catherine's house
Geraldton, Nazareth House, 89–90,
  283
Gibbs, Sir Humphrey and Dame
  Molly, 117–18
Giminez, Father William, 256
Gloucester, Henry, Duke of, 56
Goodwood Orphanage, Adelaide,
  94–6, 313
Graham (migrant), 76, 80–4
Granada Television, Lost Children
  of the Empire, 153–4
Gray, Geoffrey (migrant), 322–3

Guild, Frazer, 275–6

Haig, Harold (migrant), 15–18,
    34–5, 38–9, 45, 47–52, 73,
    139, 154, 173–83, 198, 221,
    227, 228, 248, 319
Haig, Harold, senior, and Betty (née
    Johnson), 72–3, 173
Hale, Colonel, 52, 68
Harare, Zimbabwe, 114–22
Harrison, Paul (migrant), 65, 66–7
Hayden, Bill, Governor-General,
    279, 320
Haymes/Haynes, Joan (migrant),
    see Corby, Joan
Hennessey, John (christened
    Michael, migrant), 227, 319,
    322
Hill, David, 165
Hinchliffe, David, MP, 288, 301
Holt, Harold, 243
'home children', i.e. Canadian
    migrants, 131
Home Office, 25
Humphreys, Ben, 9, 23, 93,
    111–12, 148, 239–40, 269,
    271, 285
Humphreys, Mervyn, 8–9, 23,
    27–9, 34, 38, 55–6, 102, 111,
    144–5, 147–9, 170, 221, 223,
    239–40, 266–71, 303
Humphreys, Rachel, 8, 9, 23, 93,
    111, 255, 269–71, 285
Hussey, Marmaduke, 286
Hutchinson, Judy, 102–3, 105–6,
    107–8, 150, 156, 157

Illustrated London News, advert for
    child migrants, 56
Independent, 288
Inside Edition, 276

Jacobs, Martin, 287
James, Verity, 231–2
Japan, 237
Jarman, Mike, 156, 158, 296–7

Johnson, Elizabeth Ellen (later
    Smith), mother of Harold Haig,
    66–7, 174–83
Jones, John (migrant), 128
Jones, Kevin, 225, 227
Jones, Tony (migrant), 280–2

Kathleen (Madeleine's godmother),
    27–9
Keaney, Brother Francis Paul, 87,
    240, 242–3, 264
Keaney College see Bindoon Boys'
    Town
Kerry, Joan, social worker, 186,
    249, 268

Lady Northcote Emigration Fund,
    235, 259
The Leaving of Liverpool, 222,
    225–6, 227, 248, 249–54, 268,
    286–9, 298–9, 300–1
Leigh, Day & Co, solicitors, 200,
    225
Liverpool, City Council and Social
    Services, 297
Llewellyn, Lord, 305
Lockerbie disaster, 147–8
Lost Children of the Empire, 153–4,
    159, 161, 165, 199, 253
    see also Domino films; Mack,
    Joanna; Melville, Joy

McAllistair family, 209
McDaid, Desmond (migrant),
    203–17, 238–47, 283, 319, 322
McGee, Brother, 265
MacGregor, Caroline, 172
Mack, Joanna, 64, 74, 112, 161
    in Australia, 88, 91, 110,
    139–40, 144
McMullen, Dessie (migrant), 207
Madeleine (migrant), 13–14, 20–3,
    24–5, 26, 27–9, 31–3
Major, John, MP, 301–2
Malta, child migrant schemes, 201
Marcelle (migrant), 279–80, 281

Marie, 15–18, 34–5, 39, 47–8, 50, 52, 66, 72–3, 174–83
Martin, Margaret (migrant), 323
Melbourne, 45, 185, 221–2, 225–6, 270–1
Melbourne Daily Sun, 37
Melville, Joy
  in Zimbabwe, 116, 118, 121–2
  in South Africa, 123
  in Canada, 124, 126–7, 132
Meredith, Anthony, 171
Michael (migrant), 190–7
Miller, Juanita, 256–7
Minister for Immigration, Federal, 263–4
Molloy, Revd Neale, 51
Molong, Fairbridge Farm School (New South Wales), 42, 46, 61, 103, 164, 187, 235, 259
  reunion attended by MH, 103–9
Myles, John, 158, 268
  in Australia, 161, 225–32, 248
Myles, Penny, 158, 268
  in Australia, 161, 162–3, 166–7, 227

National Children's Home, 56, 155, 259
National Council of Social Services, 305–6
New Zealand, child migrant schemes, 56, 170–1
Northcote Children's Emigration Fund, 259
  farm school, 235
Nottingham Evening Post, 286
Nottinghamshire County Council, 268–9, 286, 288, 299
Nottinghamshire Social Services Department, 8, 9, 61, 224

Observer, 59, 102, 103
  see also Ferriman, Annabel
O'Gorman, Dr George, 4
Old Fairbridgians Association, 102–9, 164–5, 219

Otranto, SS, 236
Orange see Molong
Order of Australia Medal (OAM), 278–9, 282, 301–2
  investiture, 319–21
Ormonde, SS, 187, 313
orphans, migrants told they were, 47, 90, 133, 198, 208, 311–12
Osbourne, Alan (migrant), 213–15, 275, 282–3
Ottawa, 126–7
Oversea Migration Board, 306–8

Paterson, Mr, Fairbridge Farm School, 303
Pendal, Philip, MP, 253
Perth, 74–85, 86–92, 143–9, 185, 186, 190–3, 210–13, 218–21, 230–7, 268–70, 271–84
Perth, Archbishops of, xi, 233–4, 236
Picton Farm School (New South Wales), 235
Pinjarra, Fairbridge Farm School, 87, 103, 219, 235, 302
Pittard, Mr, 261
Presbyterian Church, 56
Pritchard, Ann see Bennett, Sandra
Project Anna, 276

Quarrier Homes, 56
Quigley, Jimmy (migrant), 204–5

Ray, Robert, 184–5
Reagan, President Ronald, 12, 124
The Record, 233, 236, 237, 253, 278
Rhodesia, child migration schemes, 56, 115, 117, 119–22
  see also Zimbabwe
Robinson, Mrs, 123
Rockhampton (Queensland), St Joseph's Orphanage, 41, 293
Royal Overseas League, 170
Rutter, Beverly, 268

St Catherine's House (General
    Register Office), 19, 65, 66,
    158, 173–4, 267
St Joseph's Orphanages *see*
    Clontarf; Rockhampton
Salvation Army, 16, 48, 56, 59,
    68–9, 155–8, 174–5, 259
7.30 Report (ABC TV), 275
Shanahan, Tony, 292
Silver, Dennis, 104–5, 165
Sinclair, Dr Rob, 165
Sixty Minutes, 276
Skidmore, David, 296
Smedley, Pamela (christened
    Elizabeth, migrant), 96–9,
    135–7, 140–2, 152–3, 319, 322
Smith, Lionel Maulever Worsop, 178
Smith, Sue, 187
South Africa
    Joy Melville in, 123
Spicer, David (lawyer), 57–8, 104,
    106, 107, 108, 110, 144, 151,
    155–7, 174–5
    in Perth, 74, 75, 76, 79, 84–5,
    86, 87–8, 90, 91–2
    in Adelaide, 93, 96, 99–100
    in Sydney, 101
Spycatcher case, 12, 20
Stanhope, Albert (migrant), 313–18
Stanhope, Patricia (later Archer),
    314–18
Stephens, Marjorie and Grace, 180
Stephenson, Syd (migrant), 42–3
Strathcaird, 233, 236
Strathnaver, 236
Sunday Times, 275–6, 296
Susan (friend in Melbourne),
    219–20, 221
Sussex County Council
    and Harold Haig, 50, 68
Swaine, Frances (lawyer), 224,
    248–9
Sydney, 44–5, 101–9, 139–40,
    226–9
Sydney Morning Herald, 101

Tardun
    orphanage, 87, 263
    St Mary's Farm School, 264
Taylor, Hon. Joan, 61–2, 269, 282,
    286, 288, 296
Temple, Shirley, 153
Termanbacca (Ireland), Nazareth
    House, 203–4
Thatcher, Margaret, 69, 124
Thorn, Mr, Minister for
    Immigration, 237
The Times, 1934, 134; 1948, 303
Tom (migrant), 119–20
Tormey, Lawrie (migrant), 207
Toronto, 124–6
Tremarco, Christine, 225
Triangle (organization), 10–11, 13,
    34–6

University of Western Australia, 75

Vancouver, 129–31
Vera (Madeleine's mother), 24–5,
    26, 27, 29, 31–2, 33
VOICES organization, 276, 282, 292
Voigt, Louise, 44

Walter (migrant), 167–8
West Australian, 240, 256
Western Australia
    and child migration schemes, 260,
    262–3, 264
    orphanages, 88
Wilkins, George (migrant), 45–7,
    102–4, 109, 154
Wilkins, Rita (migrant), 47
Winston Churchill Trust, 36
Wogan, 153
Wright, Peter, 13

Yentob, Alan, 286, 287
Yeo, Tim, MP, 286

Zimbabwe, MH in, 114–22